Lecture Notes in Artificial Intelligence   11669

Subseries of Lecture Notes in Computer Science

More information about this series at http://www.springer.com/series/1244

Kouzou Ohara · Quan Bai (Eds.)

Knowledge Management and Acquisition for Intelligent Systems

16th Pacific Rim Knowledge Acquisition Workshop, PKAW 2019
Cuvu, Fiji, August 26–27, 2019
Proceedings

Springer

Editors
Kouzou Ohara
Aoyama Gakuin University
Tokyo, Japan

Quan Bai ⓘ
University of Tasmania
Tasmania, Australia

ISSN 0302-9743   ISSN 1611-3349   (electronic)
Lecture Notes in Artificial Intelligence
ISBN 978-3-030-30638-0   ISBN 978-3-030-30639-7   (eBook)
https://doi.org/10.1007/978-3-030-30639-7

LNCS Sublibrary: SL7 – Artificial Intelligence

This Springer imprint is published by the registered company Springer Nature Switzerland AG
The registered company address is: Gewerbestrasse 11, 6330 Cham, Switzerland

Preface

This volume contains the papers presented at the 2019 Pacific Rim Knowledge Acquisition Workshop (PKAW 2019) held in conjunction with the 16th Pacific Rim International Conference on Artificial Intelligence (PRICAI 2019), during August 26–27, 2019, in Fiji.

Since the 1990s, PKAW has provided researchers with opportunities to present ideas and have intensive discussions on their work related to knowledge acquisition, which is one of core fields of Artificial Intelligence (AI). The scope of PKAW is not limited to traditional knowledge acquisition approaches such as human (expert) centric ones, but also covers diverse areas closely related to knowledge acquisition such as knowledge engineering, knowledge management, machine learning, data mining, etc. We need to choose appropriate techniques for knowledge acquisition, depending on its type and the task addressed. In fact, the scope changes over time so that it can cover novel, newly emerged techniques and application areas in which knowledge acquisition plays an important role. Especially, now, we live in the era of the third wave of AI, in which the availability of high-performance computing and massive electronic data generated from various sensors and texts on the Web make it possible to devise novel data-driven methodologies such as Deep Learning and its variants. These advanced technologies could help us acquire tacit knowledge that has been difficult to learn by human-centric approaches, while they also remind us of the importance of the understandability of knowledge, leading to a new field of Explainable AI.

Within this context, we invited submissions in the above broad fields and finally selected 9 regular papers and 7 short papers from 38 submitted papers. All papers were peer-reviewed by three reviewers. These papers demonstrate advanced research work from the practical viewpoint and make contributions in technical and theoretical aspects to the fields of intelligent systems/agents, natural language processing, and applications of machine learning techniques including Deep Learning to real world problems.

The workshop co-chairs would like to thank all the people who supported PKAW 2019, including the PKAW Program Committee members and sub-reviewers who spent their precious time reviewing papers, the PRICAI Organizing Committee who appropriately dealt with our requests and all of the administrative and local matters. Thanks to EasyChair for providing the online platform to efficiently handle submissions and to Springer for publishing the proceedings in the *Lecture Notes in Artificial Intelligence* (LNAI) series. Of course, we would like to give a special thanks to all authors who submitted papers, all presenters, and all attendees.

August 2019

Kouzou Ohara
Quan Bai

Organization

Organizing Committee

Honorary Chairs

Paul Compton   The University of New South Wales, Australia
Hiroshi Motoda   Osaka University, Japan

Workshop Co-chairs

Kouzou Ohara   Aoyama Gakuin University, Japan
Quan Bai   University of Tasmania, Australia

Publicity Chair

Soyeon Caren Han   University of Sydney, Australia

Advisory Committee

Maria R. Lee   Shih Chien University, Taiwan
Kenichi Yoshida   University of Tsukuba, Japan
Byeong-Ho Kang   University of Tasmania, Australia
Deborah Richards   Macquarie University, Australia

Program Committee

Xiongcai Cai   The University of New South Wales, Australia
Zehong Cao   University of Tasmania, Australia
Tsung-Teng Chen   NTPU, Taiwan
Akihiro Inokuchi   Kwansei Gakuin University, Japan
Toshihiro Kamishima   National Institute of Advanced Industrial Science
     and Technology (AIST), Japan
Alfred Krzywicki   The University of New South Wales, Australia
Weihua Li   Auckland University of Technology, New Zealand
Toshiro Minami   Kyushu Institute of Information Sciences, Kyushu
     University Library, Japan
Tsuyoshi Murata   Tokyo Institute of Technology, Japan
Hayato Ohwada   Tokyo University of Science, Japan
Tomonobu Ozaki   Nihon University, Japan
Hye-Young Paik   The University of New South Wales, Australia
Mira Park   University of Tasmania, Australia
Ulrich Reimer   University of Applied Sciences St. Gallen, Switzerland
Kazumi Saito   University of Shizuoka, Japan
Derek Sleeman   University of Aberdeen, UK

Xing Su	Beijing University of Technology, China
Vojtěch Svátek	University of Economics Prague, Czech Republic
Hiroshi Uehara	Akita Prefectural University, Japan
Shuxiang Xu	University of Tasmania, Australia
Takahira Yamaguchi	Keio University, Japan
Tetsuya Yoshida	Nara Women' University, Japan

Additional Reviewer

Hahn, Heiko

Contents

Estimating Difficulty Score of Visual Search in Images for Semi-supervised Object Detection

Dongliang Ma, Haipeng Zhang, Hao Wu, Tao Zhang, and Jun Sun[✉]

JiangSu Provincial Engineering Laboratory of Pattern Recognition
and Computational Intelligence, JiangNan University, Wuxi, China
mdl.viper@gmail.com, zhpmatrix@gmail.com, wuhao940917@gmail.com,
{taozhang,junsun}@jiangnan.edu.cn

Abstract. Humans can intuitively understand the content of images, and often reach a consensus that some images are more difficult to visual search tasks than others. However, this is quite challenging for computers as it is a subjective task which may be influenced by human emotional factors. Instead of focusing on how the models make reactions on datasets, our method has a capability of assigning scores to samples respectively within a dataset that estimating the difficulty of visual search tasks. Our model shows better performance for predicting visual search difficulty scores of samples produced by human annotators in PASCAL VOC2012. Eventually, we demostrate with experiments that our method has an ability of selecting suitable samples to improve the performance of detectors in a semi-supervised task.

Keywords: Visual search · Semi-supervised object detection

1 Introduction

Since its development two decades ago, Convolutional Neural Networks have promoted the development of computer vision. Various network architectures [4,7,11] all prove the power of CNNs. On the other hand, cognitive research [1,13,16] shows that for tasks that search for patterns in images, response time of users make effects on visual search difficulty, and visual search difficulty may vary from image to image. Salient objects could be quickly found in images, while others are more difficult, requiring humans to perform intensive visual processing as shown in Fig. 1. Regrettably, CNNs still can't think and analyze problems in human way.

In previous work [5,9,14], they addressed the issue of estimating image difficulty defined as the response time of human for visual search tasks. The task may be affected by the following factors, i.e. the background, complexity of scene, amount of objects, and possible occlusion. In this work, we have established a new end-to-end neural network regression model to predict the difficulty scores

© Springer Nature Switzerland AG 2019
K. Ohara and Q. Bai (Eds.): PKAW 2019, LNAI 11669, pp. 1–9, 2019.
https://doi.org/10.1007/978-3-030-30639-7_1

Fig. 1. Some figures captured by PASCAL VOC2012 are shown in visual search tasks. The object to be identified in the first line is the aircraft, the second birds, the third people. For the same object, we can easily find it in the left image, which is difficulty to find in the image on the right. The difficulty of the picture increases from left to right in our mind. Obviously, the time it takes to find the specified object in the above images are not the same.

of images, so that the model can automatically predict the human's assessment of the difficulty of images.

Moreover, almost all of the existed works investigate only the models and ignore the relationship between models and samples, estimating the difficulty of images can be used as a criterion for distinguishing images. It has been employed in some previous works for weakly supervised object detection [10, ?], semi-supervised object classification [5], and potential application in object detection [12,15]. In order to verify the strength of our work, we use the difficulty score of image represents both confidence and·interpretability that we can select some particular samples to improve model detection accuracy.

In terms of the difficulty estimation for visual search in images, this paper has the following two contributions. Firstly, Kendall RankLoss is designed for optimizing the Kendall's τ correlation coefficient [3] which evaluates the neural network to estimate the difficulty scores of images. Secondly, we utilize our score of difficulty as a indication to label the unlabeled data during training in semi-supervised object detection.

The rest of the paper is organized as follows. Section 2 introduces related works and Sect. 3 presents our proposed work. In Sect. 4, the experimental results are reported and analyzed. Lastly, some concluding remarks are given in Sect. 5.

2   Related Work

At present, there are few researches conducted on image difficulty [5,9,14]. Russakovsky et al. [9] measured difficulty by the size and the number of bounding-boxes (even at test time). Grauman and Vijayanarasimhan [14] attempted to evaluate the difficulty of an image based on the time it takes for humans to segment it. However the task of image segmentation [14] is fundamentally different from our visual search task. For example, a truncated object can be easily segmented but difficult to be found and identified. Radu et al. [5] used the specially established PASCAL VOC2012 dataset close to human visual level to estimate the difficulty of images. The process of dataset labelling was performed on a crowd-sourcing platform named CrowdFlower, after 736 trusted annotators observe the information in the image, and the time required to answer the question was used as a measure of the image difficulty and convert it into image difficulty score. They designed a series of related processing methods including clearing outliers to ensure the validity of the data. Based on the usual visual search tasks, they proposed an explanation of the difficulty of the image close to the human cognitive level. Since the background of each image in the PASCAL VOC2012 dataset is different, the densities, numbers, sizes and appearances of the objects are different, which can meet the demand of experimental validation. They built a regression model based on deep features learned by convolutional neural network. Importantly, they used MSE (Mean Squared Error) and Kendall's τ correlation coefficient to evaluate the difficulty generalization performance of the model. In our work, we designed the Kendall RankLoss for optimizing the Kendall's τ correlation coefficient [3]. In addition to what is different that they regarded the neural network as a feature extractor to get information, we employ the same CNN as an end-to-end regression model directly. We validate our model with the same dataset and evaluation criteria as they do.

3   Our Approach

3.1   Kendall RankLoss

When the model is trained, if the batch size of the neural network is large enough, we can back-propagate the information to the network with the difference between the rank information of the predicted difficulty scores and the ground-truth rank information in each batch as the error, and resultantly the entire network can continuously reduce the error. By the definition of Kendall's τ correlation coefficient, the range of its value is between -1 and 1. When the rank information of all samples is exactly the same as the rank information of the real values, Kendall's τ correlation coefficient takes a value of 1, and vice versa. Supposedly, there are n samples for each mini-batch $\{x_i, y_{t_i}\}_{i=1}^{N}$, where x_i represents the i th image in the batch, y_{t_i} denotes the true label and y_{p_i} is known as the corresponding predicted difficulty score by model, and the sgn function is denoted by f. Therefore, we can define Kendall's τ correlation coefficient on the batch as follows

$$\tau = \frac{\sum_{i \in N} \sum_{(j<i) \in N} f(y_{t_i} - y_{t_j}) f(y_{p_i} - y_{p_j})}{n(n-1)/2} \tag{1}$$

and design the Kendall RankLoss for optimizing Kendall's τ correlation coefficient as

$$1 - \tau = 1 - c \sum_{i \in N} \sum_{(j<i) \in N} f(y_{t_i} - y_{t_j}) f(y_{p_i} - y_{p_j}) \tag{2}$$

As shown in Eq. (2), since the batch size is determined, we can replace it with a constant term. Besides, from the equation, the range of the RankLoss function is [0, 2], and we should minimize loss function during the model training. Here, if we represent the entire network parameters by ω, the network update process is given by

$$\frac{\partial rankloss}{\partial \omega} = -c \sum_{i \in N} \sum_{(j<i) \in N} f'(\frac{\partial y_{p_i}}{\partial \omega} - \frac{\partial y_{p_j}}{\partial \omega}) \tag{3}$$

$$\omega = \omega - \eta \frac{\partial rankloss}{\partial \omega} \tag{4}$$

It is the most important that the loss function not only needs to meet the target task, but also should be derivative, so that the purpose of updating the network parameters can be achieved in the back propagation phase by the gradient descent method. As shown in Fig. 2(a), the sgn function is non-differentiable, and thus Kendall RankLoss is not suitable for the network learning. To tackle this problem, we make the modification to Kendall RankLoss by replaced the sgn function with the hardtanh function (as shown in Fig. 2(b)), so that $rankloss \approx rankloss_{modified}$.

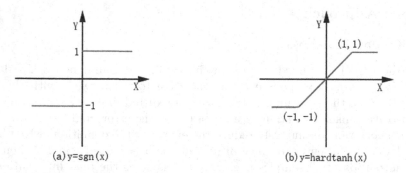

(a) y=sgn(x)   (b) y=hardtanh(x)

Fig. 2. (a) The sign function of a real number x is -1 when x is negative, 0 when x is zero, or $+1$ when x is positive. (b) The hardtanh function of a real number x is -1 when x is less than -1, or $+1$ when x is greater than $+1$. Otherwise the hardtanh function is equivalent to the function $y = x$.

3.2   Multi-loss Alternative Strategy

According to experience, when the MSE (Mean Squared Error) between the predicted values and the ground-truth becomes smaller, the difference of model which has the same trend between the rank information of the predicted values and the ground-truth. It is expected that the generalization ability of the model is consistently good, whether it is reflected by the MSE or the Kendall's τ correlation coefficient or other measures. However, there are also differences between MSE and Kendall's τ correlation coefficient. For example, we suppose that there are three items in our set whose true value label is $\varphi_{true} = \{2, 3, 4\}$, for the two different models $\{\mu_1, \mu_2\}$, the predicted values for the sets are $\varphi_1 = \{2, 4, 3\}$ and $\varphi_2 = \{6, 8, 10\}$, respectively. It is clear that μ_2 is better than μ_1 in the performance of the rank, but in terms of MSE, the performance of μ_1 is better. Usually, multi-object tasks with certain correlations are trained in the same network, and better generalization performance can be achieved as a general result. Therefore, in this paper, we employ multi-loss training strategy to improve the generalization performance of our model.

Algorithm 1. Learning Algorithm for our model.

1: Input: training data $\{(x_1, y_1), \ldots, (x_m, y_m)\}$
2: Parameter: number of iterations T, learning rate η
3: Initialize parameters ω, set of loss functions $\{loss_{mse}, rankloss_{modified}\}$, batch size n, alternative frequency f
4: **for** $t = 1$ to T **do**
5:     **if** $t\%f = 0$ **then**
6:         $loss = loss_{mse}$
7:     **else**
8:         $loss = rankloss_{modified}$
9:     **end if**
10:     **for** n to m **do**
11:         input training data $\{(x_1, y_1), \ldots, (x_n, y_n)\}$ and compute the difficulty score with current ω
12:         compute gradient $\Delta\omega$
13:         update $\omega = \omega - \eta\Delta\omega$
14:     **end for**
15: **end for**

However, for $\forall(i, j) \in N$, the Kendall RankLoss designed in this paper can only be used for backpropagation under the condition of $|y_{p_i} - y_{p_j}| \leq 1$. This $rankloss_{modified}$ does not completely solve the non-differentiable problem. In addition, the range of the designed Kendall RankLoss is $[0, 2]$, whereas the range of MSE is $(0, +\infty)$. Furthermore, Kendall RankLoss is affected by the interrelationship between the predictions in the same batch, which slow down its convergence. Because of the fact that polynomial weighted loss function does not meet our needs, motivated by the previous work which solves the ranking problems by using the gradient [2], we adopt multi-loss alternative strategy to train our image difficulty estimation model. Algorithm 1 shows the model that estimaties difficulty scores for images.

4   Experiments

4.1   Model for Estimating Difficulty Score

Implementation Details. As Radu et al.'s work [5], we use VGG16 [11] as our network for estimating the difficulty score of images. The proposed model is implemented on PyTorch [6], which is an open source deep learning library. When the model is trained with a batch size of 400 on 8 GPUs (Tesla K80), the whole training processing takes about 8 h. The SGD was employed with momentum = 0.9 and weight decay = 5×10^{-4} for adjusting learning rate. Learning rate was set to 1×10^{-3} for the first 160 iterations, and decayed by 10 at 200 and 240 iterations. Just as most computer vision tasks, we also used data augment to prevent the overfitting of the model in the image preprocessing stage. The data augment was conducted by randomly changing the contrast, brightness, hue, saturation of the image, flipping the image, and perturbing each pixel to add noise in the image. Noticeably, we set the alternative frequency to 3, which means 2 epochs for training Kendall RankLoss and 1 epoch for MSE repeatedly. This parameter is found by grid search. Quantitative results on PASCAL VOC2012 estimating scores of images are shown in Table 1.

Table 1. Performance evaluation on PASCAL VOC2012 estimating difficulty scores of images.

Methods	MSE	Kendall's τ
Radu's work	0.231	0.472
Ours	0.206	0.476

Ablation Study. As shown in Table 2, ablation experiments have been conducted to analyze models. Exp.9 of the best end-to-end model was used as the basic setting for comparison.

(1) Kendall RankLoss is essential

In Exp.2, we used Kendall RankLoss to optimize Kendall's τ correlation coefficient. The RankLoss is very important because it uses rank information for the model optimization. With RankLoss, we can increase Kendall's τ correlation coefficient to 6.0%.

(2) Multi-object Learning contributes to a better model

In Exp.3–Exp.6, we used a multi-loss joint training network, with which we can increase the Kendall's τ correlation coefficient by 2.0% with a slight increase in MSE.

(3) Multitask alternative strategy matters

In Exp.7–Exp.9, we employed multi-loss alternative strategy for training, resulting in an obvious improvement on Kendall's τ correlation coefficient but leading to a slight improvement on MSE. Since Kendall's τ correlation coefficient is difficult to optimized, it is verified that this operation is effective.

Table 2. Ablation study on PASCAL VOC2012 estimating difficulty scores of images. "MSE": the loss of Mean Squared Error, "KRL": the loss of Kendall RankLoss we proposed in this paper. "MSE + λ*KRL": Polynomial loss function, λ is the weight of Kendall RankLoss. "MSE/KRL": Multi-loss Alternative Strategy, f means the frequency of Kendall RankLoss

Methods	MSE	Kendall's τ
VGG16 (MSE)	0.211	0.405
VGG16 (KRL)	17.040	0.464
VGG16 (MSE + λ*KRL), λ = 0.2	0.210	0.415
VGG16 (MSE + λ*KRL), λ = 0.5	0.213	0.422
VGG16 (MSE + λ*KRL), λ = 0.7	0.225	0.425
VGG16 (MSE + λ*KRL), λ = 1.0	0.228	0.435
VGG16 (MSE/KRL), f = 1	0.210	0.425
VGG16 (MSE/KRL), f = 2	0.207	0.467
VGG16 (MSE/KRL), f = 3	0.206	0.476

4.2   Application of Estimating Difficulty Score

When it comes to semi-supervised learning tasks, a fundamental approach is to train the model on the annotated data firstly and then employ the model to annotated the unlabeled parts of the dataset to enlarge the train subset. After that, we retrained the model with the above steps iteratively. However, our experiments have displayed that it has poor effect to introduce CNN for this method. We make a conclusion that the accomplishment failed due to some of the features contained in the unlabeled data were not extracted during training. Therefore, the unlabeled data are predestinated to be incorrectly labeled and may weaken our model upon added into training set. To address the above issue, we use the difficulty score of images to pick up some particular samples to improve model detection accuracy. Samples with low difficulty scores are assumed to be interpretable and experiments have shown that they are also trustworthy.

In this section, we apply SSD300 [8] on Pascal VOC datasets. Both the VOC2007 and VOC2012 datasets have similar forms: each image in the dataset has bounding box which belongs to one of the twenty categories. In our work, we refer the VOC2007 as the labeled dataset and VOC2012 is considered as unlabeled dataset to do semi-supervised learning. The implementation details are as follows.

We use an ImageNet pre-trained VGG16 network, and train the model on VOC2007 dataset for 60000 iterations, then use the model to make labels on VOC2012 dataset. After that, we use the difficulty model to predict scores of images in VOC2012 dataset, and select images with the lowest 30% score. After VOC2007 dataset and selected VOC2012 samples with predicted labels are participated by re-training process last for another 10000 iterations. Lastly, we test on VOC2007 test subset.

Table 3. Mean AP of SSD300 model. They have exactly the same setting except that they have different samples to train. Data: "07": VOC2007 trainval, "07 + 12 (groundtruth)": union of VOC2007 and VOC2012 with groundtruth. "07 + 12 (predicted)": union of VOC2007 and VOC2012 with predicted labels. "07 + 12 (proportion 30%)": union of VOC2007 and VOC2012 samples with predicted labels selected by our difficulty score model with easiest 30%.

Dataset	Mean AP
07	68.0%
07 + 12 (groundtruth)	74.3%
07 + 12 (predicted)	66.13%
07 + 12 (proportion 30%)	71.6%

From Table 3 we could observe that our semi-supervised training method increases mAP about 4%. Our final accuracy lays somewhere in between Exp2 and Exp3. This is exactly what we expected. Our method works better than the baseline, and since we only use 30% (possibly mislabeled) data from the VOC2012 trainval dataset. It is reasonable that samples with low difficulty scores are assumed to be interpretable and experiments have shown that they are also trustworthy.

5   Conclusion

Semi-supervised leaning has proven to be efficient in multiple scenarios. However, when applied to deep learning, the traditional and naive ways do not work well. In this work, we design a simple loss function to optimize Kendall's τ correlation coefficient, and apply it with multi-loss alternative training strategy to train an end-to-end neural network for estimating difficulty scores. Unlike softmax score which only encodes confidence, image with low difficulty score represents both interpretability and confidence proved by experiments. We could therefore select explainable and trustworthy samples from additional datasets to apply semi-supervised learning on object detection.

Acknowledgements. This research was partly supported by Open Fund of Key Laboratory of Urban Land Resources Monitoring and Simulation, Ministry of Land and Resources (KF-2018-03-065) and National Science Foundation, China (No. 61702226).

References

1. Arun, S.P.: Turning visual search time on its head. Vision Res. **74**, 86–92 (2012)
2. Caruana, R.: Using the future to "sort out" the present: rankprop and multitask learning for medical risk evaluation. Proc. NIPS' **8**, 959–965 (1996)
3. Croux, C., Dehon, C.: Influence functions of the Spearman and Kendall correlation measures. Stat. Methods Appl. **19**(4), 497–515 (2010)
4. He, K., Zhang, X., Ren, S., Sun, J.: Deep residual learning for image recognition. In: Proceedings of the IEEE Conference on Computer Vision and Pattern Recognition, pp. 770–778 (2016)
5. Tudor Ionescu, R., Alexe, B., Leordeanu, M., Popescu, M., Papadopoulos, D.P., Ferrari, V.: How hard can it be? Estimating the difficulty of visual search in an image. In: IEEE Conference on Computer Vision and Pattern Recognition, pp. 2157–2166 (2016)
6. Ketkar, N.: Introduction to PyTorch. Deep Learning with Python, pp. 195–208. Apress, Berkeley (2017). https://doi.org/10.1007/978-1-4842-2766-4_12
7. Krizhevsky, A., Sutskever, I., Hinton, G.E.: Imagenet classification with deep convolutional neural networks. Adv. Neural Inf. Process. Syst. 1097–1105 (2012)
8. Liu, W., et al.: SSD: single shot multibox detector. In: Leibe, B., Matas, J., Sebe, N., Welling, M. (eds.) ECCV 2016. LNCS, vol. 9905, pp. 21–37. Springer, Cham (2016). https://doi.org/10.1007/978-3-319-46448-0_2
9. Russakovsky, O., et al.: Imagenet large scale visual recognition challenge. Int. J. Comput. Vis. **115**(3), 211–252 (2015)
10. Shi, M., Ferrari, V.: Weakly supervised object localization using size estimates. In: Leibe, B., Matas, J., Sebe, N., Welling, M. (eds.) ECCV 2016. LNCS, vol. 9909, pp. 105–121. Springer, Cham (2016). https://doi.org/10.1007/978-3-319-46454-1_7
11. Simonyan, K., Zisserman, A.: Very deep convolutional networks for large-scale image recognition. arXiv preprint arXiv:1409.1556 (2014)
12. Soviany, P., Ionescu, R.T.: Optimizing the trade-off between single-stage and two-stage object detectors using image difficulty prediction. arXiv preprint arXiv:1803.08707 (2018)
13. Trick, L.M., Enns, J.T.: Lifespan changes in attention: the visual search task. Cogn. Dev. **13**(3), 369–386 (1998)
14. Vijayanarasimhan, S., Grauman, K.: What's it going to cost you?: predicting effort vs. informativeness for multi-label image annotations. In: 2009 IEEE Conference on Computer Vision and Pattern Recognition, CVPR 2009, pp. 2262–2269 (2009)
15. Wang, K., Yan, X., Zhang, D., Zhang, L., Lin, L.: Towards human-machine cooperation: self-supervised sample mining for object detection. In: Proceedings of the IEEE Conference on Computer Vision and Pattern Recognition, pp. 1605–1613 (2018)
16. Wolfe, J.M., Palmer, E.M., Horowitz, T.S.: Reaction time distributions constrain models of visual search. Vis. Res. **50**(14), 1304–1311 (2010)

Improving Named Entity Recognition with Commonsense Knowledge Pre-training

Ghaith Dekhili[✉], Ngoc Tan Le, and Fatiha Sadat

University of Quebec in Montreal, 201 President Kennedy Avenue,
Montreal, QC H2X 3Y7, Canada
{dekhili.ghaith,le.ngoc_tan,sadat.fatiha}@uqam.ca

Abstract. Commonsense can be vital in some applications like Natural Language Understanding, where it is often required to resolve ambiguity arising from implicit knowledge and under-specification. In spite of the remarkable success of neural network approaches on a variety of Natural Language Processing tasks, many of them struggle to react effectively in cases that require commonsense knowledge.

In the present research paper, we take advantage of the availability of the open multilingual knowledge graph ConceptNet, by using it as an additional external resource in a Named Entity Recognition system (NER). Our proposed architecture involves BiLSTM layers combined with a CRF layer that was augmented with some features such as pre-trained word embedding layers and dropout layers. Moreover, apart from using word representations, we used also character-based representation to capture the morphological and the orthographic information. Our experiments and evaluations showed an improvement in the overall performance with +2.86 in the F1-measure.

To the best of our knowledge, there is no study relating the integration of a commonsense knowledge base in NER.

Keywords: Deep neural networks · Word embeddings · Commonsense · ConceptNet

1 Introduction

Natural Language Processing (NLP) and Machine Learning (ML) communities have long been interested in developing models capable of commonsense reasoning. This has been accentuated by the proliferation of Artificial Intelligence (AI) technologies like dialogue systems, recommendation systems and information retrieval tools, which renewed interest in commonsense reasoning (Trichelair et al. 2018) [20]. Trichelair et al. (2018) [20] confirm that the progress of these technologies and the general societal reaction toward them, greatly depend on advances in commonsense reasoning, to the point that we say that systems can seem glaringly unintelligent when they lack commonsense. In addition to that,

© Springer Nature Switzerland AG 2019
K. Ohara and Q. Bai (Eds.): PKAW 2019, LNAI 11669, pp. 10–20, 2019.
https://doi.org/10.1007/978-3-030-30639-7_2

commonsense can be vital in some applications like Natural Language Understanding (NLU), where it is often required to resolve ambiguity arising from
implicit knowledge and under-specification.

ConceptNet (Speer et al. 2016) [17] is a knowledge graph that connects words
and phrases of natural language (terms) with labeled, weighted edges (assertions). Its knowledge is collected from many sources that involve experts who
created manually this resource, crowd-sourcing and games with a purpose. It
is designed to represent the general knowledge involved in understanding languages, improving natural language applications by allowing the application to
better understand the meanings behind the words people use (Speer et al. 2016)
[17]. This new version of the linked open data resource is particularly well suited
with advanced NLP techniques and approaches such as word and graph embeddings. When ConceptNet is combined with word embeddings acquired from distributional semantics such as Word2Vec (Mikolov et al. 2013) [14], it provides
applications with understanding that they would not acquire from distributional
semantics alone, nor from narrower resources such as WordNet or DBPedia.

The present research aims at integrating commonsense knowledge, by using
ConceptNet, into a Named Entity Recognition (NER) task in order to learn
more entities and improve the efficiency and effectiveness of the NER. This
research relies on the work presented by Speer et al. [17] who created a robust
set of embeddings that represents both ConceptNet and distributional word
embeddings learned from text by concatenating the columns of the pre-trained
matrices provided by Word2Vec and GloVe [16], with word embeddings extracted
from Conceptnet. This set of embeddings represents different domains and has
complementary strengths as word embeddings extracted from ConceptNet are
incorporated.

Commonsense reasoning has been employed in other studies related to different NLP applications such as question answering, sentiment analysis and text
summarization. To the best of our knowledge, there is no study relating the
integration of a commonsense knowledge base in NER.

This paper is presented as follows: Sect. 2 presents previous relevant research.
Section 3 presents some relevant background on supervised learning algorithms
and models including deep neural networks. Section 4 presents our proposed
model followed by a brief description of the input embeddings used in our model.
Section 5 presents the tools and data sets used, along with the results of our
experiments. Section 6 concludes this research paper and presents some ideas for
future work.

2   Related Work

To solve the problem of systems who lack commonsense reasoning, Zhong et al.
[24] believe that a desirable way is to pre-train a generic model from external
commonsense knowledge about the world. Their results show that incorporating a commonsense-based function improves the state-of-the-art on two question
answering tasks that require commonsense reasoning. Wang et al. [22] present

Three-way Attentive Networks (TriAN) to model interactions between the passage, question and answers, in multiple-choice commonsense reading comprehension. In their work they used relation embedding from the graph of general knowledge ConceptNet as additional features to explicitly model commonsense knowledge. Amplayo et al. [1] propose Entity2Topic (E2T) to improve the performance of a text summarizer. E2T which is a module that encodes the entities extracted from an original text by an entity linking system (ELS). These entities hold commonsense information once they are linked to a knowledge base such as Wikipedia. In their paper they show that by applying E2T to a simple sequence-to-sequence model with an attention mechanism as a base model, they get significant improvements in a text summarizer performance.

Balahur et al. [3] presented a method to build a commonsense knowledge base EmotiNet representing situations that trigger emotions. In their research, they showed that using this resource helps the emotion detection in textual contexts in which no explicit mention of affect is present. Unsupervised learning has been also used to discover commonsense relationships. Trinh et Le [21] presented a simple method for commonsense reasoning with neural networks, using unsupervised learning. Their results showed an improvement in key features of the question that is related to the correct answer, indicating good understanding of the context and commonsense knowledge. Mikolov et al. [14] and Mikolov et al. [15] used also unsupervised learning and showed that by learning to predict adjacent words in a sentence, word vectors can be used to answer analogy questions such as: Man:King::Woman:?. Their work uses a similar intuition that language modeling can naturally capture commonsense knowledge. Elkan and Greiner [7] built an ontology of commonsense knowledge in predicate logic form over the decades. Zhang et al. [23] presented the Reading Comprehension with Commonsense Reasoning Dataset (ReCoRD), a large-scale dataset, for machine reading comprehension (MRC) requiring commonsense reasoning. DBPedia (Auer et al. [2] extracted knowledge from Wikipedia infoboxes, providing a large number of facts, largely focused on named entities that have Wikipedia articles.

The Google Knowledge Graph [9] is perhaps the largest and most general knowledge graph, though its content is not freely available. It focuses largely on named entities that can be disambiguated, with a motto of "things, not strings". ConceptNet's role compared to these other resources is to provide a sufficiently large, free knowledge graph that focuses on the commonsense meanings of words as they are used in natural language. This focus on words makes it particularly compatible with the idea of representing word meanings as vectors [17].

Trichelair et al. [20] proposed a new evaluation protocol for the WSC. Their protocol accounts for the WSC's limited size and variable instance difficulty, properties common to other commonsense benchmarks. In their work they augmented the existing dataset by switching candidates in sentences whenever possible. Their evaluation protocol provides a new perspective on state-of-the-art methods for commonsense reasoning.

To the best of our knowledge, there is no study relating the integration of a commonsense knowledge base in NER.

3   Background on Some Supervised Machine Learning Models

In this section we present some used supervised machine learning models used in this research, such as the Long Short-Term Memory (LSTM) operating model, BiLSTM which is the combination of two LSTMs, followed by a brief description of the Conditional random field (CRF) modelling model and its usefulness.

3.1   The Long Short-Term Memory Model

LSTM [8] is an artificial recurrent neural network (RNN) architecture used in the field of deep learning. This powerful family of connectionist models can capture time dynamics via cycles in the graph [13].

RNNs take as input a sequence of vectors $(x_1, x_2, ..., x_n)$ at time t and return another sequence $(h_1, h_2, ..., h_n)$, the hidden state, which stores all the useful information at (and before) time t. Although RNNs can, in theory, learn long dependencies, in practice they fail to do so and tend to be biased towards their most recent inputs in the sequence [4]. LSTMs have been designed to combat this issue by incorporating a memory cell and have been shown to capture long-range dependencies. They do so using multiplicative gates which control the amount of information from the previous state to forget and the information from the inputs to pass on to the memory cell LSTM [8]. As in the work presented by Lample et al. [11], we use the following implementation:

$$i_t = \sigma(W_{xi}x_t + W_{hi}h_{t-1} + W_{ci}c_{t-1} + b_i) \tag{1}$$

$$c_t = (1 - i_t) \odot c_{t-1} + i_t \odot tanh(W_{xc}x_t + W_{hc}h_{t-1} + b_c) \tag{2}$$

$$o_t = \sigma(W_{xo}x_t + W_{ho}h_{t-1} + W_{co}c_t + b_o) \tag{3}$$

$$h_t = o_t \odot tanh(c_t) \tag{4}$$

where σ is the element-wise sigmoid function, $\odot$ is the element-wise product and c_t and o_t are the cell state and the output at the step t, respectively.

3.2   Bidirectional LSTM

For each sentence $(x_1, x_2, ..., x_n)$ containing n words, each represented as a d-dimensional vector, an LSTM computes a representation $\overrightarrow{h_t}$ of the left context of the sentence at every word t [11]. As information that we can get from reading the same sequence in reverse can be beneficial to understand the sentence in a better way, an effective solution proven by Dyer et al. [6], is Bidirectional LSTM (BiLSTM). The idea is to compute, using a second LSTM, a representation $\overleftarrow{h_t}$ of the right context of the word. So that we will be able to capture past and future information. The representation of a word using this model is obtained by concatenating the two hidden states, to form the final output ht $= [\overrightarrow{h_t}; \overleftarrow{h_t}]$. These representations effectively include a representation of a word in context, which is useful for numerous tagging applications [11].

3.3   CRF

A very simple but surprisingly effective tagging model is to use the h_t's as features to make independent tagging decisions for each output y_t [12]. For sequence labeling tasks, it is beneficial to consider the correlations between labels in neighborhoods and jointly decode the best chain of labels for a given input sentence, since the "grammar" that characterizes interpretable sequences of tags imposes several hard constraints, such as an adjective is more likely to be followed by a noun than a verb, which can be equivalent in NER with standard BIO2 annotation [19] to I-ORG cannot follow I-PER [13].

Therefore, as in the research presented by Lample et al. [11], we model label sequence jointly using a CRF, instead of modeling them independently.

4   The Proposed Approach

In this section we present our NER model followed by a brief description of the input embeddings used.

4.1   Our Proposed NER Model

We investigate the idea of using pre-trained word embeddings extracted from an external resource such as ConceptNet to initialize the look-up table and to enrich our training data in NER. As in Lample et al. [11], we used in our architecture a Bi-directionnal Long Short-Term Memory (BiLSTM) layers, combined with a Conditional Random Field (CRF) [10] layer augmented with some features such as dropout layers.

Figure 1 represents our proposed architecture. Apart from using word representations, we used also character-based representation to capture the morphological and the orthographic information. As shown in Fig. 1, word embeddings are given to a bidirectional LSTM. l_i represents the word i and its left context, r_i represents the word i and its right context. Concatenating these two vectors yields a representation of the word i in its context c_i [11].

This study aims to compare word embeddings that represent only relational knowledge (ConceptNet PPMI) [17]) and their combination with word embeddings that represent only distributional semantics (word2vec and GloVe). The latter combination is known as ConceptNet Numberbatch [17].

In this section we present more in detail the architecture of the model used in this research.

4.2   Input Embeddings

The input layers of our model are vector representations of individual words. Learning independent representations for word types from the limited NER training data is a difficult problem: there are simply too many parameters to reliably estimate [11]. In our study, we use pre-trained word embeddings to initialize our look-up table and to enrich our training dataset. As in Speer et al. [17],

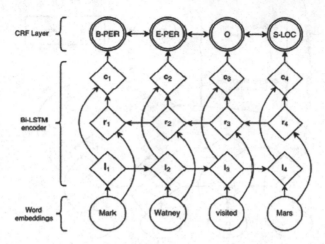

Fig. 1. The main architecture of the NER system using combined Bi-LSTM with CRF

we used ConceptNet PPMI extracted from ConceptNet, which contains over 21 million edges and over 8 million nodes, its English vocabulary contains approximately 1.5 million nodes, and ConceptNet Numberbatch, which is the concatenation of ConceptNet PPMI embeddings with Word2Vec embeddings trained on 100 billion words of Google News using skip-grams with negative sampling [14] and GloVe 1.2 embeddings trained on 840 billion words of the Common Crawl [16]. Learning character-level embeddings has the advantage of learning representations specific to the task and domain at hand. Following Lample et al. [11], we use a forward and a backward LSTM to derive a representation of each word from its characters. A character look-up table initialized randomly contains an embedding for every character had been used too. The word embedding deduced from its characters is the result of the concatenation of the resultant vectors from the bidirectional LSTM. Other approaches like Convolutional Neural Networks (CNN) have been used in other works for the same purpose [5]. Figure 2 describes an architecture involving the characters embeddings of the word "Mars" that were given to a bidirectional LSTMs. Their last outputs were concatenated to an embedding from a look-up table to obtain a representation for this word, as in [11].

5   Experiments and Evaluations

In this section we describe the data we used in this research, an overview of the features and parameters used in our NER system as well as the evaluations and results.

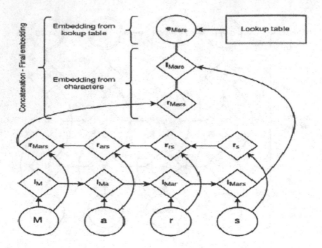

Fig. 2. An architecture using character embeddings of the word "Mars" in Bi-LSTM [11]

5.1 Dataset

Our experiments are based on the CoNLL-2003 datasets [18]. The dataset contains four types of named entities: location (LOC), person (PER), organization (ORG) and miscellaneous (MISC) which do not belong to the previous types of entities. The data was taken from the Reuters Corpus,[1] which consists of Reuters news stories between August 1996 and August 1997.

For the training and development set, ten days' worth of data were taken from the files representing the end of August 1996. For the test set, the texts were from December 1996 [18].

Table 1 provides the statistics of the datasets.

Table 1. Statistics of the CoNLL-2003 English Datasets

Datasets	#Tokens	#Types	#Sentences
Train	204,562	23,624	14,985
Dev	51,573	9,966	3,464
Test	46,624	9,485	3,682

5.2 Training

As in Lample et al. [11], we used in our experiments the IOBES tagging schema, a variant of IOB commonly used for NER, which encodes information about singleton entities (S) and explicitly marks the end of named entities (E). We

---

[1] http://www.reuters.com/researchandstandards/.

used a dropout training of 0.5 to encourage the model to depend on character level embeddings and pretrained word representation.

To train our network, we used the back-propagation algorithm using stochastic gradient descent (SGD) with a learning rate of 0.01. We used a single layer for both LSTMs whose dimensions are 100 each. We did not use language-specific knowledge or external resources such as gazetteers. Except replacing every digit with a zero in the dataset, we neither perform any data preprocessing.

In our experiments, we re-implemented the architecture inspired from Lample et al. [11][2].

5.3   Evaluations and Results

Tables 2, 3 and 4 show a comparison of results obtained with our model. We also present in these tables, the support which is the number of occurrences of each class in the test dataset.

According to the results presented in Table 3 we notice, on the one hand, that the use of ConceptNet PPMI embeddings improves the F1-score of two NE categories, LOC and PER. On the other hand, the increase of precision of these two entities brought an increase of the overall precision of all NE categories. In contrast, the use of ConceptNet PPMI embeddings did not improve the results of the ORG NE category, which is a common problem in the NER task as organizations can be expressed by acronyms, which are highly ambiguous. However if we analyze Table 4, we notice an increase in the precision of the ORG NE category. This can be explained by the use of Glove and Word2Vec embeddings. Moreover, the precision of the PER category increased remarkably, which led to an improvement of the overall precision.

To conclude, ConceptNet embeddings (PPMI) combined with Glove and Word2Vec performs better than using them independently. The use of this hybrid embeddings showed a significant improvement with +2.86 in the F1-measure of the overall NER system. A combination of the strength of the three pre-trained embeddings, constructed from different domains and data, helped increase the performance of the overall system. Moreover, the small amount of data from which we extracted ConceptNet PPMI embeddings (21 million edges and over 8 million nodes, its English vocabulary contains approximately 1.5 million nodes) comparing to Glove (840 billion words of the Common Crawl) and word2vec (100 billion words of Google News) can explain the improvement in the performance, especially when using all embeddings. Moreover, as shown in the three tables, using ConceptNet Numberbatch embeddings improved remarkably the performance of each of the four entities taken separately.

---

[2] https://github.com/glample/tagger.

Table 2. NER results with no external pre-trained embeddings used (only embeddings constructed from our dataset are used)

Entity	Precision (%)	Recall (%)	F1-score (%)	Support	Accuracy (%)
LOC	89.56	88.97	89.26	1657	
MISC	79.82	74.36	76.99	654	
ORG	84.66	77.06	80.68	1512	
PER	81.10	92.08	86.24	1836	
Average	84.38	84.54	**84.46**		**96.73**

Table 3. NER results with ConceptNet PPMI embeddings + embeddings constructed from our dataset

Entity	Precision (%)	Recall (%)	F1-score (%)	Support	Accuracy (%)
LOC	**91.83**	87.59	**89.66**	1591	
MISC	75.73	73.79	74.75	684	
ORG	81.44	79.53	80.48	1622	
PER	**85.81**	88.62	**87.19**	1670	
Average	**85.02**	83.80	**84.40**		**96.70**

Table 4. NER results with ConceptNet numberbatch embeddings + embeddings constructed from our dataset

Entity	Precision (%)	Recall (%)	F1-score (%)	Support	Accuracy (%)
LOC	89.03	91.97	**90.47**	1723	
MISC	76.94	77.49	**77.22**	707	
ORG	**86.06**	81.40	**83.66**	1571	
PER	**92.08**	92.08	**92.08**	1617	
Average	**87.56**	87.09	**87.32**		**97.27**

6   Conclusion

Prior research on NER has focused on the effectiveness of the combination of BiLSTM and CRF models [11]. However this research did not try to integrate a commonsense knowledge base to help solve frequent problems in NER such as the ambiguity. A key aspect in our proposed research is the use of the robust ConceptNet Numberbatch in NER. Our results showed an improvement for the LOC and PER NE categories. Using ConceptNet PPMI embeddings, without those of Glove and Word2Vec, improved LOC's and PER's performance. Apart from using word representations, we used also character-based representation to capture the morphological and the orthographic information. Most notably, this is the first study, to the best of our knowledge, which evaluated the effectiveness of the use of relational knowledge embeddings combined to distributional semantics embeddings in an English NER task.

As a future work, we aim to investigate the usefulness of adding additional layers such as CNN layer to enhance our model structure. Moreover, we would like to investigate the unsupervised learning to train a language model on a massive amount of unlabeled data as done in Trinh et al. [21] and deal with the challenge of implicit entities.

References

1. Amplayo, R.K., Lim, S., Hwang, S.: Entity commonsense representation for neural abstractive summarization. In: CoRR (2018)
2. Auer, S., Bizer, C., Kobilarov, G., Lehmann, J., Cyganiak, R., Ives, Z.: DBpedia: a nucleus for a web of open data. In: Aberer, K., et al. (eds.) ASWC/ISWC-2007. LNCS, vol. 4825, pp. 722–735. Springer, Heidelberg (2007). https://doi.org/10.1007/978-3-540-76298-0_52
3. Balahur, A., Hermida, J.-M., Montoyo, A.: Detecting implicit expressions of sentiment in text based on commonsense knowledge. In: Proceedings of the 2nd Workshop on Computational Approaches to Subjectivity and Sentiment Analysis, pp. 53–60. Association for Computational Linguistics (2011)
4. Bengio, Y., Simard, P., Frasconi, P.: Learning long-term dependencies with gradient descent is difficult. IEEE Trans. Neural Netw. 5(2), 157–166 (1994)
5. Chiu, J.-P.-C., Nichols, E.: Named entity recognition with bidirectional LSTM-CNNs. Trans. Assoc. Comput. Linguist. 4, 357–370 (2016)
6. Dyer, C., Ballesteros, M., Ling, W., Matthews, A., Smith, N.-A.: Transition-based dependency parsing with stack long short-term memory. In: Proceedings of ACL-2015 (vol. 1: Long Papers), pp. 334–343, China (2015)
7. Elkan, C., Greiner R.: Building large knowledge-based systems: representation and inference in the cyc project: D.B. Lenat and R.V. Guhae. In: Artificial Intelligence (1993)
8. Hochreiter, S., Schmidhuber, J.: Long short-term memory. Neural Comput. 9(8), 1735–1780 (1997)
9. Introducing the knowledge graph: things, not strings. https://googleblog.blogspot.com/2012/05/introducing-knowledge-graph-things-not.html
10. Lafferty, J., McCallum, A., Pereira, F.-C.N.: Conditional random fields: probabilistic models for segmenting and labeling sequence data. In: ICML (2001)
11. Lample, G., Ballesteros, M., Subramanian, S., Kawakami, K., Dyer, C.: Neural architectures for named entity recognition. In: CoRR (2016)
12. Ling, W., et al.: Finding function in form: compositional character models for open vocabulary word representation. In: Proceedings of the Conference on Empirical Methods in Natural Language Processing (EMNLP) (2015)
13. Ma, X., Hovy, E.: End-to-end sequence labeling via bi-directional LSTM-CNNs-CRF. In: Proceedings of the 54th Annual Meeting of the Association for Computational Linguistics, pp. 1064–1074, Berlin (2016)
14. Mikolov, T., Chen, K., Corrado, G., Dean, J.: Efficient estimation of word representations in vector space. In: CoRR (2013)
15. Mikolov, T., Sutskever, I., Chen, K., Corrado, G., Dean, J.: Distributed representations of words and phrases and their compositionality. In: CoRR (2013)
16. Pennington, J., Socher, R., Manning, C.-D.: GloVe: Global vectors for word representation. In: 12th Proceedings of the Empiricial Methods in Natural Language Processing (EMNLP 2014), pp. 1532–1543 (2014)

17. Speer, R., Chin, J., Havasi, C.: ConceptNet 5.5: an open multilingual graph of general knowledge. In: CoRR (2016)
18. Tjong Kim Sang, E.-F., De Meulder, F.: Introduction to the CoNLL-2003 shared task: language-independent named entity recognition. In: CoNLL (2003)
19. Tjong Kim Sang, E.-F., Veenstra, J.: Representing text chunks. In: Proceedings on EACL 1999, pp. 173–179, Norway (1999)
20. Trichelair, P., Emami, A., Cheung, J.-C.-K., Trischler, A., Suleman, K., Diaz, F.: On the evaluation of common-sense reasoning in natural language understanding. In: CoRR (2018)
21. Trinh, T.-H., Le, Q.V.: A simple method for commonsense reasoning. In: CoRR (2018)
22. Wang, L., Sun, M., Zhao, W., Shen, K., Liu, J.: Yuanfudao at SemEval-2018 Task 11: three-way attention and relational knowledge for commonsense machine comprehension. In: CoRR (2018)
23. Zhang, S., Liu, X., Liu, J., Gao, J., Duh, K., Van Durme, B.: ReCoRD: bridging the gap between human and machine commonsense reading comprehension. In: CoRR (2018)
24. Zhong, W., Tang, D., Duan, N., Zhou, M., Wang, J., Yin, J.: Improving question answering by commonsense-based pre-training. In: CoRR (2018)

Neurofeedback and AI for Analyzing Child Temperament and Attention Levels

Maria R. Lee, Anna Yu-Ju Yen[✉], and Lun Chang

Shih Chien University, Taipei 104, Taiwan
{maria.lee,h0562001,mookk}@g2.usc.edu.tw

Abstract. One of the common problems among preschool children is attention ability development. It is important to detect and identify earlier the attention problems which may minimize the harmful impact of childhood disorders. The purpose of this research is to predict and analyze the attention levels of children aged 4–7. Using parental report or subjective report to analyze the children's psychological dimensions of temperament is a common approach for temperament research, but it may be bias. Electroencephalography (EEG) is a method to illustrate the brain electrical activity. We proposed a Neurofeedback Technology (NFT) system to amalgamate the collection of EEG signals data and Behavior Style Questionnaire (BSQ) for child temperament data by applying k-means algorithm, an Artificial Intelligence (AI) unsupervised machine learning, clustering analysis method, to observe children's attention levels. The experimental results not only infer that the value of temperament with EEG classification could be consistent, but also provide a valid way to classify attention levels in specific time period. The combination of the parental subjective report with EEG data demonstrates a novel and valuable approach for resolving child attention problems. The results facilitate earlier identification of attention problems and support better parent-child understanding and interactions.

Keywords: Neurofeedback · Artificial Intelligence · EEG · Big data analysis · Attention · Temperament

1 Introduction

One of the common problems among preschool children is attention ability development. Inattention among preschoolers may cause a variety of alternatives or co-existing conditions, such as Attention-deficit/Hyperactivity Disorder (ADHD), language disorders, low intellectual functioning, or other forms of problems. It is important to detect and identify earlier the attention problems and doing so may minimize the harmful impact of childhood disorders [2, 11, 13, 17, 22].

The purpose of this research is to predict and analyze the attention levels of children who are 4–7 years old. Using parental report or subjective report to analyze the children's psychological dimensions of temperament is a common approach for temperament research [1, 18]. However, parental memory bias, contrast effects, and the possibly different understanding of the questions by parent or caregiver are the limitation of this approach [10].

© Springer Nature Switzerland AG 2019
K. Ohara and Q. Bai (Eds.): PKAW 2019, LNAI 11669, pp. 21–31, 2019.
https://doi.org/10.1007/978-3-030-30639-7_3

When a brain is functioning, the brain nerve cells continually having electrical discharge activity, forming brain waves. Electroencephalography (EEG) is a method to illustrate the brain electrical activity. It is a very small signal to be observed on any instruments. EEG measures the voltage changes that are caused due to the ionic movement within the neurons of the brain [5, 7, 8, 12, 24]. BRAINLINK is a tool that works just like a simple EEG based brain-computer interface, analyzing and classifying EEG signals with the help of a neural network [6].

We proposed a Neurofeedback Technology (NFT) system to amalgamate the collected data of EEG signals data and Behavior Style Questionnaire (BSQ) for child temperament data by applying Artificial Intelligence (AI) clustering analysis method, k-means algorithm, to observe children's attention levels. K-means clustering as one of the simplest unsupervised machine learning algorithms is able to classify similar data points together and discover underlying patterns [9, 16]. The EEG data provide valuable and reliable information while analyzing children's attention levels with the outcomes of parental reports. Combining the subjective report with EEG data for analysis produces a valuable and reliable approach for children's attention levels. The experimental results not only infer that the value of temperament with EEG classification could be consistent, but also provide a valid way to classify attention levels in specific time period. The results facilitate earlier identification of attention problems and support better parent-child understanding and interactions.

2 Literature Review

With the development of information technology and the rise of artificial intelligence, the 21st century is called the "century of the brain" [19]. Neurofeedback technology has become one of the new innovative technologies. We apply the Research Fronts of the Essential Science Indicators (ESI) database developed by Clarivate Analytics [4] to explore trends in the field of neurofeedback (shown in Fig. 1). The information selected for this research is that from 1990/01/01 to 2018/12/15, obtaining 4,723 highly cited papers in the field of neurofeedback. Leading papers can help to distinguish the most influential academic papers, while at the same time uncovering breakthrough research directions in a subject area, including the field of neuroscience (40.77%, 1,926), biomedical engineering (20%, 1,373), computer science artificial intelligence (10.35, 489), recovery (10%, 473), clinical neuropathy (8.7%, 411), Electrical Engineering (8.32%, 393), Interdisciplinary Science (6.183%, 292), Psychology (5.844%, 276), Mathematical Computer Biology (5.082%, 240) and related papers on interdisciplinary applications in computer science (3.557%, 168).

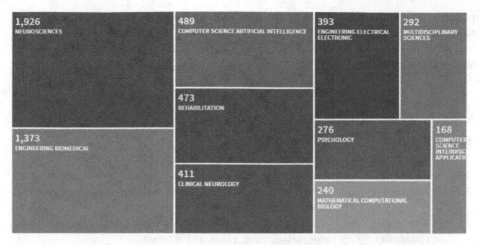

Fig. 1. Trends in the field of neurofeedback

An EEG signal is measured in the range of micro volts (µV). EEG measures the voltage changes that are caused due to the ionic movement within the neurons of the brain. EEG signals are divided into different types of signals based on the frequency of the signal: delta (0.5–4 Hz), theta (4–7 Hz), alpha (8–15 Hz), beta (13–30 Hz), and gamma (30–200 Hz). Table 1 shows the EEG band names, frequency range (Hz) and activity status [5, 7, 8, 12, 24].

Table 1. Bands of EEG signals

EEG band name	Frequency range (Hz)	Activity status
Delta (δ)	0.5–4 Hz	Deep sleep
Theta (θ)	4–7 Hz	Pressure, depression
Alpha (α)	8–15 Hz	Relax and calm
Beta (β)	12–16 Hz	Relax but concentrate
	16.5–20 Hz	Thinking, processing audiovisual messages
	20.5–28 Hz	Excitement, anxiety
Gamma (γ)	30–200 Hz	Meditation

The study of child temperament includes psychological and physiological approaches, and these approaches influence how researchers classify and interpret child temperament. Using parental report or subjective report to analyze the children's psychological dimensions of temperament is so far a common approach for temperament research [1, 18]. By answering the temperament questionnaires, parents or caregivers provide their perspective and observation on child behavior or reaction under numerous real situation. However, parental memory bias, contrast effects, and the possibly different understanding of the questions by parent or caregiver are the limitation of such an approach [10]. We employ and modify the child temperament survey and produce Behavior Style Questionnaire (BSQ) [20, 21]. A total of 72 BSQ survey are created (Table 2).

Table 2. Child temperament – Behavior Style Questionnaire [20, 21]

Item	Activity	Activity status
1	Activity amount	The frequency of activities is high or low of a child
2	Regularity	A child is easy or not easy to be influenced by the environment
3	Adaptability	Child's adaptation to the difficulty and duration of new people, things, places and situations
4	Approaching (avoidance)	A child's acceptance or rejection when the first time to contact a new person, thing, place, and situation
5	Mood nature	Whether a child is pleasant and friendly every day
6	Attention distraction	Whether the child is easily disturbed by the surrounding environments
7	Persistence	When a child is engaged in or wants to do something, suffering difficulties or frustrations, he/she overcomes the obstacles and continues the activity
8	Reaction strength	The intensity of the child's response to internal and external stimuli
9	Reaction threshold	The amount of stimulation required to cause a child to respond, in addition to visual, tactile, audible, odorous, olfactory, and the ability of observing

On the other hand, the behavioral observation and physiological measures as physiological approaches are developed in modern research. Behavioral observation executed in a controlled and independent laboratory could be more objective than parental report. However, the restriction of time and space, and the cost of the experiment are relatively high. Physiological measures include electroencephalographic (EEG), autonomic measures and neuroendocrine measures. EEG is a relatively noninvasive measure among physiological measures, and is able to trace the central brain activity by event-related potentials (ERPs). Since the limitation of recording children's EEG and immature possibility of children's ERP components, combining the subjective report or behavioral observation with EEG data for analysis could be a valuable and reliable approach in temperament research [3, 10].

In this research, we focus on predicting and analyzing the attention levels of 4–7 year-old children. The attention span/persistence is defined as the "capacity for attentional focusing and control as basis for voluntary behavior including persistence", which is related to effortful control and distractibility. The effortful control includes attentional control and inhibitory control that the former is about "the capacity to maintain attention on tasks as well as to shift attention when desired", and the latter is "the capacity to plan and to suppress inappropriate action" [14, 15, 23].

K-means clustering as one of the simplest unsupervised machine learning algorithms is able to classify similar data points together and discover underlying patterns [9, 16]. We adopt AI clustering analysis method, k-means algorithm, to cluster and observe children's attention levels. The novelty of this research is its feature engineering, adopting NFT combined with BSQ. Another one is the combination of these two features by using AI clustering to discovery the consistency in terms of children's cognitive reactions.

3   Research Method

The proposed NFT system combines two kinds of data, EEG signal data and the temperament BSG data. Figure 2 shows the NFT system architecture and process. The system includes 5 process stages, which are data acquisition, data collection, data storing, data analytics, and data visualization. We follow Institutional Review Board (IRB) regulations for human subjects research ethics. Parents and young children are volunteers for the experiment.

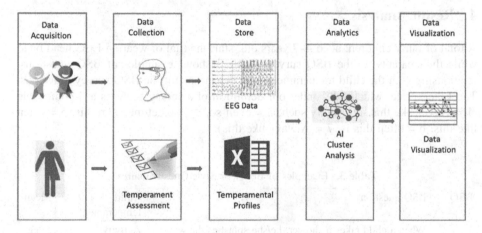

Fig. 2. The proposed NFT system process and architecture

a. In the data acquisition and the data collection stages, parents fill in the BSQ survey whereas children play games and wear EEG. A head-mounted brainwave detecting instrument is constructed to collect the EEG signals. We use a tool called BRAINLINK, shown in Fig. 3, that works just like a simple EEG based brain-computer interface – it analyzes and classifies EEG signals with the help of a neural network. EEG records the brain's spontaneous electrical activity over a short period of time. In our research, there is only a two-minute recording of EEG data for each case.

Fig. 3. Head-mounted brainwave detecting instrument (BrainLink)

b. In the data storing stage, the EEG data store records in the EEG data files (.bdf files) and BSQ records in excel.
c. In the data analytics stage, AI unsupervised learning, k-means algorithm, is applied to analyze children's attention levels. K-means clustering is one of the simplest unsupervised machine learning algorithms. The algorithm classifies similar data points together and discover underlying patterns. To achieve this objective, K-means looks for a fixed number (k) of clusters in a dataset. We combine the EEG data and BSQ survey data for better parent-child understanding and interactions.
d. What follows is IBM SPSS Modeler for data analytics and visualization.

4   Result Analysis

A total of thirty children, aged 4–7 years old, start the trial of wearing EEG head band while their parents do the BSQ survey. Table 3 shows examples of BSQ questions, relationship with the child temperament, and the means for the BSG survey questions. The Likert scale, which falls under our definition of a survey scale, is a 7-point scale (1 = Never like this, 2 = rarely such, 3 = even so, 4 = sometimes like this, 5 = often like this, 6 = often this is, 7 = Always like this).

Table 3. Examples of Behavior Style Questionnaires

BSQ #	BSQ question	Child temperament	Mean
1	When a child takes a shower, he/she splashes the water and play it very lively	Activity amount	5.63
2	A child is very happy when he/she plays with other children	Mood nature	1.88
3	The sense of smell is sensitive, and the taste of a little bit of bad smell is quickly felt	Reaction threshold	2.63
4	A child feels shy when he/she meets strangers	Approaching (avoidance)	2.63
5	When doing something, for example, drawing, puzzling, modeling, etc., no matter how long it takes, he/she insist to finish it	Persistence	3.63
6	A child has regular stools every day	Regularity	3.00
7	Things that a child didn't like to eat before, he/she is willing to eat now	Adaptability	3.38

After parents fill in seventy-two BSQ questions, the responses are stored in Excel. We compile the BSQ responses with child temperament. Examples of results are shown in Fig. 4.

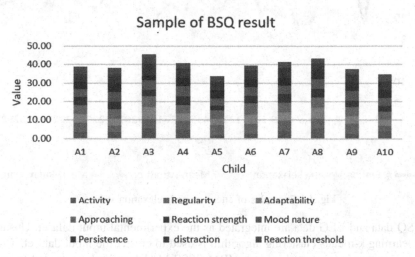

Fig. 4. Examples of results for BSQ questions

When parents fill in BSQ survey, young children wear EEG head band and play games. EEG, the spontaneous electrical activity, is recorded over a short period of time. The data are collected at a sampling frequency close to 1 kHz for every second with 512 EEG band data set collected. In our example, about 2 min, which gives a total of 61,440 EEG band data set collected in each sample. EEG produces brain band data set with attention and relaxation value. We pre-process the EEG band data set and employ the average of the EEG data set in each sample.

Figure 5 shows the attention and relaxation reference scale for the examples of EEG data. The horizontal axis refers to the child samples and the vertical axis represents the attention and relaxation reference scale. As shown in Fig. 5, the solid blue line represents the individual average attention reference scale, while the dotted gray line represents the group average attention reference scale. The solid red line represents the individual average relaxation reference scale, while the dotted orange line represents the group average relaxation reference scale. Between the individual average reference scale and the group average reference scale, the attention scale is lower than the relaxation reference scale.

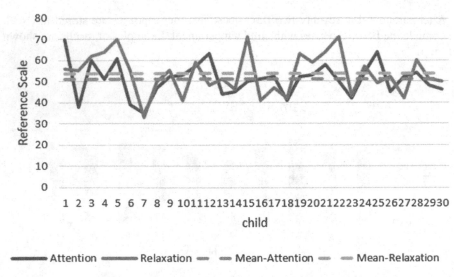

Fig. 5. Examples of attention and relaxation value

BSQ data and EEG data are integrated as the experimental input dataset. Unsupervised learning k-means clustering algorithm is used to cluster the input dataset. The k-means algorithm is computed using an IBM SPSS Modeler. We have trailed the clustering for 3-classes, 4-classes and 5-classes. However, the results for 4-classes seemed more suitable for the identification of attention and relaxation levels. The results for 4-classes are summarized in Table 4. The classification is done for 4 classes, including class-1, class-2, class-3, and class-4. Class-2, of ten children, shows lower attention and relaxation levels. Class-4, of two children, has the highest attention and relaxation levels.

Table 4. Classified subjects using k-means clustering for 4-classes

	Class -1	Class - 2	Class -3	Class -4
Size	46.7% (14)	33.3% (10)	13.3% (4)	6.7% (2)
Reaction strength	3.90	4.58	3.06	3.81
Approaching (avoidance)	3.84	4.76	5.50	6.19
Persistence	4.46	4.38	4.38	3.12
Reaction threshold	3.20	2.90	3.16	4.62
Activity amount	3.34	3.95	4.38	5.00
Regularity	4.28	4.34	5.69	4.19
Adaptability	4.52	4.97	5.41	5.19
Attention distraction	4.61	4.64	4.94	5.62
Mood nature	4.63	4.55	4.94	5.19
Attention	54.29	43.50	54.75	56.50
Relaxation	57.57	46.40	54.00	60.50

In the temperament data part, class-4 has the highest approaching, activity amount, attention distraction and mood nature. Class-2 has the lowest reaction threshold. The experimental results infer the consistency in the value of temperament with EEG classification, and a valid approach for classifying attention levels in specific time period.

5 Conclusions

This research proposes an NFT system which has been developed with the objective of predicting and analyzing children's attention levels. The combination of the parental subjective reports with EEG data has been demonstrated as a novel and valuable approach for resolving problems of child attention levels. Unsupervised machine learning k-means algorithm reveals to be a useful and effective technique for data cluster analysis. The experimental results that demonstrated the temperament activities, including reaction strength, approaching (avoidance), persistence, reaction threshold, activity amount, regularity, adaptability, attention distraction, and mood nature, can be identified and EEG data that classified the attention and relaxation value in specific time period can be asserted. The contribution of this paper is to find implicit clusters of children who might have hidden cognitive disorders. One of novelties of this research is its feature engineering, adopting NFT combined with BSQ. Another one is the discovery of clusters indicating consistency between these two features in terms of childrens' cognitive reactions. The discovery is practically valuable, because finding childrens' cognitive disorder in their early stage is very difficult.

For further research, we would like to extend the predicting and analyzing of the attention levels to preteens, i.e. children that are 8–11 years old. Most preteens show great gains in their cognitive development and mark a growth spurt—physically, emotionally, and mentally. They are in child developmental milestones. We are interested to observe not only attention levels, but also their creativity. Creativity is especially important for preteens because together with their mood, it facilitates their ability of expression. Moreover, creativity fosters mental growth in preteens by providing opportunities for new ways of thinking and problem-solving.

Acknowledgement. This research is supported by the Ministry of Education, Taiwan and Shih Chien University under grant USC-107-03-04010, USC-107-05-04006 and USC-108-08-04005.

References

1. Carey, W.B., McDevitt, S.C.: Revision of the infant temperament questionnaire. Pediatrics **61**(5), 735–739 (1978). https://doi.org/10.1037/t05932-000
2. Capsi, A., Silva, P.A.: Temperamental qualities at age three predict personality trait in young adulthood: longitudinal evidence from a birth cohort. Child Dev. **66**(2), 486–498 (1995). https://doi.org/10.2307/1131592

3. Cheng, S.-C., Cheng, Y.-P., Huang, C.-H., Huang, Y.-M.: Exploring the correlation between attention and cognitive load of students when attending different classes. In: Wu, T.-T., Huang, Y.-M., Shadicva, R., Lin, L., Starčič, A.I. (eds.) ICITL 2018. LNCS, vol. 11003, pp. 205–214. Springer, Cham (2018). https://doi.org/10.1007/978-3-319-99737-7_21
4. Clarivate Analytics, Essential Science Indicators. https://clarivate.com.tw/products/essential-science-indicators/
5. Desai, J.: Electroencephalography (EEG) Data Collection and Processing through Machine Learning, University of Arkansas, Theses and Dissertations (2014)
6. Felzer, T., Freisleben, B.: BRAINLINK: a software tool supporting the development of an EEG-based brain-computer interface. Proc. METMBS 2, 329–335 (2002)
7. Heilmeyer, F.A., Schirrmeister, R.T., Fiederer, L.D., Volker, M., Behncke, J., Ball, T.: A large-scale evaluation framework for EEG deep learning architectures. In: 2018 IEEE International Conference on Systems, Man, and Cybernetics (SMC), pp. 1039–1045. IEEE (2018). https://doi.org/10.1109/smc.2018.00185
8. Hegde, N.N., Nagananda, M.S., Harsha, M.: EEG signal classification using k-means and fuzzy c means clustering methods. Int. J. Sci. Technol. Eng. 2(1), 1–5 (2015)
9. Kanungo, T., Mount, D.M., Netanyahu, N.S., Piatko, C.D., Silverman, R., Wu, A.Y.: An efficient k-means clustering algorithm: analysis and implementation. IEEE Trans. Pattern Anal. Mach. Intell. 24(7), 881–892 (2002). https://doi.org/10.1109/TPAMI.2002.1017616
10. Mathewson, K.J., Miskovic, V., Schmidt, L.A.: Individual differences in temperament: definition, measurement, and outcomes. In: Ramachandran, V.S. (ed.) Encyclopedia of Human Behavior (Second Edn.), pp. 418–425. Academic Press, San Diego (2012). https://doi.org/10.1016/b978-0-12-375000-6.00203-2
11. Mahone, E.M., Schneider, H.E.: Assessment of attention in preschoolers. Neuropsychol. Rev. 22(4), 361–383 (2012). https://doi.org/10.1007/s11065-012-9217-y
12. Orhan, U., Hekim, M., Ozer, M.: EEG signals classification using the k-means clustering and a multilayer perceptron neural network model. Expert Syst. Appl. 38(10), 13475–13481 (2011). https://doi.org/10.1016/j.eswa.2011.04.149
13. Palfrey, J.S., Levine, M.D., Walker, D.K., Sullivan, M.D.: The emergence of attention deficits in early childhood: a prospective study. J. Dev. Behav. Pediatr. 6(6), 339–348 (1985). https://doi.org/10.1097/00004703-198512000-00004
14. Reed, M.A., Pien, D.L., Rothbart, M.K.: Inhibitory self-control in preschool children. Merrill-Palmer Q. 30(2), 131–147 (1984)
15. Rothbart, M.K., Bates, J.E.: Temperament. In: Damon, W., Lerner, R. (Series eds.) (eds.) Handbook of Child Psychology, vol. 3, Social, Emotional, and Personality Development, 6th edn., pp. 99–166. Wiley, New York (2006)
16. Singh, D., Reddy, C.K.: A survey on platforms for big data analytics. J. Big Data 2(1), 8 (2015). https://doi.org/10.1186/s40537-014-0008-6
17. Sonuga-Barke, E.J., Koerting, J., Smith, E., McCann, D.C., Thompson, M.: Early detection and intervention for attention-deficit/hyperactivity disorder. Expert Rev. Neurother. 11(4), 557–563 (2011). https://doi.org/10.1586/ern.11.39
18. Thomas, A., Chess, S.: Temperament and Development. Brunner/Mazel, New York (1977)
19. Wang, L.: Mu-ming Poo: China brain project and the future of Chinese neuroscience. Nat. Sci. Rev. 4(2), 258–263 (2017). https://doi.org/10.1093/nsr/nwx014
20. Wang, P.L. (ed.): Children's Temperament: Basic Characteristics and Social Composition. Psychological Publishing, Taiwan (2003)
21. Wang, P.L.: A literature review of child temperament research from 1980 to 2011. Res. Appl. Psychol. 61, 52–112 (2014)

22. Wilens, T.E., et al.: Psychiatric comorbidity and functioning in clinically referred preschool children and school-age youths with ADHD. J. Am. Acad. Child Adolesc. Psychiatry **41**(3), 262–268 (2002). https://doi.org/10.1097/00004583-200203000-00005
23. Zentner, M., Bates, J.E.: Child temperament: an integrative review of concepts, research programs, and measures. Int. J. Dev. Sci. **2**(1–2), 7–37 (2008). https://doi.org/10.3233/dev-2008-21203
24. Zhu, G., Li, Y., (Paul) Wen, P., Wang, S., Zhong, N.: Unsupervised classification of epileptic EEG signals with multi scale k-means algorithm. In: Imamura, K., Usui, S., Shirao, T., Kasamatsu, T., Schwabe, L., Zhong, N. (eds.) BHI 2013. LNCS (LNAI), vol. 8211, pp. 158–167. Springer, Cham (2013). https://doi.org/10.1007/978-3-319-02753-1_16

Finding Diachronic Objects of Drifting Descriptions by Similar Mentions

Katsuaki Tanaka[1]([⊠]) and Koichi Hori[2]

[1] Faculty of Human and Social Studies, Saitama Institute of Technology,
Fukaya, Japan
pkaw2019@katsuaki-tanaka.net
[2] School of Engineering, The University of Tokyo, Tokyo, Japan
hori@computer.org

Abstract. In this paper, we propose that document sets consist of two types, drift descriptions that record actions on diachronic objects that could be regarded as the same over time and diversity descriptions that record actions on different objects. This research finds diachronic objects to extract a document subset of drift descriptions. We assumed that a diachronic object would be mentioned similarly and have different time-distribution appearances. Consequently, we proposed a method to find words that represent diachronic objects by similar mentions and applied it to three different document sets. The results show that it is possible to extract document objects for drift descriptions.

Keywords: Time series documents · Word co-occurrence patterns · Knowledge and elapsed time

1 Introduction

Documents are used to record various things. Documents include descriptions about some actions that are performed on objects (an observation is also an action) by some subjects, and the number of documents has increased over time. As an example of descriptions in documents, consider a case where plants are observed and recorded in different documents over time. For example, some sentences from different documents such as "Hibiscus bloomed (A)," "The orchid's bud grew (B)," "The orchid bloomed (C)," and "Orchids are often epiphytes (D)" could be considered. Among (A), (B), (C), and (D), (A) and (B) describe different hibiscus and orchid plants and comprise a set of documents describing actions for different objects (Fig. 1). Hereinafter, the set is referred to as diversity description documents. In contrast, (B) and (C) describe orchids at different times and comprise a set of documents describing actions for objects that could be regarded as the same object (Fig. 2). Such an object is a diachronic object, and documents that describe a diachronic object are drift description documents. Note that (C) and (D) are both documents describing orchids, but (D) presents a constant fact regardless of time, so they are not actions at different

© Springer Nature Switzerland AG 2019
K. Ohara and Q. Bai (Eds.): PKAW 2019, LNAI 11669, pp. 32–43, 2019.
https://doi.org/10.1007/978-3-030-30639-7_4

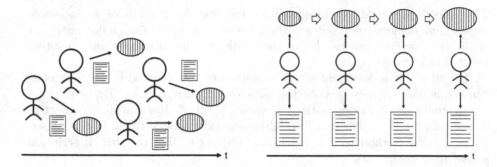

Fig. 1. Diversity description documents

Fig. 2. Drift description documents

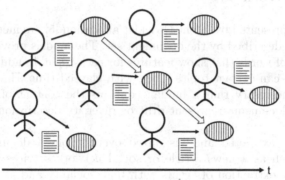

Fig. 3. General document set (The diversity and drift description types are mixed)

times. Therefore, the combination of (C) and (D) is a set of diversity description documents.

The passage of time can be read from drift description documents because they describe actions at different times on a diachronic object. In contrast, the passage of time cannot be read from diversity description documents because they describe actions on different objects; i.e., the diachronic object discussed in this paper plays the role of "something has not changed" as in "If something changed, it is essential that something has not changed." [11]

Next, consider an example of growing a new plant based on the knowledge obtained from documents written by observing plants. From diversity description documents, it is possible to know what kinds of plants exist and help to decide which plant to grow. From drift description documents, it is possible to obtain knowledge about how plants grow and help the plants grow over time.

Thus, the types of knowledge obtained from document sets of drift and diversity descriptions differ. Knowledge about diversity such as "what kinds of plants exist" could be obtained by using methods such as topic models. In contrast, knowledge about "how to solve a problem," such as "how to grow a plant," could be obtained by observing documents about the plants based on elapsed time.

This knowledge could be obtained by extracting descriptions of a diachronic object from documents. Besides, if the knowledge acquired from a document set of diversity descriptions can be applied while growing plants, a novel planting method can be developed.

In general, in a document set, documents are not recorded under clear classifications whether they describe the same object such as "(A), (B), or (C)," or are diversity and drift descriptions as shown in Fig. 3. If a diachronic object in documents can be specified, drift descriptions exist around them. In this paper, we propose a method to find diachronic objects to find the drift description subset from documents.

2   Related Work

Topic models represented by latent Dirichlet allocation [5] are methods of grasping the contents described by the document set. The models provide a probability distribution of words that show features for each topic. In addition, dynamic topic models [4] can extract topics along with elapsed time. However, in these methods, it is necessary that a human confirms the content of each topic to judge whether documents represent drift or diversity descriptions with similar features.

Studies have extracted and visualized events from a document set with elapsed time such as a news article or social network services [15]. However, it deals with the extraction of events with high sociality and assumes that the users of the research results have common knowledge of the events in the document set.

Concept drift is a research issue in machine learning that handles changes in the meaning of data over time. For example, studies have investigated handling words that appear in tweets and switching between calculation methods of appearance probability to separate stationary words that do not change along with time and bursty words that have significant changes in a short time [12]. There are also studies tracking semantic changes in vocabulary over decades using semantic networks between words [8], performing named entity recognition over long periods [3].

Anaphora resolution is resolving what a pronoun refers to for an object in a discourse as one document. Centering theory [6] is one of the major methods of resolving anaphora. There have been many studies of anaphora resolution [13].

3   Finding Diachronic Objects

3.1   Overview

In drift description documents (Fig. 2), it is difficult for readers of documents to recognize a diachronic object that has existed in older documents if the expressions that mention the object are significantly different. Therefore, diachronic objects would have similar mentions in other documents (Fig. 4). In contrast,

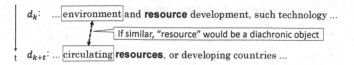

Fig. 4. Example of mentions of a diachronic object

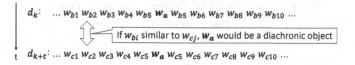

Fig. 5. Mentions of a diachronic object

in diversity description documents (Fig. 1), it is not necessary to be aware of whether the object has been described previously. Therefore, even if the same object has been mentioned in diversity descriptions, whether the mentions are similar is unclear.

Because diachronic objects would have similar mentions, we propose a method to find a diachronic object using a similar mention ratio (SMR). In this paper, it is assumed that each object is expressed by one word. Furthermore, mentions of an object are the words co-occurring with it (Fig. 5). The higher similarity of co-occurring words for an object would indicate that it is diachronic. As mentioned, documents containing a diachronic object are a document set of drift descriptions.

3.2   Similar Mention Ratio

SMR is calculated as follows. Select a word w_a as a target. Let $w_{bi}(i = 1, \ldots, m)$ be words co-occurring with w_a in a document. For a given w_{bi}, let $w_{cj}(j = 1, \ldots, n)$ be words co-occurring with w_a in another document at different times from w_{bi}. Find the maximum similarity of w_{bi} and all w_{cj}, and the average of them is the SMR of w_a.

$$\text{SMR}(w_a) = \frac{\sum_{i=1}^{m} (\max \{\text{sim}(w_{bi}, w_{cj}) \ ; \ j \in 1, \ldots, n\})}{m} \tag{1}$$

w_a co-occurring with w_b means that w_a and w_b are within five words. To check w_c and w_b co-occurring with w_a at different times in chronological order, the following procedure was used. First, based on creation times of all documents where w_a and w_b co-occur, its second and third quartile ranges are defined. Then, based on creation times of all the documents where w_a and w_c co-occur, its second and third quartile ranges are defined. If there was no overlap between the two ranges, w_b and w_c are judged to be words appearing at different times.

In this paper, we used documents written in Japanese as experimental targets. We used nouns that were acquired from documents with the Japanese morphological analysis engine MeCab [9].

Table 1. Target document sets

Records of the Global Environment Committee (D_e)	
Period	Feb 16, 2001 – Oct 24, 2012
Documents	5,910 (remarks)
Different words	12,991
Records of CubeSat XI-IV Design/Operation (D_c)	
Period	Jan 5, 2000 – Dec 12, 2002
Documents	580
Different words	7,879
Tweets Containing "artificial intelligence" (D_t)	
Period	Dec 25, 2013 – Jun 6, 2014
Documents	43,862 (one-third of collected tweets)
Different words	22,251

The similarity between words was calculated by cosine similarity using word vector representation if the words were different.

$$
\text{sim}(w_b, w_c) = \begin{cases} 0 & (w_b = w_c) \\[2mm] \dfrac{\overrightarrow{w_b} \cdot \overrightarrow{w_c}}{|\overrightarrow{w_b}||\overrightarrow{w_c}|} & (w_b \neq w_c) \end{cases}
\tag{2}
$$

The word vector representation $\overrightarrow{w}$ for w was obtained from the 300-dimensional vector model of the Wikipedia Entity Vectors [2]. It is a pre-trained model with word2vec [10] based on a skip-gram algorithm using the Japanese version of Wikipedia texts as the corpus.

Words that existed in the experiment target document sets but are not in the Wikipedia Entity Vectors were excluded from the calculation of SMR. There is a study that uses the ratio of w_{bi} that satisfies $\text{sim}(w_{bi}, w_{cj}) \geq 0.5$ for each w_a instead of the $\text{SMR}(w_a)$ to find diachronic objects [14].

4   Experiments

4.1   Target Document Sets

The proposed method was applied to the three document sets shown in Table 1. All documents were written in Japanese. The first document set comprises records of the Global Environment Committee, Central Environment Council, and Ministry of Environment, Japan [1] (hereinafter called D_e). The set contains discussions of climate change. The minutes are composed of date and time, attendance members, proceedings, list of handouts, and records of remarks, and are described in almost the same form every meeting. The same committee members attend meetings each time, and outside guests often attend to give presentations on topics. The proceeding of each meeting is in the form of guests' presentations and the committee members asking questions and discussing the contents of the presentations. Because the contents of a meeting are described in the records of remarks, only the remarks part was the subject of calculating SMR. The purpose of each remark was considered different, and one remark was regarded as one document, of which there were 5910 remarks obtained from 83 min.

The second document set consists of documents of a small satellite design and operation project, CubeSat XI-IV, which was performed at Nakasuka Laboratory, Graduate School of Engineering, the University of Tokyo (hereinafter D_c). Documents comprised meeting records, records of experiments, and guidelines of the project. The project was divided into sections for each satellite function and minutes were created by each team. Therefore, although the date, title, and document creator's name are described in a unified format in each proceeding, the meeting contents are described slightly differently.

The third document set comprised tweets containing "artificial intelligence" collected from Twitter from December 2013 to June 2014 (hereinafter called D_t). During this time, the cover of the Magazine of Artificial Intelligence published in January 2014 became a trending topic and many related tweets were sent. We processed about one-third of all the collected tweets and removed retweets and URLs.

4.2   Results

Tables 2, 3, and 4 show the top 10 words of SMR and the top 10 words of word appearance ratio for comparison. Word appearance ratio was calculated by dividing the frequency of the word by the frequency of all words in each document set.

Words classified as adjective nouns (e.g., make adverbs with "...ly") and action nouns (e.g., make sense with "do ...") by the morphological analyzer were excluded from the results because they are unlikely to be an object in documents. rel_i is described in Sect. 5.3.

5   Evaluation and Analysis

5.1   Distribution of Word Similarity

First, we checked how often there are similar mentions of words. For each word $w_{bi}(i = 1, \ldots, m)$ co-occurring with w_a, we graphed the distribution of the maximum value of similarity with word $w_{cj}(j = 1, \ldots, n)$ co-occurring with w_a at a different time from w_{bi} (Fig. 6). Figure 6 (a) and (b) show that "law" had more similar mentions than "member" in D_e.

Figure 6(d) shows the distribution of mentions of similarities of "DeepMind" in D_t that was acquired by Google during the tweet collection period. Compared with "human" in Fig. 6(c), there were many mentions with low similarity.

Table 2. Top 10 words of D_e

	Similar mention			Appearance		
	Word	Ratio	rel_i	Word	Ratio	rel_i
1	law	0.5969	3	member	0.0101	0
2	overseas	0.5916	3	environment	0.0095	2
3	rule	0.5910	3	energy	0.0088	2
4	air	0.5908	2	Japan	0.0073	3
5	resource	0.5899	2	handout	0.0072	0
6	purpose	0.5897	1	target	0.0065	2
7	efficiency	0.5895	2	Earth	0.0047	2
8	condition	0.5886	0	technology	0.0047	2
9	home	0.5883	3	committee	0.0044	0
10	public	0.5883	3	system	0.0044	2

Table 3. Top 10 words of D_c

	Similar mention			Appearance		
	Word	Ratio	rel_i	Word	Ratio	rel_i
1	heat	0.5733	3	XI	0.0095	3
2	structure	0.5726	1	power supply	0.0090	0
3	other	0.5653	0	antenna	0.0082	3
4	CUBE	0.5642	3	month	0.0077	0
5	method	0.5633	0	substrate	0.0072	3
6	cycle	0.5628	2	data	0.0067	2
7	clean room	0.5627	3	voltage	0.0062	1
8	board	0.5625	3	solar cell	0.0061	3
9	image	0.5619	3	temperature	0.0060	2
10	vacuum	0.5613	2	ground	0.0058	2

Table 4. Top 10 words of D_t

	Similar mention			Appearance		
	Word	Ratio	rel_i	Word	Ratio	rel_i
1	human	0.5850	2	AI	0.0684	1
2	robot	0.5830	0	front cover	0.0375	2
3	myself	0.5801	1	JSAI[a]	0.0320	0
4	man/woman	0.5776	1	woman	0.0309	0
5	base	0.5741	0	robot	0.0292	0
6	society	0.5726	0	man	0.0225	0
7	form	0.5719	1	housework	0.0220	0
8	machinery	0.5708	1	feeling	0.0218	0
9	(academic) society	0.5705	3	summary	0.0214	0
10	mankind	0.5701	1	NAVER	0.0201	0

[a]The Japanese Society for Artificial Intelligence

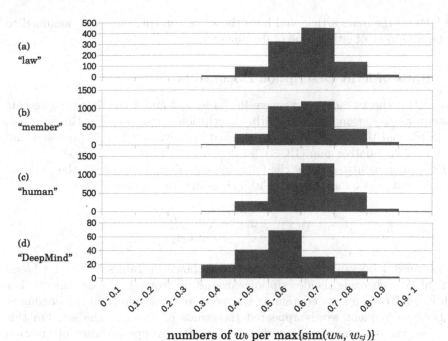

numbers of w_b per max{sim(w_{bi}, w_{cj})}

Fig. 6. Histograms of numbers of w_b per max{sim(w_{bi}, w_{cj})}, (a) w_a= "law" in D_e, (b) w_a= "member" in D_e, (c) w_a= "human" in D_t, (d) w_a= "DeepMind" in D_t

5.2   Appearance of the Words

In this section, we check the mentions in the document sets for some words in Tables 2, 3 and 4. For example, "Law" in D_e was mentioned slightly differently over time in the treatment of laws, such as "enforcement of the law," "applicability of the law," and "law system (legal system)."

"(Academic) society" was a diachronic object that indicated drift descriptions such as "we wondered if it is appropriate for a cover of the society's magazine," "an official opinion of the society on the cover of the magazine," and "the special feature of the society's magazine is good."

There were words that represented some diachronic objects with other words. For example, "air" in D_e was used such as "air pollution" and "concentration of carbon dioxide in the air." "Human" in D_t has various meanings such as "human shape" and "human consciousness."

There were also words that represented the operation of meetings in the document. For example, "member," "handout," "Earth," "committee" in D_e, and "month" ("月," Japanese counter word for each month) in D_c. We assumed that these are not objects of diversity or drift description documents.

The words following "JSAI" in Table 4 were acquired from the tweets that indicated the same news article title. Because the tweets contain only the title and URL of the news article and have the same content, they were assumed to not be an object of either type of document set.

5.3   Ratio of Drift Description Documents

This section checks each word shown in Tables 2, 3 and 4 whether it represents a diachronic object and indicates drift description documents. For this purpose, the words and their mentions were checked and evaluated with precision and discounted cumulative gain (DCG)[7].

DCG was calculated using the following equation. k represents the range to be evaluated, and we adopted $k = 10$. rel_i is the ith relevance score.

$$\mathrm{DCG}_k = rel_1 + \sum_{i=2}^{k} \frac{rel_i}{\log_2 i} \tag{3}$$

We assigned a relevance score to each word shown in Tables 2, 3 and 4 based on Table 5 by checking the descriptions around the words in the documents. For each word, 20 documents containing the word were selected from the document set because frequent words appeared thousands of times in the set. On this selection, the document set was divided into five groups in order of creation time, and four documents were selected from each group because a diachronic object appears over time, as shown in Fig. 3.

A word with a relevance score of one or more could be used as a key for searching drift description documents. Therefore, we calculated the precision of ratio words with $rel_i \geq 1$. Table 6 shows the precision and DCG for the top 10 words obtained by the SMR and word appearance ratio from each document set.

DCG_{10} is larger for SMR than for word appearance ratio in all document sets. However, in D_c, the precision value is the same, and the difference between the values of DCG_{10} is also small. One reason for these results is that the design of a small satellite was discussed in D_c, and a large number of words representing specific things such as parts of the satellite were diachronic objects. Another reason is that words such as method do not have a concrete meaning and they have fewer changes in usage in the sentences used in the document.

The difference in precision scores is large with D_t. This difference is because there were many tweets with the same contents showing the title of the same news article, and we assumed that they were not drift or diversity descriptions, as explained in Sect. 5.2.

6   Discussion

In the proposed method, we assumed that a word whose co-occurring words are similar at different times in different documents indicates a diachronic object in a document set of drift descriptions. However, even in a document set of diversity descriptions, similar mentions might exist for the same object at different times. Figure 7 shows the distribution of document sets according to the similarity of

Table 5. Policy of relevance scoring

Score	Description
3	Drift description documents
2	Word w_a means multiple objects, more than two groups of drift description documents
1	Word w_a means multiple objects, one group of drift and some diversity description documents
0	Diversity description documents or word is not an object

Table 6. Precision (P) and DCG_{10} of each document set

	D_e		D_c		D_t	
Method	P	DCG_{10}	P	DCG_{10}	P	DCG_{10}
SMR	0.9	12.70	0.8	9.891	0.7	5.068
Word Appearance	0.7	7.517	0.8	9.548	0.2	3.000

co-occurring words and elapsing time of documents. The distribution of drift and diversity description documents overlaps. By distinguishing this overlap of documents, diachronic objects and drift descriptions can be found with higher accuracy than by using the SMR proposed in this paper.

We assumed that an object is represented by a word in this paper, but the same word may be used with different meanings. It is possible to cope with this situation using an n-gram.

To evaluate the experimental results, we compared the word appearance ratio (frequency of the word divided by the frequency of all words) in document sets with SMR. The words w_b and w_c that co-occur in different documents with the word w_a are connected via the word w_a when the co-occurrence relation between

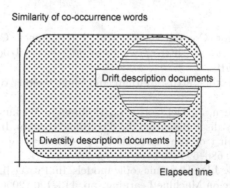

Fig. 7. Distribution of drift and diversity description documents

the words is considered a network. As a result, future research will compare the mediation centrality of w_a against SMR.

We used the vector representation of words from the Wikipedia Entity Vectors based on the text of Japanese Wikipedia to calculate similarities between words. Therefore, words that were included in the target document set but not included in the Wikipedia Entity Vectors were excluded from the similarity calculation. By obtaining a vector representation from the document set itself, similarity calculations can be performed for all the words in the document. However, because the word co-occurrence relation is used when obtaining the vector representation with word2vec, it is necessary to evaluate whether the SMR conflicts with co-occurring words used in the similarity calculation.

7   Conclusions

In this paper, we discussed two types of document sets, i.e., drift description documents, which describe actions on a diachronic object over time and diversity description documents, which describe actions on various objects.

Next, we proposed the SMR, which indicates words with similar but not the same co-occurring words at different times with the assumption that a diachronic object in drift description documents has similar mentions. We applied the SMR to three document sets with different contents and formats and evaluated the results. The results show that it is possible to find a subset of drift description documents from the document sets with the SMR results.

Based on the points described in the discussion, future work will compare the nature of the document set and the methods for extracting diachronic objects and clarify the difference in the knowledge obtained from drift description documents and diversity description documents.

Acknowledgment. This work was supported by JSPS KAKENHI Grant Number JP16K00702.

References

1. Global Environment Committee, Central Environment Council, Ministry of the Environment, Japan. https://www.env.go.jp/council/06earth/yoshi06.html. Accessed 25 Feb 2019
2. Wikipedia entity vectors. https://github.com/singletongue/WikiEntVec. Accessed 25 Feb 2019
3. Agarwal, P., Strötgen, J., Del Corro, L., Hoffart, J., Weikum, G.: Dianed: time-aware named entity disambiguation for diachronic corpora. In: Proceedings of the 56th Annual Meeting of the Association for Computational Linguistics (Short Papers), vol. 2, pp. 686–693 (2018)
4. Blei, D.M., Lafferty, J.D.: Dynamic topic models. In: Proceedings of the 23rd International Conference on Machine Learning, pp. 113–120 (2006)
5. Blei, D.M., Ng, A.Y., Jordan, M.I.: Latent dirichlet allocation. J. Mach. Learn. Res. **3**, 993–1002 (2003)

6. Grosz, B.J., Joshi, A.K., Weinstein, S.: Providing a unified account of definite noun phrases in discourse. In: 21st Annual Meeting of the Association for Computational Linguistics (1983)
7. Järvelin, K., Kekäläinen, J.: Cumulated gain-based evaluation of IR techniques. ACM Trans. Inf. Syst. **20**(4), 422–446 (2002)
8. Kenter, T., Wevers, M., Huijnen, P., De Rijke, M.: Ad hoc monitoring of vocabulary shifts over time. In: Proceedings of the 24th ACM International on Conference on Information and Knowledge Management, pp. 1191–1200 (2015)
9. Kudo, T.: Mecab: Yet another part-of-speech and morphological analyzer. http://taku910.github.io/mecab/. Accessed 25 Feb 2019
10. Mikolov, T., Chen, K., Corrado, G., Dean, J.: Efficient estimation of word representations in vector space. In: 2013 Proceedings of International Conference on Learning Representations (2013)
11. Mizoguchi, R.: Theory and Practice of Ontology Engineering. Ohmsha, Tokyo (2012)
12. Nishida, K., Hoshide, T., Fujimura, K.: Improving tweet stream classification by detecting changes in word probability. In: Proceedings of the 35th International ACM SIGIR Conference on Research and Development in Information Retrieval, pp. 971–980 (2012)
13. Poesio, M., Stuckardt, R., Versley, Y. (eds.): Anaphora Resolution: Algorithms, Resources, and Applications. TANLP. Springer, Heidelberg (2016). https://doi.org/10.1007/978-3-662-47909-4
14. Tanaka, K.: Extract object of changes from documents using similarities of co-occurrence word and its time distribution. In: Proceedings of the 33rd Annual Conference of the Japanese Society for Artificial Intelligence (2019)
15. Wanner, F., Stoffel, A., Jäckle, D., Kwon, B.C., Weiler, A., Keim, D.A.: State-of-the-art report of visual analysis for event detection in text data streams. In: EuroVis - STARs, pp. 125–139 (2014)

A Max-Min Conflict Algorithm
for the Stable Marriage Problem

Hoang Huu Viet[1], Nguyen Thi Uyen[1], Pham Tra My[1], Son Thanh Cao[1],
and Le Hong Trang[2(✉)]

[1] School of Engineering and Technology, Vinh University, Vinh City, Vietnam
{viethh,uyennt,mypt,sonct}@vinhuni.edu.vn
[2] Faculty of Computer Science and Engineering,
Ho Chi Minh City University of Technology, VNU-HCM, Ho Chi Minh City, Vietnam
lhtrang@hcmut.edu.vn

Abstract. In this paper we present a max-min conflict algorithm to find
a stable matching rather than the man- and woman-optimal matchings
for the stable marriage problem. We solve the problem in terms of a
constraint satisfaction problem, i.e. find a complete assignment for men
in which every man is assigned to a woman so that the assignment does
not contain any blocking pairs. To do this, we apply a local search method
in which a max-conflict heuristic is used to choose the man making the
maximum number of blocking pairs in a matching, while a min-conflict
heuristic is used to remove all the blocking pairs formed by the chosen
man. Experiments showed that our algorithm is efficient for finding a
stable matching of large stable marriage problems.

Keywords: Constraint satisfaction problem · Local search ·
Max-min-conflicts · Stable marriage problem

1 Introduction

The stable marriage (SM) problem, introduced by Gale and Shapley [6] in 1962,
is a well-known problem of matching an equal number men and women to satisfy
a certain criterion of stability. Recently, this problem has been attracting much
attention from the research community due to its important role in a wide range
of applications such as the Evolution of the Labor Market for Medical Interns
and Residents [15], the Student-Project Allocation problem (SPA)[1] and the
Stable Roommates problem (SR) [5,11].

An SM instance of size n consists of a set of n men and a set of n women
in which each person ranks all members of the other set in a strict order of
preference. A matching M is a set of n disjoint pairs of men and women. If a
man m and a woman w are a pair $(m, w) \in M$, we say that m and w are partners
in M, denoted by $m = M(w)$ and $w = M(m)$. If m prefers w to $M(m)$ and w
prefers m to $M(w)$, then we say that m and w form a *blocking pair* in M. A

© Springer Nature Switzerland AG 2019
K. Ohara and Q. Bai (Eds.): PKAW 2019, LNAI 11669, pp. 44–53, 2019.
https://doi.org/10.1007/978-3-030-30639-7_5

matching M is said to be *stable* if it has no any blocking pairs, otherwise it is said to be *unstable*.

Gale and Shapley showed that there exists at least one stable matching for every instance of SM and proposed an algorithm, called Gale-Shapley algorithm, to find a stable matching of SM instances of size n in time $O(n^2)$ [6]. This algorithm is a sequence of proposals either from the men to the women or from the women to the men. In the former case, it finds the so-called *man-optimal* stable matching, in which each man has the best partner, but each woman has the worst partner compared to their partners in any other stable matchings. In the latter case, it finds the *woman-optimal* stable matching, in which the men's and women's properties are interchanged. For some SM instances, there may be many other stable matchings between the *man-* and *woman-optimal* stable matchings. Moreover, the *man-* (respectively *woman-*) *optimal* stable matching is the "*selfish*" matching for the men (respectively women), i.e. the proposers always get their best partners but the responders get their worst partners. Therefore, it is appropriate to seek other optimal stable matchings to give a more balanced preference for both the men and women.

In this paper, we present a max-min conflict algorithm to seek a stable matching rather than the man- and woman-optimal matchings of SM instances. The algorithm starts from a random matching and tries to search a better one by mean of reducing the number of blocking pairs. At each search step, the algorithm chooses a man making the maximum number of blocking pairs and a woman in blocking pairs formed by the man such that her rank is minimum in the chosen man's preference list. To avoid getting stuck in a local optimum, the algorithm also chooses a random woman in blocking pairs formed by the chosen man in a small probability. Then, the algorithm removes the blocking pair formed by the man and the woman in the matching and repeats for the matching until the matching is stable. The experiments show that our approach is efficient in terms of computational time for large SM problems.

The rest of this paper is organized as follows: Sect. 2 describes the related work, Sect. 3 presents the proposed algorithm, Sect. 4 discusses the experiments and evaluations, and Sect. 5 concludes our work.

2   Related Work

In the last few years, there were several approaches to find a stable matching rather than the man- and woman- optimal matchings. Nakamura et al. proposed a genetic algorithm (GA) for finding the *sex-fair* matching of SM instances [14]. In their approach, the problem is first transferred into a directed graph and the GA is used to find the solution in the graph. Vien et al. applied the ant colony system (ACS) algorithm [3] for finding the *man-optimal, woman-optimal, egalitarian* and *sex-equal* stable matchings of SM instances [16]. Unfortunately, the ACS algorithm finds the matching under a given criterion only for small SM instances because it has to find n^2 pairs (man, woman) to form a stable matching. Zavidovique et al. [18] presented three zigzag algorithms, named ZZ,

OZ and BZ, to find matchings that meet three criteria of stability, sex equality and egalitarian. In $O(n^2)$ time, the ZZ algorithm finds the egalitarian, while the OZ algorithm finds both the egalitarian and sex equality, but they are not guaranteed that they will find stable matchings. In $O(n^3)$ time, the BZ algorithm is designed to meet all three criteria rather than the egalitarian or sex-equal matching. Everaere et al. [4] proposed a Swing algorithm for finding the sex-equal matching of SM instances, in which the men and women alternatively play the role of proposers and responders in iterations. When the Swing stops, it takes $O(n^3)$ time to obtain a stable matching other than the sex-equal matching. Giannakopoulos et al. [10] provided an ESMA algorithm [10] which the idea is similar to that of Swing. However, in the ESMA the proposers are men when the sign of the function $sin(k^2)$ is positive and women when the sign of the function is negative, where k is the iteration counter of the algorithm.

Recently, a local search approach has been applied to deal with the SM problem. Gelain et al. [7] proposed three local search algorithms, named SML, SML1 and SML2, for finding an arbitrary stable matching of SM instances. Starting at a randomly generated matching, M, these algorithms produce a set of the neighbor matchings of M, where a neighbor is determined by removing one of the blocking pairs in M, and moves M to the neighbor matching which has the smallest number of blocking pairs. This process iteratively performs until the stability in M is obtained. Viet et al. [17] developed an empirical local search algorithm for finding an approximation solution in terms of the egalitarian or sex-equal matching. This algorithm uses the breakmarriage operation [12] to find all the stable neighbor matchings of the current stable matching and then move the current matching to the best matching in the stable neighbor matchings. Besides, Gent et al. [8] proposed two algorithms to formulate an SM instance to a constraint satisfaction problem. Codognet and Diaz proposed a generic, domain-independent local search method, called adaptive search (AS), for solving constraint satisfaction problems [2]. Accordingly, Gent et al. [9] and Munera et al. [13] proposed local search algorithms to deal with the stable marriage problem with ties and incomplete lists, a variant of the SM problem, based on constraint satisfaction problems.

3   Max-Min Conflict Algorithm

In this section, we propose a max-min conflict algorithm, so called MMC, to find a stable matching for the SM problem. Our approach is based on a local search method for solving a constraint satisfaction problem, in which men are considered as variables, women are considered as the domain of each variable and constraints are that there exists no blocking pair in matchings. According to this approach, a stable matching is a complete assignment in which every variable is assigned to a value so that the matching does not violate constraints. To find a stable matching, our search strategy is that at each search step we choose the most constrained variable, i.e. a man making the maximum number of blocking pairs, and select the least constrained value, i.e. a woman having the

---

Algorithm 1. *Max-Min Conflict Algorithm*

    Input   : An SM instance of size n,

                    max_iters, the maximum number of iterations.

    Output: M, a stable matching.

1. $M :=$ a randomly generated matching;
2. $iter := 1$;
3. **while** *(iter $\leq$ max_iters)* **do**
4.   **if** *(there exists no blocking pair in M)* **then**
5. | break;
6.   **end**
7. $X := \{(m,w) \mid (m,w)$ is a blocking pair in $M\}$;
8. $error(m) :=$ counting the number of man m appearing in X;
9. $Y := \{(m',w') \in X \mid m' = \mathrm{argmax}(error(i)), i = 1, 2, \cdots, n\}$;
10.   **if** *(a small probability of p)* **then**
11. | $w'' :=$ a random woman $w' \in Y$;
12.   **else**
13. | $w'' := \mathrm{argmin}(mr(m',w'))$, where $(m',w') \in Y$;
14.   **end**
15. $M :=$ removing the bloking pair $(m', w'') \in M$;
16. $iter = iter + 1$;
17. **end**
18. **return** M;

---

minimum rank in the chosen man's preference list. This is because that choosing the most constrained variable is able to remove the largest number of blocking pairs, while selecting the least constrained value of the chosen variable removes all the blocking pairs formed by the chosen man and therefore, our algorithm accelerates the search of a stable matching.

We let $mr(m,w)$ denote the rank of a woman, w, in a man m's preference list. For a man, m, we define an error function, $error(m)$, to be the number of blocking pairs formed by m in a matching M. Our MMC algorithm is shown in Algorithm 1. Starting from a randomly generated matching, M, the algorithm performs as follows. First, the algorithm checks if there exists no blocking pair in M, meaning that M is stable, then it returns the matching M. Otherwise, the algorithm determines all the blocking pairs $(m,w) \in M$ (line 7) and finds a man, m', making the maximum number of blocking pairs in M, i.e., the man has the maximum number of conflicts in terms of blocking pairs (line 9). If a small probability of p is accepted, the algorithm chooses a random woman, w'', who is making a blocking pair with m'. Otherwise, the algorithm chooses a woman, w'', to whom man m' most prefers in the set of the women making blocking pairs with m'. Then, the algorithm removes the blocking pair (m', w'') by mean of replacing two pairs of $(m', M(m'))$ and $(M(w''), w'')$ by two pairs of (m', w'') and $(M(w''), M(m'))$ in M. The algorithm repeats until either the matching M has no blocking pairs or a maximum number of iterations is reached.

Table 1. Preference lists of eight men and eight women

Man	Preference list	Woman	Preference list
m_1	4 7 3 8 1 5 2 6	w_1	1 3 5 4 2 6 8 7
m_2	5 3 4 2 1 8 6 7	w_2	8 2 4 5 3 7 1 6
m_3	3 8 2 4 6 7 5 1	w_3	5 8 1 4 2 3 6 7
m_4	5 6 8 3 4 7 1 2	w_4	2 4 3 6 5 8 1 7
m_5	1 3 5 2 8 6 4 7	w_5	6 5 4 8 1 7 2 3
m_6	8 6 2 5 1 7 4 3	w_6	7 4 2 5 6 8 1 3
m_7	2 5 8 3 6 4 7 1	w_7	3 8 6 5 7 2 1 4
m_8	5 7 4 1 6 2 8 3	w_8	4 7 1 3 5 8 2 6

Considering an SM instance consists of eight men and eight women with their preference lists given in Table 1. Suppose that given a probability $p = 0$ and a random matching $M = \{(1,3), (2,1), (3,2), (4,8), (5,7), (6,4), (7,5), (8,6)\}$, the algorithm runs as follows. Because the matching M is unstable, the algorithm continues to find all the blocking pairs in M: $X = \{(2,2), (2,4), (4,5), (4,6), (5,1), (5,2), (5,3), (5,5), (5,6), (6,5), (6,6), (6,7), (8,5), (8,7)\}$ (the number of blocking pairs in M is 14). Then, it counts the number of blocking pairs in M, i.e. $error(m)$, formed by man m, that is $error(2) = 2$, $error(4) = 2$, $error(5) = 5$, $error(6) = 3$, $error(8) = 2$. Next, the algorithm takes the set of blocking pairs $Y = \{(5,1), (5,2), (5,3), (5,5), (5,6)\}$ corresponding to the man, $m = 5$, who is making the maximum number of blocking pairs. Because man $m = 5$ most prefers woman $w = 1$ to the other women in his blocking pairs, the algorithm removes the blocking pair $(5,1)$ in M by replacing two pairs of $(5,7)$ and $(2,1)$ by two pairs of $(5,1)$ and $(2,7)$ in M to obtain the matching $M = \{(1,3), (2,7), (3,2), (4,8), (5,1), (6,4), (7,5), (8,6)\}$. Because the number of blocking pairs in M is 10, i.e. not zero, the algorithm continues repeating until the stability of M is obtained. Specifically, after four iterations, the algorithm terminates and gives a matching $M = \{(1,3), (2,4), (3,2), (4,5), (5,1), (6,6), (7,8), (8,7)\}$, which is a stable matching.

4 Experiments

In this section we presents the experiments implemented by Matlab software on a Core i7-8550U CPU 1.8 GHz computer with 16 GB RAM. To evaluate the performance of our algorithm, we randomly produced 100 SM instances of 10 difference sizes from 20 to 200 with step 20 and 10 variants per size.

First, we ran experiments to determine the best value of probability p for the SM instances of size n, where $n = 20, 40, 60, 80$ and 100. Figure 1 shows our experimental results. For the SM instances of size 40, the average number of iterations to find stable matchings is highest when $p = 0$. For the SM instances of the other sizes, the average number of iterations to find stable matchings when

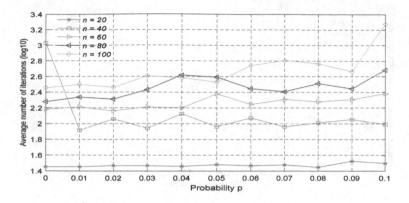

Fig. 1. The average number of iterations found by MMC algorithm with probability p

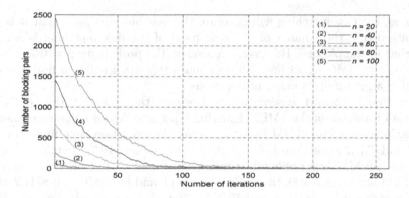

Fig. 2. The number of blocking pairs found in iterations of MMC algorithm

$p = 0$ is almost the same as that when $p = 0.02$. Therefore, we choose $p = 0.02$ to be the best value in our experiments.

Second, we performed experiments to consider the behavior of the max-min conflict heuristics. To do this, we considered the variation of the number blocking pairs of matchings in iterations of MMC algorithm. Figure 2 shows experimental results for the sizes of SM instances consisting of $n = 20, 40, 60, 80$ and 100. Specifically, to find a stable matching, MMC needs 32 iterations for $n = 20$, 132 iterations for $n = 40$, and 252 iterations for $n = 100$. It is easy to see that for an SM instance of size n, the number of pairs (man, woman) is n^2, therefore when the sizes of SM instances increases from 20 to 100, the number of pairs (man, woman) increases from 400 to 10000. However, for MMC, the number of iterations increases only from 32 to 252, i.e. MMC is efficient for large SM instances. Figure 2 also shows that the number of blocking pairs found by MMC algorithm does not monotonically decrease, i.e. there exist local minimum values. This is because when removing a blocking pair in a matching to obtain a new

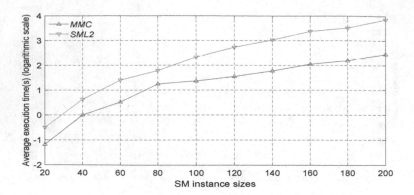

Fig. 3. The average execution time (sec.) of MMC algorithm

matching, the new matching will generate the new blocking pairs that it is not guaranteed that the number of blocking pairs of the new matching is smaller than that of the old one. However, even when the probability $p = 0$ as shown in Fig. 1, our MMC algorithm also overcomes this weak point to find a stable matching after a finite number of iterations.

Next, we performed experiments to compare the execution time of MMC algorithm with that of the SML2 algorithm [7]. Figure 3 shows the experimental results. When the size of SM instances is 20, the execution time found by the MMC and SML2 algorithms is about $10^{-1.15} \approx 0.07$ and $10^{-0.5} \approx 0.31$ s, respectively, i.e. our MMC runs about 4.5 times faster than SML2 algorithm. When the size of SM instances is 100, the execution time found by MMC and SML2 algorithm is about $10^{1.35} \approx 22.38$ and $10^{2.30} \approx 199.52$ s, respectively, i.e. our MMC runs about 9 times faster than SML2 algorithm. Especially, when the size of SM instances is 200, the execution time found by our MMC is about $10^{2.42} \approx 263.02$ s, but the execution time found by SML2 algorithm is about $10^{3.9} \approx 7943.30$ s, i.e. our MMC runs about 30 times faster than SML2 algorithm. This means that the larger SM instances is, the faster MMC runs compared to SML2 algorithm. The experimental results are explained as follows. At each iteration, SML2 keeps at least n neighbor matchings and for each neighbor matching, it has to take $O(n^2)$ time to determine the number of blocking pairs. This means that at each iteration, SML2 has to take $O(n^3)$ time to find the best matching in the neighbor matchings. Meanwhile, our MMC algorithm keeps only one neighbor matching to determine the number of blocking pairs, i.e. MMC needs only $O(n^2)$ time for each iteration and therefore, our MMC algorithm runs much faster than SML2 algorithm, especially for large SM problems.

It should be noted that in the MMC algorithm, the roles of men and women can be interchanged at iterations as in [4,10]. This means that the max-min conflict heuristics are applied for the men at the odd iterations, but applied for the women at the even iterations of the algorithm. However, we think that it is better if we improve MMC algorithm as follows: At each iteration, after we

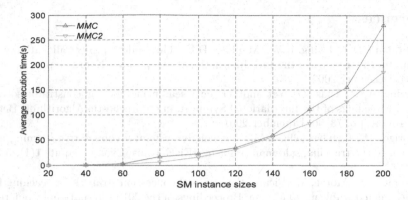

Fig. 4. The average execution time (sec.) of MMC and MMC2 algorithms

found all the blocking pairs in M, we find both a man m' and a woman w' who are having the maximum number of conflicts by mean of blocking pairs. Then, we apply the max conflict heuristic for only either m' or w' who is making the maximum number of blocking pairs in M. Next, we apply the min conflict heuristic for the chosen person. We call the improved algorithm the MMC2 algorithm. Figure 4 shows experimental results to compare the runtime of MMC algorithm with that of MMC2 algorithm. Obviously, MMC2 algorithm is an efficient variant of MMC algorithm, especially for SM instances of large sizes.

5 Conclusions

This paper proposed a max-min-conflict algorithm to find a stable matching which is different from the man- and woman-optimal matchings of the SM problem. Starting a randomly generated matching, the algorithm finds a man making the *maximum* number of blocking pairs. Once a man has been found, the algorithm chooses a woman in blocking pairs formed by the man such that her rank is *minimum* in the man's preference list. The algorithm then removes the blocking pair formed by the man and the woman in the matching and repeats for the matching until it is stable. Experiments showed that our MMC algorithm outperforms the SML2 algorithm in terms of execution time for finding a stable matching of large stable marriage problems. In the future, we plan to extend the proposed approach to the stable marriage problem with ties and incomplete lists [7,13].

Acknowledgment. This research is funded by the Vietnam National Foundation for Science and Technology Development (NAFOSTED) under **grant number 102.01-2017.09**.

References

1. Abraham, D.J., Irving, R.W., Manlove, D.F.: The student-project allocation problem. In: Proceedings of the 14th International Symposium, Kyoto, Japan, pp. 474–484, December 2003
2. Codognet, P., Diaz, D.: Yet another local search method for constraint solving. In: Proceedings of the International Symposium on Stochastic Algorithms, Berlin, Germany, pp. 73–90, December 2001
3. Dorigo, M., Gambardella, L.M.: Ant colony system: a cooperative learning approach to the traveling salesman problem. IEEE Trans. Evol. Comput. **1**(1), 53–66 (1997)
4. Everaere, P., Morge, M., Picard, G.: Minimal concession strategy for reaching fair, optimal and stable marriages. In: Proceedings of the 2013 International Conference on Autonomous Agents and Multi-agent Systems (AAMAS), St. Paul, MN, USA, pp. 1319–1320, May 2013
5. Fleiner, T., Irving, R.W., Manlove, D.F.: Efficient algorithms for generalized stable marriage and roommates problems. Theor. Comput. Sci. **381**(1–3), 162–176 (2007)
6. Gale, D., Shapley, L.S.: College admissions and the stability of marriage. Am. Math. Monthly **9**(1), 9–15 (1962)
7. Gelain, M., Pini, M.S., Rossi, F., Venable, K.B., Walsh, T.: Local search approaches in stable matching problems. Algorithms **6**(1), 591–617 (2013)
8. Gent, I.P., Irving, R.W., Manlove, D., Prosser, P., Smith, B.M.: A constraint programming approach to the stable marriage problem. In: Proceedings of the 7th International Conference on Principles and Practice of Constraint Programming, Berlin, Heidelberg, vol. 1, pp. 225–239, December 2001
9. Gent, I.P., Prosser, P.: An empirical study of the stable marriage problem with ties and incomplete lists. In: Proceedings of the 15th European Conference on Artificial Intelligence, Lyon, France, pp. 141–145, July 2002
10. Giannakopoulos, I., Karras, P., Tsoumakos, D., Doka, K., Koziris, N.: An equitable solution to the stable marriage problem. In: 2015 IEEE 27th International Conference on Tools with Artificial Intelligence (ICTAI), Vietri sul Mare, Italy, pp. 989–996, November 2015
11. Irving, R.W.: An efficient algorithm for the "stable roommates" problem. J. Algorithms **6**(1), 577–595 (1985)
12. McVitie, D.G., Wilson, L.B.: The stable marriage problem. Commun. ACM **14**(7), 486–490 (1971)
13. Munera, D., Diaz, D., Abreu, S., Rossi, F., Saraswat, V., Codognet, P.: Solving hard stable matching problems via local search and cooperative parallelization. In: Proceedings of the Twenty-Ninth AAAI Conference on Artificial Intelligence, pp. 1212–1218 (2015)
14. Nakamura, M., Onaga, K., Kyan, S., Silva, M.: Genetic algorithm for sex-fairstable marriage problem. In: 1995 IEEE International Symposium on Circuits and Systems, (ISCAS 1995), Seattle, WA , pp. 509–512, April 1995
15. Roth, A.E.: The evolution of the labor market for medical interns and residents: a case study in game theory. J. Polit. Econ. **92**(6), 991–1016 (1984)

16. Vien, N.A., Viet, N.H., Kim, H., Lee, S., Chung, T.: Ant colony based algorithm for stable marriage problem. In: Advances and Innovations in Systems, Computing Sciences and Software Engineering, pp. 457–461 (2007)
17. Viet, H.H., Trang, L.H., Lee, S.G., Chung, T.C.: An empirical local search for the stable marriage problem. In: Booth, R., Zhang, M.-L. (eds.) PRICAI 2016. LNCS (LNAI), vol. 9810, pp. 556–564. Springer, Cham (2016). https://doi.org/10.1007/978-3-319-42911-3_46
18. Zavidovique, B., Suvonvorn, N., Seetharaman, G.: A novel representation and algorithms for (quasi) stable marriages. In: 2005 Proceedings of the Second International Conference on Informatics in Control, Automation and Robotics (ICINCO), Barcelona, Spain, pp. 63–70, September 2005

Empirical Evaluation of Deep Learning-Based Travel Time Prediction

Mengyan Wang[1](✉), Weihua Li[1], Yan Kong[2], and Quan Bai[3]

[1] Auckland University of Technology, Auckland, New Zealand
{mengyan.wang,weihua.li}@aut.ac.nz
[2] Nanjing University of Information Science and Technology, Nanjing, China
kongyan4282@163.com
[3] University of Tasmania, Hobart, Australia
quan.bai@utas.edu.au

Abstract. Travel time prediction is critical in the urban traffic management system. Accurate travel time prediction can assist better city planning and reduce carbon footprints. In this paper, we conducted an empirical work on deep learning-based travel time prediction. The objective of this study is to compare the prediction performance of different machine learning methods. Meanwhile, through the comparison, a neural network module with high prediction accuracy can be offered for alleviating traffic congestion. In addition, to eliminate the influence of nonlinear external factors, a variety of extrinsic data with abrupt properties will be acquired in real time and become part of the research considerations.

Keywords: Intelligent Transport Systems · Travel time prediction · Deep learning

1 Introduction

With the drastic growth of car ownership, traffic congestion has become an essential problem that people are faced with [1]. To control and reduce traffic jams, traditional approaches, like building more transportation infrastructures, generally require huge cost [7]. By contrast, Intelligent Transportation Systems (ITSs), employ a variety of modern technologies to alleviate traffic congestion, turning out to be more efficient and effective than that of traditional approaches [2]. Motivated by this background, many studies have been dedicated to travel time forecasting [7]. High-efficient and real-time prediction of travel time is a crucial factor determining the performance of ITSs. Accurate and punctual travel time predictions can not only produce proactive traffic scheduling but also enable to avoid waste of resources and reduce carbon emissions. In addition, a precise forecast of travel time assists travellers with arranging their trips reasonably and subsequently reduces the chance of traffic congestion.

There are two major challenging issues for the traffic-time forecast. First, traffic data collection for congestion analysis and prediction turns out to be a

© Springer Nature Switzerland AG 2019
K. Ohara and Q. Bai (Eds.): PKAW 2019, LNAI 11669, pp. 54–65, 2019.
https://doi.org/10.1007/978-3-030-30639-7_6

non-trivial task. Many research works manage traffic congestion by collecting the data using sensor-equipped gates, which are installed on the main trunk roads [13]. Whereas, such approaches require hardware and appear to be limited as the data cannot be collected for the roads without sensors. Second, it is challenging to explore an appropriate neural network module to achieve high accuracy of travel-time forecasting when various factors are presented.

In this research, an empirical study has been conducted to predict travel time using deep learning approaches. Different from the shallow neural network, the deep neural network can improve prediction accuracy by superimposing multiple layers of hidden layers [6]. Moreover, Koesdwiady et al. have ever believed that in order to deal with the complex and nonlinear traffic state, the proposed of deep neural networks can discover and characterise complex structural features within a problem [6]. A travel time prediction method with using LSTM based Recurrent Neural Networks (RNNs) is proposed in this paper and is created according to multiple factors, such as time, date, weekend, workday, weather and event. Additionally, in this paper, a Deep Belief Network (DBN) and a Back Propagation Neural Network (BPNN) based travel time prediction methods are also researched. The principal purpose is to compare the different prediction performances between deep neural networks and shallow neural networks, and then demonstrate and highlight the advantages of the LSTM based RNNs module under the situation of this paper.

The rest of the paper is organised as follows. Related works on travel time prediction are reviewed in Sect. 2. Section 3 presents a deep learning-based travel time prediction framework. In Sect. 4, experiments and experimental results are introduced. Finally, the conclusion is given in Sect. 5.

2   Related Works

In recent years, a bulk of studies have been conducted to estimate travelling time since it is essential for travellers to plan traffic routing strategies, as well as alleviating the traffic congestion. Traditionally, the shallow learning has been widely adopted to estimate travel time. Mendes-Moreira et al. leverage a shallow machine learning architecture of Support Vector Machine (SVM) to predict the travel time [9]. Similarly, Goudarzi utilises a shallow artificial neural network for the travel-time forecasting [3]. However, comparing the shallow learning, the accuracy of deep learning is becoming more and more apparent. For example, Kim et al. have ever compared the shallow method and deep learning method on distinguishing the regional pattern of lung disease diffusion [5]. In their study, they claim that as a shallow neural network module that requires the use of predefined features to train the classifier. Compared to shallow neural network module, the deep learning module is able to learn and retrieve features from the data sets automatically. They admit the deep learning has a high-performance ability and they believe that deep learning modules are robust in many aspects [5].

To overcome the limitations of shallow learning, a wide range of deep learning approaches for travel-time have been investigated. Wang et al. propose an end-to-end deep learning framework for travel time estimation [11]. Similarly, Siripanpornchana et al. adopt one of the deep learning modules, i.e., Deep Belief Network (DBN), for the travel-time prediction [10]. Moreover, other deep learning modules, LSTM based RNNs also can effectively model time series data. These proposed deep learning modules prove to some extent that the deep learning module has high accuracy in predicting travel time. Whereas, in the aforementioned studies, few of them compare different deep learning modules in predicting travelling time when multiple factors presented.

Data collection and pre-processing for travel-time prediction turn out to be very challenging. Wu et al. predict the traffic flow by using a hybrid deep learning approach, where latitude and longitude are not utilised directly but have been converted to distance as input [12]. To some extent, it has weakened the characteristics of latitude and longitude in predicting travel time. Wu et al. obtain traffic data through GPS on taxis and train the model with external factors potentially affecting the travel-time prediction, such as weather, the day of the week. However, such a study can only conduct at those countries with well-developed transportation system [12].

In our empirical research study, an automatic traffic data collection and pre-processing framework is proposed, which can capture the traffic data in real-time and suiting the input scheme of deep learning modules.

3 Deep Learning-Based Traffic Prediction Framework

The primary objective of this research is to provide a high accuracy model for predicting travel time and contribute to alleviating traffic pressure. The proposed approach consists of three modules, i.e., the data collection module, the data processing module and the neural network prediction module (see Fig. 1).

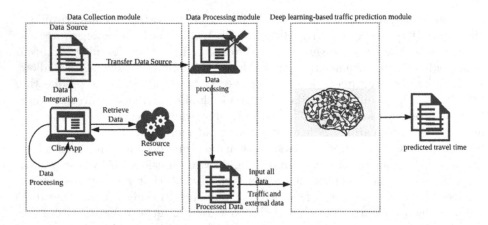

Fig. 1. Our approach architecture.

The data collection module gathers data from a variety of authorised sources through customised client apps. Then, the collected data is pushed to the data pre-processing module for further data preparation and formatting. The neural network predictive module can make full use of these data sets to predict travel time. These three modules in the proposed approach are elaborated in the following subsections.

3.1   Data Collection Module

The data collection module is the first part of the travel time prediction model and is the basis of the entire method. It should be noted that all the collected data in this study are obtained in real time by using different web APIs.

There are three types of information considered in the proposed approach, i.e., spatial information, temporal information, and external factors. The spatial information and the temporal information incorporate the given route (latitude and longitude), distance, the minimum travel time, the actual travel time, the day of the week and the time of the day. In this study, a total of 19 routes of New Zealand are selected. Due to the limitation of the Google Map API, all chosen routes are shown separately in Figs. 2 and 3.

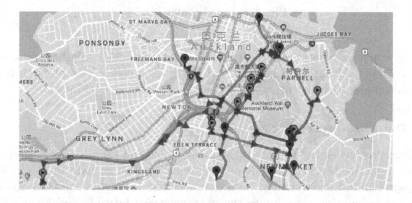

Fig. 2. Selected routes (1).

There are 10 routes in Fig. 2 and 9 routes in Fig. 3, respectively. All of these routes were selected by the following two principles. The first principle is to select sections of different distances, as distance affects the traveling time significantly. The second route selection principle is that all roads should be closed to an event venue. The purpose of this principle is to highlight the impact of event factors in predicting travel time.

As aforementioned, non-linear factors like weather and event can have a significant influence on the performance of predicting travel time. Therefore, in order to improve the prediction accuracy of the proposed model in this research, different external factors need to be incorporated into data sets, including weather and event. Real-time information of temperature, humidity and

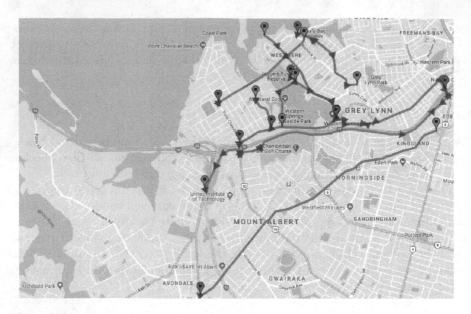

Fig. 3. Selected routes (2).

weather condition were collected through Dark Sky[1]. All weather data were retrieved every 30 min. Another external factor obtained in this research is the information about the event, which was acquired from EventFinda[2].

3.2   Data Pre-processing Module

The data pre-processing module is the second phase in the proposed approach. Firstly, the latitude and longitude of both ends for a given path are addressed. After some initial experiments, we are aware that the neural network module has a low recognition rate due to the untransformed latitude and longitude of the route, which leads to the failure of travel time prediction. Through further investigations, most of the related studies have utilised converted geographical coordinates. For example, Wang et al. have ever converted their latitude and longitude coordinates to distance by using Convolutional Neural Networks (CNNs). However, the data sets with distance information still cannot improve our neural network model to a high prediction rate. In this case, we replace those values with three-dimensional coordinates to represent the same point on the map. Longitude and latitude sometimes may have difficulties to indicate a point inside the three-dimensional space. Two positions can be extremely near each other while the values of the longitude are completely opposite, for example, (66.828393, 179.970129 and 66.828393, −179.970129). The conversion aims to eliminate the possibility of such kind of issue and ensure there is no dramatic value change

---

[1] https://darksky.net/dev.
[2] https://www.eventfinda.co.nz/.

through modeling. The locations are represented in three-dimensions, which are mathematically formulated in Eqs. 1–3.

$$x = cos(latitude) * cos(longitude) \qquad (1)$$

$$y = cos(latitude) * sin(longitude) \qquad (2)$$

$$z = sin(latitude) \qquad (3)$$

Temporal information is critical for traffic prediction. To yield better prediction result, there are two features added to each time stamp. As the traffic condition in the weekdays is entirely different with weekends, a boolean value is used to represent weekdays and weekends. Besides, in response to the ever-changing traffic volume of the day, using "hour" as a fundamental unit and convert into binary format. For example, 9 pm can be converted to the value of binary 10101.

To meet the requirements of the deep learning models and get accurate results, the input data need to be normalised. Therefore, in this research, the min-max normalization [4] has been utilised, which is formulated in Eq. 4.

$$S = \alpha * \frac{x - min(x)}{max(x) - min(x)} , \qquad (4)$$

where $\alpha = 1$, so that the weather data can be normalized in the range of 0 and 1.

Finally, regarding the event data, whether a record is affected by the event is defined by both event time and the actual traffic time. For example, the Lantern Festival in Auckland starts from Feb 16, 2019 to Feb 17, 2019 and the event time is from 16:00 to 23:00. If a record has a longer actual travel time than normal travel time within the event time, it is considered as affected and is marked as 1, non-affective record is marked as 0.

3.3   The Travel Time Prediction Module

The processed data is imported into the travel time prediction module. In this study, we applied two deep learning methods and one shallow neural network method in the prediction module to compare the performances of different neural network methods. For the deep learning approach, we selected RNNs and DBNs. For the shallow neural network, we chose BPNNs.

LSTM Based Recurrent Neural Networks. Researchers have found that compared to other deep learning modules, RNNs are more suitable for modeling sequential data. For example, the data of time series and the data of video or audio [8]. Moreover, the RNN method is more appropriate to obtain the traffic condition evolution on temporal and spatial [14]. However, the traditional RNN is not competent to capture the long-term evolution. Furthermore, due to the gradient vanish phenomenon and gradient explode phenomenon, it cannot easily achieve to train an RNN model with roughly 5 to 10 min. Therefore, we combine LSTM with RNNs to enlarge the memory of RNNs (see Fig. 4).

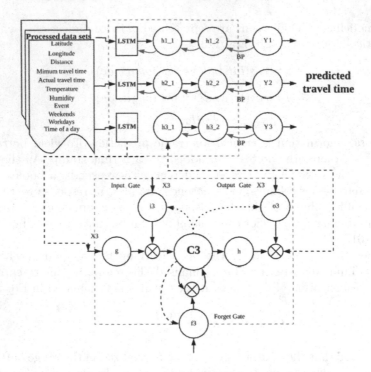

Fig. 4. An LSTM based RNN approach.

In Fig. 4, an LSTM based RNN module used in our deep learning traffic prediction module is described. Firstly, all processed data sets should be input into RNN, including the column of latitude, longitude, distance, minimum travel time, actual travel time, temperature, humidity, event, weekends, workdays and time of a day. After importing the data, as the first layer of the whole traffic prediction module, LSTM needs to perform a series of processing on incoming data sets using the input gate, the forget gate and the output gate. Then, the output from LSTM can be pushed to the next hidden layer.

After the forward propagation is performed, the module needs to propagate back. The purpose of backpropagation is to reduce errors by continuously adjusting the bias and weights parameters to build a more accurate module. The travel time prediction performance is demonstrated by using three criteria, i.e., Mean Absolute Error (MAE), Mean Absolute Percent Error (MAPE) and Root Mean Square Error (RMSE) (see Equations from 5 to 7).

$$MAE = \frac{1}{n} \sum_{i=1}^{n} |x - x_{pre}| \tag{5}$$

$$MAPE = \frac{1}{n} \sum_{i=1}^{n} \frac{|x - x_{pre}|}{x} \times 100\% \tag{6}$$

$$RMSE = \sqrt{\frac{1}{n}\sum_{i=1}^{n}(x - x_{pre})^2} \qquad (7)$$

In the above equations, x denotes the actual travel time, x_{pre} is the value of travel time prediction. In addition, n refers to the number of training epochs. As the error gets smaller, it shows that deep learning module is getting improved.

Deep Belief Networks. DBNs is a widely used deep neural network module in traffic-related prediction. A classic DBN combines a series of restricted Boltzmann machine (RBM) layers with one back propagation layer. We use DBN module as another deep learning traffic prediction module, which has a series of hidden layers and a reverse adjustment layer to better express a complex relationship between input and output. Figure 5 describes the application of DBN method in the whole proposed travel time prediction model.

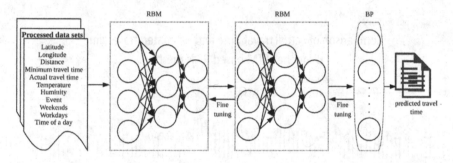

Fig. 5. The application of DBN method in the proposed travel time prediction model.

It can be observed from Fig. 5 that the data set obtained from the data processing model has been imported into our DBN module. Same as the LSTM based RNN module, the data set covers the attribute of latitude, longitude, distance, minimum travel time, actual travel time, temperature, humidity, event, weekends, workdays and time of a day. These data are forwarded through a series of stacked RBM modules until meeting the BP layer, which is set at the end of the entire DBN module. The BP layer adopts the BP algorithm, which can process the trained module through back propagation and fine-tuning. The main motivation for using the algorithm of backpropagation is to improve prediction accuracy by adjusting weights and bias. When the loss gets the minimum value by continually changing weights and bias, the whole training process is completed. Finally, a series of predicted travel time records can be verified with the ground truth, and subsequently gives the rate of accuracy after testing. Additionally, BPNN is also adopted as a portion of the proposed prediction model. However, due to its simple architecture as well as the uncomplicated method of training model, there is no detailed description of it here.

4   Experiment Results and Discussion

After completing the steps of data collection and data processing, we adopt the LSTM based RNN module, the DBN module and the BPNN module to predict travel time. All traffic prediction modules are trained by using the same data set. Before importing the data, the entire data set is divided into training data sets and testing data sets at a ratio of 80% and 20%. In our case, 4000 training data and 1000 test data are imported into the traffic prediction module. After all three neural network modules complete the predictions, a criterion is provided to decide whether the prediction result is valid. For example, if the estimated result is floating within plus or minus fifteen percent of the actual result, then this prediction is considered to be accurate. Conversely, if the value of estimated data is not in this range, the prediction result is failed. Through this calculation, we can obtain the final accuracy of the entire prediction result. First of all, prediction results of LSTM based RNNs are recorded and compared to the actual travel time data (see Fig. 6).

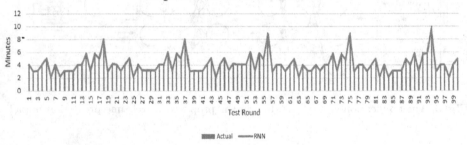

Fig. 6. The comparison between actual travel time and the estimated travel time using the LSTM based RNN method.

Figure 6 illustrates the perfect match between the curve and the clustering column based on the LSTM-based RNN method. The highest point of most clustering columns is consistent with the curve, and only a very small number of predicted travel times are inaccurate with the actual travel time. For instance, in the 73rd, the 92nd and 94th rounds have a lower forecasting time than their actual travel time. However, it still can be seen from the Fig. 6, the proposed model using the LSTM-based RNN method has very high accuracy in predicting travel time. In order to reflect the performance of the LSTM based RNNs module more intuitively in this study, another graph is plot in Fig. 7.

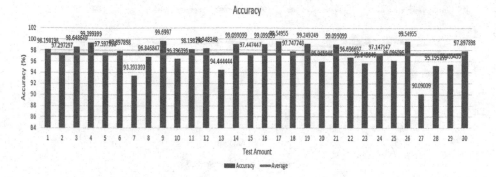

Fig. 7. The prediction accuracy of LSTM based RNNs.

The histogram in Fig. 7 can fully demonstrate the predictive power of the LSTM based RNNs module. As mentioned before, if the prediction error is floating within the range of plus or minus fifteen percent of the actual result, the prediction is considered as a valid result. Conversely, the result is taken as invalid. Using this as the criterion, we can calculate the accuracy of the module based on valid estimate travel time. However, since the accuracy of each module testing may vary, the experiment has been run for 30 times and all results are recorded in order to gain the average accuracy of the LSTM based RNNs module prediction. Figure 7 also indicates that the prediction accuracy of the modules trained by the provided data set are all over 90%. The lowest accuracy rate is 90.09, while the highest accuracy is close to 100%. Then, an average prediction accuracy is given in Fig. 7 for providing a balance point for the predictive power of the LSTM based RNN module.

In addition, in order to highlight and prove the high accuracy of the LSTM based RNN module, the DBN and BPNN modules are conducted in the experiment as well to predict the travel time. It can be noted that the same data sets and processing methods are used for all three neural networks. The parameters such as the hidden layer of the neural network, the learning rate, and the number of training times are all set to the same as well. In order to better intuitively understand the performance of three different neural networks in travel time prediction, we combine the 30 experiment results of each module into one figure for comparison (see Fig. 8).

Figure 8 reveals that the prediction accuracy of three neural networks in this experiment. All three curves display stable trends, which keep within a certain range without large fluctuations. The gray line represents the LSTM based RNN method, the blue curve stands for the DBN method and the orange curve is the BPNN method. The three methods with the same data set yield different predictive performances demonstrated in Fig. 8. Fundamentally, both DNNs outperform the shallow neural network. The method of LSTM based RNN gives the best performance among all three modules, with an average accuracy of 90%. In contrast, the BPNN based predictive method has the lowest accuracy (about 50% to 60%). Compared with BPNN, the DBN overall prediction has a better performance, which maintains the accuracy between 60% and 70%.

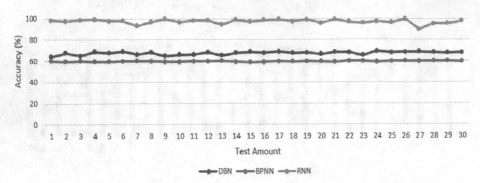

Fig. 8. The accuracy of travel time prediction with LSTM based RNN, BPNN and DBN methods.

Additionally, MAE, MAPE, and RMSE are also calculated for analysing the predictive power of proposed methods from the perspective of computational error in this research.

Table 1. The comparison of performance using MAE, MAPE and RMSE.

Comparison performance			
	LSTM based RNN	DBN	BPNN
MAE(min)	0.43	0.76	1.39
MAPE(%)	7.4	14.4	31
RMSE(min)	0.67	1.2	2.69

Table 1 describes the travel time prediction ability of three methods in terms of different standards. As shown in the table, MAE can get the minimum value of 0.43 when the LSTM based RNN approach is used in the proposed predictive model. In contrast, the BPNN method based prediction model creates the largest MAE between the actual travel time and the estimated travel time, which is about 1 min and 23 s. Besides, regardless of MAPE or RMSE, the value corresponding to BPNN and DBN is always greater than the value corresponding to the method of LSTM based RNN. It proves that the LSTM based RNN method outperforms the DBN and BPNN methods on predicting travel time.

5   Conclusion and Future Work

In this paper, three deep learning approaches have been compared and utilised in the travel time prediction. Multiple factors incorporated and processed to build the modules. The experimental results revealed that data processing has a great impact on forecast performance. For example, the processing of latitude and longitude in the data pre-processing module. In addition, the LSTM based RNN method has been proved that it has higher prediction accuracy than the other two modules, i.e., DBNs and BPNNs. In the future, a neural network module with more higher accuracy will be developed. Additionally, more related external data are supposed to taken into consideration.

References

1. Alam, M., Ferreira, J., Fonseca, J. (eds.): Intelligent Transportation Systems: Dependable Vehicular Communications for Improved Road Safety. SSDC, vol. 52. Springer, Cham (2016). https://doi.org/10.1007/978-3-319-28183-4
2. Cheng, J., Li, G., Chen, X.: Research on travel time prediction model of freeway based on gradient boosting decision tree. IEEE Access **7**, 7466–7480 (2019)
3. Goudarzi, F.: Travel time prediction: comparison of machine learning algorithms in a case study. In: 2018 IEEE 20th International Conference on High Performance Computing and Communications; IEEE 16th International Conference on Smart City; IEEE 4th International Conference on Data Science and Systems (HPCC/SmartCity/DSS), pp. 1404–1407. IEEE (2018)
4. Jakaria, A.H.M., Hossain, M.M., Rahman, M.: Smart weather forecasting using machine learning: a case study in Tennessee (2018)
5. Kim, G.B., et al.: Comparison of shallow and deep learning methods on classifying the regional pattern of diffuse lung disease. J. Digit. Imaging **31**(4), 415–424 (2018)
6. Koesdwiady, A., Soua, R., Karray, F.: Improving traffic flow prediction with weather information in connected cars: a deep learning approach. IEEE Trans. Veh. Technol. **65**(12), 9508–9517 (2016)
7. Li, D., Deng, L., Cai, Z., Franks, B., Yao, X.: Intelligent transportation system in macao based on deep self-coding learning. IEEE Trans. Ind. Inf. **14**(7), 3253–3260 (2018)
8. Liu, Y., Wang, Y., Yang, X., Zhang, L.: Short-term travel time prediction by deep learning: a comparison of different LSTM-DNN models. In: 2017 IEEE 20th International Conference on Intelligent Transportation Systems (ITSC), pp. 1–8. IEEE (2017)
9. Mendes-Moreira, J., Jorge, A.M., de Sousa, J.F., Soares, C.: Comparing state-of-the-art regression methods for long term travel time prediction. Intell. Data Anal. **16**(3), 427–449 (2012)
10. Siripanpornchana, C., Panichpapiboon, S., Chaovalit, P.: Travel-time prediction with deep learning. In: 2016 IEEE Region 10 Conference (TENCON), pp. 1859–1862. IEEE (2016)
11. Wang, D., Zhang, J., Cao, W., Li, J., Zheng, Y.: When will you arrive? Estimating travel time based on deep neural networks. In: Thirty-Second AAAI Conference on Artificial Intelligence (2018)
12. Wu, Y., Tan, H., Qin, L., Ran, B., Jiang, Z.: A hybrid deep learning based traffic flow prediction method and its understanding. Transp. Res. Part C Emerg. Technol. **90**, 166–180 (2018)
13. Zhang, D., Kabuka, M.R.: Combining weather condition data to predict traffic flow: a gru-based deep learning approach. IET Intell. Transp. Syst. **12**(7), 578–585 (2018)
14. Zhao, Z., Chen, W., Wu, X., Chen, P.C., Liu, J.: LSTM network: a deep learning approach for short-term traffic forecast. IET Intell. Transp. Syst. **11**(2), 68–75 (2017)

Marine Vertebrate Predator Detection and Recognition in Underwater Videos by Region Convolutional Neural Network

Mira Park[1(✉)], Wenli Yang[1], Zehong Cao[1], Byeong Kang[1],
Damian Connor[2], and Mary-Anne Lea[3]

[1] Information and Communication Technology, University of Tasmania,
Sandy Bay, Hobart, TAS 7000, Australia
mira.park@utas.edu.au
[2] Wild Ocean Tasmania, Eaglehawk Neck, TAS 7179, Australia
[3] Ecology and Biodiversity Centre, Institute for Marine and Antarctic Studies,
College of Science and Engineering, University of Tasmania,
Hobart, TAS 7001, Australia

Abstract. In this paper, we present R-CNN, Fast R-CNN and Faster R-CNN methods to automatically detect and recognise the predators in underwater videos. We compare the results of these methods on real data and discuss their strengths and weaknesses. We build a dataset using footage captured from representative environment of the wild and devise a data model with three classes (seal, dolphin, background). Following this, we train R-CNN, Fast R-CNN and Faster R-CNN, then evaluate them on a test dataset compose of challenging objects that had not been seen during training. We perform evaluation on GPU, acquiring information about the AP and IOU for each model and network based on various proposal numbers as well as runtime speeds. Based on the results, we found that the best model of predator detection using visual deep learning models is Faster R-CNN with 2000 proposals.

Keywords: R-CNN · Fast R-CNN · Faster R-CNN · Marine vertebrate · Seal · Dolphin · Detection · Recognition · Deep learning

1 Introduction

Marine vertebrate predators such as seals, seabirds, dolphins, whales, sharks and tuna prey on seasonal aggregations of oily, small pelagic, schooling fish, such herring, sardines and pilchards worldwide [1, 2]. These prey resource pulses provide seasonal concentrations of energy which may be important pre- and post-breeding. The dynamics and kinematics (properties of motion) of marine vertebrate predation upon such mobile prey are little understood [3]. Our understanding is further hampered by the multispecies nature of such interactions and our inability to capture these interactions with conventional biotelemetry tools (e.g. time depth recorders, accelerometers and animal borne cameras) [4]. Such information underpins our understanding of ecosystem trophic linkages and calculating fisheries quotas.

© Springer Nature Switzerland AG 2019
K. Ohara and Q. Bai (Eds.): PKAW 2019, LNAI 11669, pp. 66–80, 2019.
https://doi.org/10.1007/978-3-030-30639-7_7

In Southeastern Australia and Tasmania, schooling small pelagic fish, such as redbait (*Emmelichthys nitidus*) and jack mackerel (*Trachurus declivis*), are preyed upon by commercial species such as Pacific Bluefin tuna (*Thunnus orientalis*) and vertebrate marine predators alike [5–8]. Quantifying the dynamics, frequency and species composition of predation events on schooling small pelagics will provide information critical to the sustainable management of this ecosystem.

In this developmental project we aim to detect and identify the predators (seals and dolphins) using state of the art image processing methodologies as the first step in automatically analysing how predators approach, access and exploit baitfish schools.

Object detection in images has received much attention in recent years with tremendous progress mostly due to the emergence of deep neural networks (DNN), especially deep convolutional neural networks [9–12], and their region-based descendants [13–19]. Since the 2012 ImageNet competition, and new computational power accessible through the latest GPU, Neural Network came back as a strong possibility for classification tasks [10]. Moreover, by integrating convolutional layers, DNNs can both create features of vectors and classify them. One of the advantages is that DNN algorithms can automatically learn highly effective feature representations from the input data and categorise them. These methods achieve excellent results on still image datasets, and with this success, computer vision tasks have been extended from the still image domain to the video domain because the data sources of practical applications are mostly videos. Thus, the additional challenges are a rapid camera or object movement, the quality of video clips being lower than still images and partial occlusion. The general idea is to treat a video clip as a collection of frames, as then for each frame, and feature representation could be derived.

However, detection of marine predators is not easy since small changes in the environment can cause very large changes in the appearance of an object. Object detection and recognition techniques have been commonly used on videos analysis and a few research studies have been investigated for marine animal detection and recognition [20, 21]. Additionally, the dynamic nature of the environment and the natural camouflaging of the animals poses more challenges.

In this paper, we examine the problem of detecting predators in an underwater environment. We consider several of deep learning-based visual object detection algorithms, build a dataset on which to train and evaluate them on, and compare their performance. Hence, we make the following contributions:

1. We evaluate the accuracy and performance of underwater animal detection algorithms based on R-CNN, Fast R-CNN and Faster R-CNN.
2. We produce a unique dataset of marine predator behaviors for training deep visual detection models.

2 Related Work

This work is related to numerous works that have been reported in the fields of machine learning and computer vision, specifically in deep learning. This section shortly reviews the related works, and present some fundamental concepts needed for the understanding of this work.

Marine biologists have employed the underwater video techniques in marine ecology studies for many years [22, 23]. To monitor a marine ecosystem, researchers have widely used computer vision techniques to detect underwater objects automatically [24, 25].

Traditional object detection techniques rely on discriminant features such as the texture, colour or shape and these features are usually hardly captured in underwater video images. Influence of illumination is also one of the major difficulties in the context.

Therefore, deep feature learning such as CNN can be applied since it takes little account on those features. It has achieved successful advancement of object detection by a significant margin in many vision tasks, such as ImageNet Challenge [10]. Some of the researches have shown that CNN models trained using the ImageNet can be regarded as generalised feature extractors, which powerful high level features are produced for many new related tasks [26, 27]. Therefore, currently the CNNs model has been widely used as a powerful discriminant tool for object detection and recognition [28, 29].

A CNN is an architecture formed by a stack of convolutional layers and fully connected layers to connect the input layer and the hidden layers. In this structure, the output of one layer is the input of the following layer. Each convolutional layer transforms the signal sent from the previous layer using convolutional kernels, and activation function breaks the linearity. By visualising the features of each layer, Zeiler and Fergus [30] found that the first layer of the network usually learns low-level features such as edges and corners, and further layers learn high-level features. A pooling phase reduces the image and strengthens the learning by selecting the highest pixel value from a region. The last convolutional layer eventually concatenates all the information in one feature vector and sends it to a classifier.

These models take an image and categorise the image as a certain class. However, if multiple classes of objects are presented in the image, the models cannot classify and locate the objects. To solve these multi-class and localization problems, object detection is modelled as a classification problem where we take windows of fixed size from input image at all the possible locations and feed these patches to an image classifier. The classifier predicts the class as well as a bounding box containing that object. However, it is not easy to decide the size of the window because the object can be of varying sizes. Therefore, a research work [31] of underwater live fish recognition used a spatial pyramid pooling (SPP). An image pyramid is created by scaling the image and the image is resized at multiple scales. A fixed size window will completely contain the object in one of these resized images.

However, SPP is too slow and computationally very expensive. R-CNN [16] solves this problem by using an object proposal algorithm called Selective Search [32] which reduces the number of bounding boxes that are fed to the classifier to close to 2000 region proposals [13]. Selective search uses local cues like texture, intensity, colour and/or a measure of shape to generate all the possible locations of the objects. These objects are fed to CNNs and fully connected part of CNN takes a fixed sized input (e.g., 224 x 224 for VGG16).

R-CNN is still very slow because running CNN on 2000 region proposals generated by Selective Search takes a lot of time. To fix this problem, the CNN presentation is calculated for the entire image only once and can use that to calculate the CNN representation for each patch generated by Selective Search. However, it is not trivial to perform backpropagation through spatial pooling layer. To propagate the gradients through spatial pooling, it uses a simple back-propagation calculation which is very similar to max-pooling gradient calculation with the exception that pooling regions overlap and therefore a cell can have gradients pumping in from multiple regions. This is Fast R-CNN [13] and it adds the bounding box regression to the neural network training itself. So, now the network had two heads, classification head, and bounding box regression head. This multitask objective is a salient feature of Fast R-CNN as it no longer requires training of the network independently for classification and localization.

R-CNN and Fast R-CNN do not afford end-to-end training on either the proposal or classification stage. Besides, the proposals are typically selected from sliding windows of predefined scales [33], where the boundaries are fixed and may result in imprecise localization if the windows are not dense. Selective Search is still the main reason of the slow running time, so Faster R-CNN [14, 34] replaces Selective Search with a very small convolutional network call Region Proposal Network (RPN) to generate Regions of Interests (ROI). The RPN uses the last convolutional feature map to produce region proposals, which is then fed to the fully connected layers for the final detection. Both RPN and object detection tasks are all done by the same convolution networks and they are correlated to each other. With such design, object detection is much faster and Faster R-CNN [14] has been widely adopted in object detection due to its competitive detection accuracy on public benchmark [35, 36]. The core idea is to leverage the immense capacity of deep neural networks (DNNs) to power the two processes of proposal generation and object classification. Given its success in object detection in images, there is considerable interest in employing Faster R-CNN from object localization in the video.

3 Materials and Methods

This work analyses three deep learning network algorithms for underwater animal detection. To evaluate these network algorithms, we construct a dataset for training and evaluation, define our data model, and annotate images for training. The videos were taken in Tasmania reefs and the diver was holding the camera which then slightly moves. For capturing the varied appearances across broad geographical regions, this dataset needs to include data collected from a large spread of diverse marine environments. To enable visual detection of underwater animal using a deep-learned appearance model, a large annotated dataset of underwater animal is needed.

Film footage - Documentary and amateur quality film footage can provide the context needed to interpret both the species composition and dynamics of predation events. Video and still footage of fur seals (Arctocephalus pusillus doriferus), common dolphins (Delphinus delphis) and Pacific Bluefin tuna interactions with bait balls (tightly schooled small pelagic fish) has been recorded in recent years on the east coast of the Tasman Peninsula, Tasmania by Wild Ocean Tasmania. High resolution, still images were taken underwater with a digital singe lens reflex camera (DSLR) in a waterproof housing. Film footage was taken at 1080 resolution at 120 frames per second using a YI 4k + action camera (YI Technologies Incorporated). The camera operator was at variable distance to the bait ball in each instance and snorkeling and consequently, there is some movement in the videos due the movement of the camera operator. Thirty video sequences were selected from the video collection, totaling 11522 frames.

The frames were manually labelled by following the expert instruction on identifying fur seals and dolphins from diagnostic morphology. This defined ground-truth bounding boxes of all the visible predators (seals and dolphins). This tagging is for training an object detection model and Visual Object Tagging Tool (VOTT), which is a cross platform annotation tool, was used for tagging video and image assets. There are three folders as follows:

- /negative - images used for training that don't contain any objects
- /positive - images used for training that do contain objects
- /testImages - images used for testing that do contain object

The images in the/positive folder includes two classes: seal and dolphins. There are 7682 labelled images, 6682 (6482 positives, 200 negatives) images are used for training while 1000 images are used for testing. The size of each image is 1920 x 1080 pixels and each image contains zero to many labelled predators.

All three networks were trained and tested using on Ubuntu machine, using two GPU (NVIDIA GeForce GTX 1080 Ti SC Black Edition) and CPU (Intel Xeon Processor E5-2620).

Dataset vary greatly in quality, objects in scenes, and the cameras used. They contain images captured from real-world environments, giving us a variety of objects. Additionally, the clarity of the water and quality of the light vary significantly from video to video. This allows us to create a dataset for training which closely conforms to real-world conditions. Our training data was drawn from videos labeled as containing predators. Every video was sampled at a rate of three frames per second to produce images which could be annotated to prepare them for use in learning models.

The choice of learning data is a crucial point. We worked with biology experts in the IMAS laboratory to label many videos. The data must contain examples of predators present in the scene and if no predators are presented it is labeled as "negative".

3.1 Predator Detection Using Faster-RCNN

We modelled the problem as predator classification and localization. In this section, we investigate applying the Faster R-CNN to the detection of different predators. Firstly, we use a convolutional neural network (CNN) to get the whole feature map, then use region proposal convolutional network (RPN) [13] to select region proposals. Second, ROI pooling is used to generate each small feature map mapping to the region proposal. Finally, outputs are given to the fully connected layers to try to minimize the classification loss as well as bounding box regression loss. The main workflow of classification and localization using Faster R-CNN is shown in Fig. 1. It shows the automatic predator detection and recognition tasks.

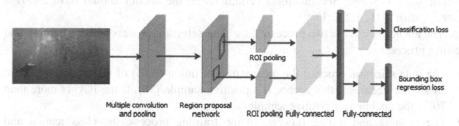

Fig. 1. The main workflow of classification and localization using Faster R-CNN

In this paper, the backbone network is the VGG16 [11], which is pre-trained on the ImageNet CLS-LOC dataset [37]. As shown in Fig. 2, the original VGG16 is a deep CNN that includes 13 convolutional layers, 4 pooling layers and 3 fully-connected layers. The training corresponds to mapping a window field 224 × 224 for VGG16 in the input image to the low-dimensional features through a convolutional neural network. In the RPN, a 3 × 3 convolutional layer is used to generate the fully-connected feature map with dimension 512. Finally, the SoftMax loss and Smooth loss are used to classification and bounding box regression respectively. The detailed network structures of Faster R-CNN used for predator detection are described in the following four sections.

3.2 Multiple Convolutional and Pooling

The architecture of our network follows the VGG16 with 13 convolutional layers, 4 pooling layers and 3 fully-connected layers, where 13 convolutional layers are used the same kernel size, pad and stride. The size of the output image after the convolution operation can be calculated as the following equation.

$$Output_{size} = \frac{input_{size} - kernel_{size} + 2 * pad}{stride} + 1 \qquad (1)$$

Each pooling layer is used to convert the size of input images (M*N) to 1/2, and the final size of the output image will be changed to (M/16, N/16). The low-resolution feature map can be generated from the high-resolution feature map by a certain convolutional layer, but the computational costs are high.

3.3　Anchor Generation

The anchors are generated on the feature maps by dense sampling. There are two parameters of the anchors in Fast R-CNN. First, Different sizes of objects, different scales of objects are detected on different feature maps. Therefore, in different feature maps, *different scales* (128^2, 256^2, 512^2) are allocated. In the feature map with low resolution, the anchor scale is large, and in the feature map with high resolution, the anchor scale is small. Second, for a certain scale, the anchor should have *different aspect ratios* (1:1, 1:2, 2:1).

The anchor is used in two processes: the data selection process and the training and testing process.

- The data selection process: the intersection of union (IOU) of the ground truth and an anchor decides if this anchor is a positive sample [38]. If the IOU is more than 70%, the anchor is a positive sample.
- The training and testing process: in the training process, the classification and location loss are computed by the anchors. In the testing process, the bounding box results are computed by the anchor location layers and, after the non-maximum suppression (NMP) of the bounding box results, the detection results are computed.

3.4　Region Proposal Network

Region Proposal Network (RPN) are used to generate proposals from an input image. The RPN overview is shown in Fig. 2.

An input image goes through the multiple convolution and pooling network layers to generate a 2D feature map (512 × 512). Then a 3 × 3 sliding window is used for each pixel over the feature map to select class-agnostic region proposals. An anchor is centred at the 3 × 3 sliding window, each sliding window has nine anchors, each anchor comes from the combination of three scales (128^2, 256^2, 512^2) and three aspect ratios (1:1, 1:2, 2:1). Then, every sliding window in maps to a 512-d figure vector. This feature vector is fed into two sibling fully-connected layers – a Bbox regression layer (*reg*) and a Classification score layer (*cls*).

A Classification score layer computes the probability of object or no_object, so it has 18 (2 × 9 anchors) outputs. A Bbox regression layer outputs the coordinates of the bounding box. It computes the coordinates of the detection boundaries for each object class: box centre coordinates (x, y), width (w) and height (h), so it has 36 (4 × 9 anchors) outputs.

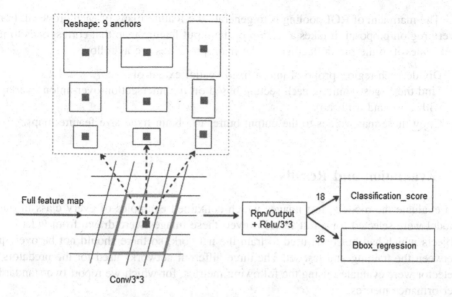

Fig. 2. The network structure of RPN

As a result, RPN output is 54 per pixel, and W × H × 54 × 9 anchors in total where W is a width and H is a height of a feature map. For training RPNs, a loss function is defined as follow:

$$L(\{p_i\}, \{t_i\}) = \frac{1}{N_{cls}} \sum_i L_{cls}(p_i, p_i^*) + \lambda \frac{1}{N_{reg}} \sum_i p_i^* L_{reg}(t_i, t_i^*) \qquad (2)$$

where i is the index of an anchor in a mini-batch, p is the probability of a proposal being an object, p^* is the true label of a proposal, N is the number of anchors and t and t^* are the coordinate of the predicated and ground-truth bounding-box. N_{cls} and L_{reg} are two normalization parameters, L_{cls} is classification loss, it's log loss over two classes (object or not object). L_{reg} is regression loss. The first term is the classification score loss over 2 classes (object or no_object) and the second term is the Bbox regression loss when there is an object ($p_i^* = 1$). Thus, RPN is to pre-check which pixel is a part of object and the corresponding pixels. The corresponding pixels and bounding boxes are produced.

3.5   ROI Pooling

For each region proposal, features within the region are first pooled into a fixed size feature map and this is called ROI pooling [13]. The pooled area goes through CNN and two full-connected branches for SoftMax classifier and bounding box regressor.

The main aim of ROI pooling is to generate the feature maps of each proposal. For every region proposal, it takes a section of the input feature map that corresponds to it and scales it to the pre-defined size. The main processes are as follows:

- Divide each region proposal into a fixed spatial extent of 7×7.
- Find the largest value in each section based on the intersection-over-union overlap with a ground truth box.
- Copy these max values to the output buffer to obtain fixed-size feature maps.

4   Evaluation and Results

To evaluate the models, test images which contained examples of every class in our model were selected for a test set. However, these images were drawn from videos of objects which had not been used to train the network, so there should not be overlap between the training and test set. The three different networks used for the predators' detector were evaluated using the following metrics, for which we report two standard performance metrics.

- AP (Average Precision) is the average of the maximum precisions at different recall values, to evaluate the model performance. Precision is the ratio precision = TP/ (TP + FP), and recall is the ratio recall = TP/(TP + FN), where TP, FP, and FN stand for True Positive, False Positive, and False Negative.
- IOU (Intersection Over Union) is a measure of how well predicted bounding boxes fit the location of an object, defined as IOU = area_of_intersection/area_of_union, where the intersection and union referred to the area of the intersection and union of the true and predicted bounding boxes. An IOU detection threshold 0.7 is used for deciding whether an object has been successfully detected. Then we compute its overlap ratio with the ground truth bounding box. If this value is over a threshold, then the detection is considered as true positive, otherwise it is labelled as false positive.

These two metrics concisely describe the accuracy and quality of object detections.

We loaded the VGG16 model as the base model described to get the full convolutional feature map. Then the output is used as the input to the RPN described in Fig. 2 to get region proposals mapping to the full feature map, and they are fed to the ROI pooling layer, which performs a pooling operation on a part of the input map that corresponds to region proposals in the original image.

Finally, all the detected ROI candidates are sorted by foreground probability, which is applied NMS to reduce the number of candidates and finally samples the desired number of ROIs for its output.

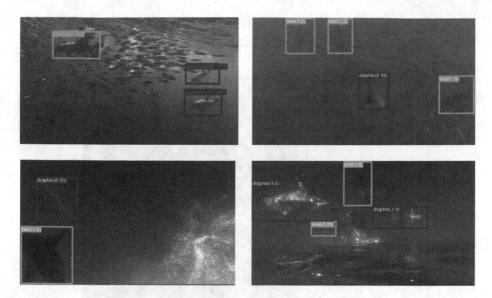

Fig. 3. Examples of results using Faster R-CNN

Figure 3 show some examples of the results. Furthermore, we also compared the different region-based object detection methods with a different number of training datasets using the 2000 proposals (dataset 1 with 500 training samples, dataset 2 with 2000 training samples and dataset 3 with 6682 training samples) shown in Table 1.

We also train the Dataset 3 using different proposals (500, 1000 and 2000), and compare the AP as shown in Table 2. We can see the more proposals will get the higher average precision of predator detections.

Table 1. Comparison of the Average Precision (AP), training time and execution time

Algorithm	Dataset 1			Dataset 2			Dataset 3		
	AP	Time[1]	Time[2]	AP	Time[1]	Time[2]	AP	Time[1]	Time[2]
R-CNN	47.79%	≈36 h	55 s/image	56.13%	≈48 h	55 s/image	68.42%	≈96 h	55 s/image
Fast R-CNN	54.14%	≈6 h	15 s/image	67.41%	≈15 h	15 s/image	74.79%	≈36 h	15 s/image
Faster R-CNN	67.49%	≈1 h	1.5 s/image	79.55%	≈3 h	1.5 s/image	87.78%	≈8 h	1.5 s/image

Time[1]: Training time, Time[2]: Testing time

Table 2. Comparation of different proposal numbers using Faster R-CNN

Proposal Numbers	AP	Examples
500	52.17%	
1000	69.23%	
2000	87.78%	

We can find the detection accuracy of Faster R-CNN is much higher than R-CNN and Fast R-CNN methods. However, it still has some problems regarding the detection of overlapping cases shown in Fig. 4, which we need to improve in the future. Dataset 3 with high proposal numbers results better performance than the other two datasets with low proposal numbers. The results show the large training samples with high proposal numbers can improve its performance.

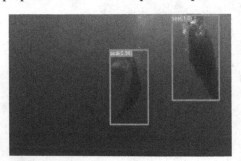

Fig. 4. Example of overlapping

Table 3 shows the comparison of the object detection in videos between different approaches including ours.

Table 3. Different approaches for detection and recognition of objects in videos

Reference/Year	Objects	Methods	Results
[39] 2015	Animal-borne video data of six green sea turtles 1280 × 720 pixels, 30 frames/s	Template matching	Accuracy (0.34 ± 0.12% and 0.52 ± 0.29% High true (86.2 ± 8.1%) and Low false (6.6 ± 8.4%).
[40] 2016	Zebras Antelope In Aerial video 4,102 ground truth	Optical flow methods	True detection 3365, False alarm 96, False positive 2.03%, False negative 17.97%
[41] 2016	13000 fish thumbnails 20 × 40 pixels to 150 × 200 pixels	HOG + SVM, CNN	Precision: 0.77 Recall: 0.69
[42] 2018	115 tropical Fish (LifeCLEF)	CNN	Recall 0.9 Precision 0.8
[43] 2015	12 coral fish	Fast R-CNN	mAP 0.81
[44] 2018	50 fish	Faster R-CNN	mAP 0.82
[45] 2018	21 tropical fish	3 layer CNN	Accuracy 96%
Our work	1000 Seal, Dolphin	R-CNN	AP 68.42%
Our work	1000 Seal, Dolphin	Fast R-CNN	AP 74.79%
Our work	1000 Seal, Dolphin	Faster R-CNN	AP 87.78%

5   Discussion and Conclusions

We have presented three R-CNN methods to detect and recognize the predators in underwater videos. We built a dataset using footage captured from representative environment of the wild and devised a data model with three classes (seal, dolphin, background). Following this, we trained R-CNN, Fast R-CNN and Faster R-CNN, then evaluated them on a test dataset compose of challenging objects that had not been seen during training. We performed the evaluation on GPU, acquiring information about the AP and IOU for each model and network based on various proposal numbers as well as runtime speeds. Based on these results, we found that the best model of predator detection using visual deep learning models is Faster R-CNN with 2000 proposals.

Great challenges are introduced by the moving camera, dynamic background, low-light, high-noise and aerial perspective of the scenes. Low illumination environments cause relatively low contrast background and that is the main reason the traditional image segmentation is not working because of weak descriptors. The objects' shapes are significantly different over various camera angles due to the freely swimming environment. Therefore, it is important to have the various shapes of the objects in the training datasets. If the number of the datasets is not enough, data augmentation can be considered [46].

The advantages of our work are to overcome the above drawbacks by using the state-of-the-art CNN methods. These methods produce abstract discriminative features from the object rather than the interesting points detected from the low-contrast image.

To improve performance, our future work can widen the database by applying rotations and symmetries in order to capture all the possible position of the objects. We also can create another class called 'part of predator' to improve the localization accuracy.

References

1. Pikitch, E.K., et al.: The global contribution of forage fish to marine fisheries and ecosystems. Fish Fish. **15**(1), 43–64 (2014)
2. Engelhard, G.H., et al.: Forage fish, their fisheries, and their predators: who drives whom? ICSE J. Mar. Sci. **71**(1), 90–104 (2013)
3. Kane, E.A., Marshall, C.D.: Comparative feeding kinematics and performance of odontocetes: belugas, Pacific white-sided dolphins and long-finned pilot whales. J. Exp. Biol. **212**(24), 3939–3950 (2009)
4. Austin, D., et al.: Linking movement, diving, and habitat to foraging success in a large marine predator. Ecology **87**(12), 3095–3108 (2006)
5. Hume, F., et al.: Spatial and temporal variation in the diet of a high trophic level predator, the Australian fur seal (Arctocephalus pusillus doriferus). Mar. Biol. **144**(3), 407–415 (2004)
6. Kirkwooe, R., Hume, F., Hindell, M.: Sea temperature variations mediate annual changes in the diet of Australian fur seals in Bass Strait. Mar. Ecol. Prog. Ser. **369**, 297–309 (2008)
7. Young, J.W., et al.: Feeding ecology and interannual variatons in diet of southern bluefin tuna, Thunnus maccoyii, in relation to coastal and oceanic waters off eastern Tasmania. Aust. Environ. Biol. Fishes **50**(3), 275 (1997)
8. Gales, R., et al.: Stomach contents of long-finned pilot whales (Globicephala melas) and bottlenose dolphins (Tursiops truncatus) in Tasmania. Mar. Mamm. Sci. **8**(4), 405–413 (1992)
9. LeCun, Y., et al.: Backpropagation applied to handwritten zip code recognition. Neural Comput. **1**, 541–551 (1989)
10. Krizhevsky, A., Sutskever, I., Hinton, G.E.: ImageNet classification with deep convolutional neural networks. In: Advances in Neural Information Processing Systems 2012, pp. 1097–1105 (2012)
11. Simonyan, K., Zisserman, A.: Very deep convolutional networks for large-scale image recoginiton. arXiv, arXiv:1409.1556 (2015)
12. Szegedy, C., et al.: Going deeper with convolutions. In: IEEE Conference on computer vision and pattern recognition, Boston, MA, USA (2015)
13. Girshick, R.: Fast R-CNN. In: IEEE International Conference on Computer Vision, Los Alamitos, CA, USA (2015)
14. Ren, S., et al.: Faster R-CNN: towards real-time object detection with region proposal networkss. IEEE Trans. Patt. Anal. **39**, 1137–1149 (2017)

15. Dai, J., et al.: R-FCN: object detection via region-based fully convolutional networks. In: Advance in Neural Information 2016, pp. 379–387 (2016)
16. Girshick, R., et al.: Rich feature hierarchies for accurate object detection and semantic segmentation. In: IEEE Conference on Computer Vision and Pattern Recognition, Columbus, OH, USA (2014)
17. Zhong, J., Lei, T., Yao, G.: Robust vehicle detection in aerial images based on cascaded convolutional neural networks. Sensors **17**, 2720 (2017)
18. Liu, W., et al.: SSD: single shot multibox detector. In: Leibe, B., Matas, J., Sebe, N., Welling, M. (eds.) ECCV 2016. LNCS, vol. 9905, pp. 21–37. Springer, Cham (2016). https://doi.org/10.1007/978-3-319-46448-0_2
19. Oh, S.I., Kang, H.B.: Object detection and classification by decision-level fusion for intelligent vehicle systems. Sensors **17**, 207 (2017)
20. Huang, P.X., Boom, B.J., Fisher, R.B.: Hierarchical classification with reject option for live fish recognition. Mach. Vis. Appl. **26**, 89–102 (2015)
21. Chuang, M.C., et al.: Tracking live fish from low-contrast and low-frame-rate stereo videos. IEEE Trans. Circ. Syst. Video Technol. **25**, 167–179 (2015)
22. Jones, D.T., et al.: Evaluation of rockfish abundance in untrawlable habitat: combining acoustic and complementary sampling tools. Fish. Bull. **110**, 332–343 (2012)
23. Pelletier, D., et al.: Comparison of visual census and high definition video transects for monitoring coral reef fish assemblages. Fish. Res. **107**, 84–93 (2011)
24. Struthers, D.P., et al.: Action cameras: Bringing aquatic and fisheries research into view. Fisheries **40**, 502–512 (2015)
25. Cappo, M., Harvey, E., Shortis, M.: Counting and measuring fish with baited video techniques - an overview. In: Australian Society for Fish Biology Workshop Proceedings, pp. 101–114 (2006)
26. Oquab, M., et al.: Learning and transferring mid-level image representations using convolutional neural networks. In: IEEE Conference on Computer Vision and Pattern Recognition (2015)
27. Donahue, J., et al.: DeCAF: a deep convolutional activation feature for generic visual recognition. arXiv, arXiv:1310.1531 (2013)
28. Zhang, N., Donahue, J., Girshick, R., Darrell, T.: Part-based R-CNNs for fine-grained category detection. In: Fleet, D., Pajdla, T., Schiele, B., Tuytelaars, T. (eds.) ECCV 2014. LNCS, vol. 8689, pp. 834–849. Springer, Cham (2014). https://doi.org/10.1007/978-3-319-10590-1_54
29. Kang, K., et al.: Object detection from video tubelets with convolutional neural networks. In: IEEE Converence on Computer Vision and Pattern Recognition, pp. 817–825 (2016)
30. Zeiler, M.D., Fergus, R.: Visualizing and understanding convolutional networks. In: Fleet, D., Pajdla, T., Schiele, B., Tuytelaars, T. (eds.) ECCV 2014. LNCS, vol. 8689, pp. 818–833. Springer, Cham (2014). https://doi.org/10.1007/978-3-319-10590-1_53
31. Qin, H., et al.: DeepFish: accurate underwater live fish recognition with a deep architecture. Neurocomputing **187**, 1–10 (2015). https://doi.org/10.1016/j.neucom.2015.10.122. (0925-2312)
32. Uijlings, J.R., et al.: Selective search for object recognition. Int. J. Comput. Vis. **104**, 154–171 (2013)
33. Shou, Z., Wang, D. Chang, S.F.: Temporal action localization in untrimmed videos via multi-stage CNNs. In: CVPR, pp. 1–10 (2016)
34. Ren, S., et al.: Faster R-CNN: Towards real-time object detection with region proposal networks. arXiv:1506.01497 (2015)
35. Everingham, M., et al.: The PASCAL visual object classes challenge: A retrospective. IJCV **111**(1), 98–136 (2015)

36. Lin, T.-Y., et al.: Microsoft COCO: common objects in context. In: Fleet, D., Pajdla, T., Schiele, B., Tuytelaars, T. (eds.) ECCV 2014. LNCS, vol. 8693, pp. 740–755. Springer, Cham (2014). https://doi.org/10.1007/978-3-319-10602-1_48

37. Russakovsky, O., et al.: Imagenet large scale visual recognition challenge. Int. J. Comput. Vis. **115**, 211–252 (2015)

38. Hosang, J., Nenenson, R., Schiele, R.: How good are detection proposals, really?. arXiv, arXiv:1406.6962 (2014)

39. Okuyama, J., et al.: Application of a computer vision technique to animal-borne video data: extraction of head movement to understand sea turtles' visual assessment of surroundings. Anim. Biotelemetry **3**, 35 (2015)

40. Fang, Y., et al.: Motion based animal detection in aerial videos. Procedia Comput. Sci. **92**, 13–17 (2016)

41. Villon, S., Chaumont, M., Subsol, G., Villéger, S., Claverie, T., Mouillot, D.: Coral reef fish detection and recognition in underwater videos by supervised machine learning: comparison between deep learning and HOG+SVM methods. In: Blanc-Talon, J., Distante, C., Philips, W., Popescu, D., Scheunders, P. (eds.) ACIVS 2016. LNCS, vol. 10016, pp. 160–171. Springer, Cham (2016). https://doi.org/10.1007/978-3-319-48680-2_15

42. Xu, W., Matzner, S.: Underwater fish detection using deep learning for water power applications. In: 5th Annual Conference on Computational Science and Computational Intelligence, Las Vegas, NV (2018)

43. Li, X., et al.: Fast accurate fish detection and recognition of underwater images with R-CNN. In: OCEANS 2015 MTS/IEEE, Washington, pp. 1–5 (2015)

44. Rathi, D., Jain, S., Indu, D.S.: Underwater fish species classification using convolutional neural network and deep learning. arXiv, arXiv:1805.10106 (2018)

45. Mandal, R., et al.: Assessing fish abundance from underwater video using deep neural networks. arXiv, arXiv:1807.05838 (2018)

46. Zhou, H., et al.: Faster R-CNN for marine organism detection and recognition using data augmentation. In: ICVIP, Singapore (2017)

Constructing Dataset Based on Concept Hierarchy for Evaluating Word Vectors Learned from Multisense Words

Tomoaki Yamazaki[1], Tetsuya Toyota[2], and Kouzou Ohara[2(✉)]

[1] Graduate School of Science and Engineering, Aoyama Gakuin University,
Sagamihara 252-5258, Japan
c5618168@aoyama.jp
[2] College of Science and Engineering, Aoyama Gakuin University,
Sagamihara 252-5258, Japan
{toyota,ohara}@it.aoyama.ac.jp

Abstract. Recently, word embedding techniques that assign a multidimensional vector to each word in a given corpus are often used in various tasks in Natural Language Processing. Although most of existing methods such as word2vec assign a single vector to each word, some advanced ones assign a multisense word with multiple vectors corresponding to individual meanings it has. However, unfortunately, it is difficult to properly evaluate those word vectors assigned to multisense words by using publicly available word similarity datasets. Thus, in this paper, we propose a novel dataset and a corresponding evaluation metric that enable us to evaluate such word vectors learned considering multisense words. The proposed dataset consists of synsets in WordNet and BabelNet that are well-known lexical databases, instead of using individual words, and incorporates the distance between synsets in the concept hierarchies of WordNet and BabelNet to evaluate the similarity between word vectors. We empirically show that the proposed dataset and evaluation metric allow us to evaluate word vectors for multisense words more properly than metrics for an existing dataset.

Keywords: Word embedding · Concept hierarchy · Multisense word · Word similarity

1 Introduction

Recently, a technique called word embedding is widely used in various tasks in Natural Language Processing (NLP), which embeds words in a given corpus into a multidimensional space by learning multidimensional vectors corresponding to them. There exist some well-known learning models including word2vec [9] and fastText [6], and most of them usually assign a single vector to each word. But, in reality, many words are used in multiple meanings in a corpus, and they cannot be properly handled by those learning models that assign only one vector to each

© Springer Nature Switzerland AG 2019
K. Ohara and Q. Bai (Eds.): PKAW 2019, LNAI 11669, pp. 81–96, 2019.
https://doi.org/10.1007/978-3-030-30639-7_8

word. To overcome this limitation, some researches proposed advanced learning models that can assign a multisense word with multiple vectors corresponding to individual meanings it has [14, 15, 18].

The ways to evaluate word vectors are roughly classified into two types: extrinsic and intrinsic ones [2]. The extrinsic evaluation indirectly assesses word vectors learned by a word embedding method under a specific application task such as document classification. More specifically, it trains another model to solve such a task by using word vectors as the input of the model, and evaluates the vectors based on its accuracy. On the other hand, the intrinsic evaluation directly assesses word vectors based on the similarity between them or the accuracy of analogical results derived directly from them. Although the intrinsic evaluation is straightforward, we have to prepare a word similarity dataset in advance. Some word similarity datasets involving evaluation metrics on them are publicly available [5, 8], but, unfortunately, they cannot properly evaluate multiple vectors learned for multisense words.

To overcome the difficulty in the intrinsic evaluation and properly evaluate word vectors for multisense words, in this paper, we focus on lexical databases involving a concept hierarchy and propose a method of constructing a word similarity dataset from them. WordNet [4] used in this work is one of representative lexical databases, in which words constitute synsets. A synset is a set of synonyms and each synset intuitively corresponds to one concept. Since each word belongs to one or more synsets according to its individual meanings, WordNet can manage words with a finer granularity than Part-of-Speech (PoS) tagging. In WordNet, the concept hierarchy is formed by manually linking those synsets to each other based on the hypernym-hyponym relationship between them, which allows us to correctly evaluate the similarity between words in each meaning.

In fact, we use another lexical database BabelNet [13] together with WordNet to construct the word similarity dataset. BabelNet is an extension to WordNet resulted from combining WordNet with Wikipedia [11] that is a well-known online encyclopedia edited by anonymous volunteer users. BabelNet reflects desirable features of Wikipedia such as the comprehensive and up-to-date vocabulary. The reason why we use BabelNet is that (1) Wikipedia is often used as a corpus for learning word vectors and (2) it includes up-to-date meanings of words used in our daily lives that are not contained in WordNet[1].

Instead of using individual words, the proposed method constructs the word similarity dataset based on synsets that are extracted from the concept hierarchies of WordNet and BabelNet because each synset is considered to represent a meaning of a word. In fact, when constructing the dataset, we remove some synsets from it if they are likely to prevent meanings of a multisense word from being correctly identified. Besides, we propose an evaluation metric on the resulting word similarity dataset to properly evaluate word vectors even if multisense words exist. We empirically show that the dataset constructed by the proposed

---

[1] Note that BabelNet can be automatically updated by using the latest Wikipedia database, while WordNet is maintained manually. And thus, it is difficult for Word-Net to include the up-to-date meanings of words.

method and our evaluation metric can assess word vectors learned for multisense words more properly than metrics on an existing dataset do.

2 Related Work

2.1 Word Embedding Methods

When learning meanings of words statistically, the distributional hypothesis [7] that states "words that occur in the same context tend to have similar meanings" is often adopted. Here note that a context for a word is defined by its peripheral words in a sentence. Indeed, in learning word vectors, each word is mapped onto a multidimensional space and assigned with a vector according to its meaning in the context derived from its peripheral words. In this section, we briefly explain word2vec [9], a well-known word embedding method, and the advanced ones that can assign multiple vectors to a multisense word.

word2vec. word2vec is a pioneering word embedding technique proposed by Mikolov et al. [9] and attracted much attention due to its usefulness in various application tasks in NLP and the interesting characteristics the resulting vectors possess such as analogy derived from addition and subtraction of them. Although there are some learning methods for word2vec, we only explain about Skip-Gram Negative Sampling (SGNS) [10] because SGNS is fast and can achieve a good accuracy in general.

Suppose that a learning corpus is represented as a sequence of words $w_1, w_2,$ $\cdots, w_T$ and that $C_{w_t} = (w_{t-ws}, \cdots, w_{t-1}, w_{t+1}, \cdots, w_{t+ws})$, the list of $2ws$ words that appear before and after the t-th word w_t, stands for the context of w_t. Then, the standard Skip-Gram decomposes the conditional probability $p(w_t|C_{w_t})$ into the product of $p(w_t|c)$ for $c \in C_{w_t}$, and learns word vectors so that they maximize the log likelihood L defined in Eq. (1).

$$L \equiv \sum_{t=1}^{T} \sum_{c \in C_{w_t}} \log p(w_t|c) \tag{1}$$

On the other hand, in order to reduce the computational cost, SGNS conducts sampling of negative examples during learning and maximizes the objective function L' defined in Eq. (2) that is an approximation of Eq. (1).

$$L' \equiv \sum_{t=1}^{T} \sum_{c \in C_{w_t}} (\log \sigma(v_c \cdot \tilde{v}_{w_t}) + \sum_{k=1}^{K} \log \sigma(-v_c \cdot \tilde{v}_{\tilde{w}_k})), \tag{2}$$

where σ is a sigmoid function, v_c is a vector assigned to the context word c, $\tilde{v}_w$ is a vector that is assigned to word w at the moment of sampling, $\tilde{w}_k$ is a negative example, and K is the total number of negative examples to sample.

Word Embedding Methods for Multisense Words. word2vec assigns a single vector to each word. This scheme is simple, but has a drawback that it cannot properly represent a word with a single vector if it has multiple meanings. This is because all contexts corresponding to individual meanings are mixed together in a single vector, which implies that the resulting vector cannot properly represent any of them. One straightforward solution to this problem is assigning multiple vectors, or *sense vectors* to a single multisense word according to its meanings. For that purpose, Trask et al. proposed sense2vec [18] that can learn different sense vectors for each PoS assigned to a multisense word by applying PoS tagging to a learning corpus before running word2vec. However, sense2vec does not work well if a word has multiple meanings for a specific PoS. Therefore, some researchers proposed word embedding methods that estimate meanings of words during the learning process. MSSG [14] proposed by Neelakantan et al. learns sense vectors for every word by estimating the meaning of a word, that is, the context in which the word occurs, during the learning process of Skip-Gram and adaptively selecting an appropriate sense vector of the word that should be trained in that context. Another line of research on learning sense vectors for multisense words is the one based on a concept hierarchy such as WordNet. DeConf [15] proposed by Pilehvar et al. can learn sense vectors for a multisense word by learning word vectors for every synset in WordNet.

2.2 Word Similarity Dataset

How well word vectors are learned is evaluated based on a word similarity database or analogical results derived from them. One of typical word similarity datasets is WordSimilarity-353 (WordSim353) [5] that consists of 353 pairs of words (with some overlaps). As shown in Table 1, a similarity score that is an average of scores given by 13 or 16 subjects is given to each pair of words. Agirre et al. pointed out that WordSim353 does not distinguish the similarity from the association [1]. For example, in WordSim353, the pair of "cup" and "coffee" has a relatively high score of 6.58, but, in reality, "cup" is not similar to "coffee" although "cup" has an association with "coffee."

To more correctly evaluate the similarity between words, Hill et al. constructed another dataset named SimLex-999 [8] consisting of 999 word pairs associated with the similarity score like WordSim353. The distribution of PoSs in SimLex-999 is shown in Table 2. Hill et al. constructed this dataset while preventing their subjects from confusing the similarity with the association between words and empirically showed that there is a correlation between the similarity and the hypernym-hyponym relationship of words.

As the evaluation metric on these datasets, the rank correlation between two ordered lists of word pairs is usually used. In one of the lists, word pairs are sorted based on the similarity between their word vectors, while, in the other list, word pairs are sorted based on the similarity scores given in the dataset. If each word w is assigned a unique vector v_w as in the case of word2vec, the similarity between word vectors can be easily computed by their inner product or cosine similarity. On the other hand, if word w is multisense and has a sense vector

Table 1. Examples of word pairs in WordSim353

word1	word2	word similarity[0,10]
cup	coffee	6.58
cup	article	2.40
tiger	tiger	10.00

Table 2. The distribution of PoSs in SimLex-999

Noun	Verb	Adjective or Adverb
666	222	111

v_{w_s} for each meaning s of w, their inner product and cosine similarity are not straightforwardly computable. In this case, three kinds of similarity metrics are considered: $globalSim$, $avgSim$, and $maxSim$. $globalSim$ is the similarity score between $global\ vectors$. A global vector of word w is given as the average of its sense vectors. $avgSim$ of two words w and w' is the average of similarity scores between all possible combinations of their sense vectors as defined in Eq. (3), while $maxSim$ is the maximum score of them as defined in Eq. (4).

$$avgSim(w, w') \equiv \frac{1}{S_w \cdot S_{w'}} \sum_{i=1}^{S_w} \sum_{j=1}^{S_{w'}} cos(\boldsymbol{v}_{w_i}, \boldsymbol{v}_{w'_j}) \qquad (3)$$

$$maxSim(w, w') \equiv \max_{1 \leq i \leq S_w, 1 \leq j \leq S_{w'}} cos(\boldsymbol{v}_{w_i}, \boldsymbol{v}_{w'_j}) \qquad (4)$$

Here, S_w and $S_{w'}$ are the number of the meanings of word w and w', respectively.

2.3 Lexical Database with Concept Hierarchy

WordNet. WordNet [4] created by Princeton University is the most famous lexical database in NLP. The version 2.1 has 155,327 words and 117,597 synsets[2]. A synset is a set of synonyms. For example, a synset that contains "play" that is a hyponym of "dramatic work" is shown as follows:

$$\{play_n^1, drama_n^1, dramatic\ play_n^1\}.$$

The superscript of each word denotes the synset ID for the word, while the subscript stands for its PoS. Since a word can be included in different synsets according to its meanings, it has different synset IDs in different synsets to distinguish them with each other. For example, $play_n^1$ in the above example means that this synset is the first synset for "play" and its PoS is noun. In fact, "play" is a multisense word and appears in 52 synsets in total, which are 17 nouns and 35 verbs. Note that there exist many words that appear only in a unique synset. Noun, verb, adjective, and adverb are available as PoS in WordNet.

Besides, three kinds of relationships between synsets are considered, which are instance-of, is-a, and part-of. Two synsets has a relation of instance-of if one

---

[2] The latest version at the time of this writing is 3.1.

of them is an instance of the other. For example, the synset including "Shake-speare" is an instance of the synset including "dramatist." On the other hand, the is-a relationship corresponds to the hypernym-hyponym relationship between synsets. For example, the synset including $play_n^1$ is a hyponym synset of the one including $dramatic\ work_n^1$ and "play" $is\ a$ "dramatic work" in that sense. In other words, the former synset is more specific than the latter one. The part-of relationship represents the part-whole relationship such as the one that exists between the synset including "chair" and the synset including "back." Basically, one synset has a unique hypernym synset, while it can have one or more hyponym synsets, which forms the hierarchical structure reflecting the general-specif relationships between synsets in WordNet.

BabelNet. BabelNet [13] is a lexical database corresponding to many languages, which is automatically generated from 2 language resources of Wikipedia and WordNet. More specifically, BabelNet expands WordNet by means of Wikipedia so that it can incorporate the good features of Wikipedia such as the multilingual support, the comprehensive vocabulary, and the promptness of the update. Due to those desirable features, it was used for the word sense disambiguation task in SemEval [12]. The process of combining Wikipedia and WordNet consists of three steps: unifying synsets of each resource while avoiding conflicts between them, collecting the vocabulary information for various languages from translation pages in Wikipedia or by using a machine translation technique, and giving new relations to collected synsets. The advantage of using Wikipedia in BabelNet is not only the 271 languages support but also that it can cover proper nouns and up-to-date senses of a word described in Wikipedia. For example, "salad" has a unique meaning as food in WordNet, but, it has another meaning as the name of a musician in Wikipedia. Note that BabelNet adopts only meanings of a word that appear in Wikipedia.

3   Proposed Dataset

3.1   Overview of the Proposed Dataset

Our objective in this paper is properly evaluating word vectors that contains sense vectors for multisense words. To this end, we construct a word similarity dataset consisting of concepts that appear in Wikipedia. The reason why we only use the concepts in Wikipedia is that (1) Wikipedia is often used as a learning corpus for word embedding and (2) they allow us to evaluate a wide range of meanings of words used in our daily lives. Indeed, we use WordNet and BabelNet together to generate our dataset so that we can incorporate the hierarchical structures in those databases to properly evaluate the similarity between word vectors. The proposed dataset has a record for each meaning or synset of a word, which is composed of the word itself, a set of its synonyms (synset), PoS, and its three hypernym synsets at the upper layers in the hierarchical structures. Table 3 shows some records in the proposed dataset, in which the hypernyms-1

Table 3. A part of the proposed dataset

word	PoS	synonyms (synset)	hypernyms-1	...
hectare	Noun	ha, hm2, ...	unit_of_measure, metric, ...	...
halve	Verb	bisect	divide, fraction	...
accomplish	Verb	action, carry_out, ...	complete, effect, ...	...
accomplish	Verb	achieve, attain, ...	succeed, win, ...	...
month	Noun	calendar_month, jfmamjjasond, ...	period, period_of_time, ...	...
month	Noun	-	time_unit, unit_of_time, ...	...
announce	Verb	denote, proclaim, ...	inform	...
announce	Verb	declare	say, state, ...	...
announce	Verb	-	name, identify	...
announce	Verb	foretell, herald, ...	tell	...

Table 4. The PoS distribution in the proposed dataset

the number of the sense	only Noun	only Verb	Noun and Verb
1	416	84	-
more than 2	317	63	120

of a word is a synset that is the parent node of the synset including the word in the concept hierarchy of WordNet or BabelNet. Similarly, the hypernyms-2 and hypernyms-3 are its grandfather node and its great-grandfather node, respectively. In Table 3, "hectare" and "halve" have a single record, which means that they have a unique meaning. On the other hand, the other three words have two or more records, which implies that they are multisense. In addition to ordinary single words, the proposed dataset includes compound words and proper nouns such as JFMAMJJASOND that is an abbreviation of 12 months consisting of their capital letters.

3.2   How to Create the Dataset

The dataset we present in this paper is created from the following three resources: The English Wikipedia dated November 20, 2018, WordNet 3.0, and BabelNet 4.0.1. We exclude adjectives and adverbs from the dataset because we cannot obtain their hypernym synsets in most cases. In fact, we limited words to be included in the dataset to those which are ones having only noun records, ones having only verb records, and ones having both records. Hereafter, we refer to those words as target words. Table 4 shows the PoS distribution in the proposed dataset.

   The construction process of the dataset is composed of two steps: the search for target words and hypernym synsets of the synsets including them and the removal of target words having inappropriate hypernym-hyponym relationships.

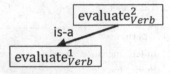

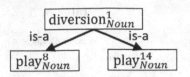

Fig. 1. An example of the parent-child (is-a) relationship between synsets that have an identical word

Fig. 2. An example of the sibling relationship between synsets that have an identical word

Through these steps, we collect only records corresponding to meanings used in Wikipedia and exclude the ambiguity in the similarity between words as much as possible.

1. **Search for target words and hypernym synsets**

   In this step, for every target word, we first search the concept hierarchies of WordNet and BabalNet for synsets including it, and then search for their hypernym synsets by traversing the hierarchies up to the 3 upper level. Note that all synsets including a target word do not always have 3 hypernym synsets. In this work, we chose the target words from ones in SimLex-999 at first, and further randomly selected from Wikipedia. It is noted that multisense words tend to more frequently appear than single-meaning words in Wikipedia, which implies that learning word vectors for single-meaning words is harder than for multisense words when using Wikipedia as a learning corpus and that the distribution of resulting target words is easily biased if we choose words uniformly at random. Thus, to alleviate such biased distribution, we divided words into three groups according to their frequency, and chose approximately the same number of multisense words and single-sense words from each group. More specifically, we adopted the medians of the frequency of multisense words and single-sense words, 132 and 2011, as the threshold values and divided words into three groups whose ranges of the frequency are $[10, 131]$, $[132, 2010]$, and $[2011, +\infty]$, respectively. However, unfortunately, since we could not obtain a sufficient number of words having only a single verb record from the last group, we chose more than half of the required number of them from the second group.

2. **Removal of target words having inappropriate hypernym-hyponym relationships**

   Between different synsets including an identical word, there may exist a parent-child relation or a sibling relation in the concept hierarchy as shown in Figs. 1 and 2. In these cases, such synsets could prevent proper evaluation of sense vectors of the word because they make it difficult to determine which synset (meaning) corresponds to which sense vector. Thus, to alleviate such ambiguity caused during evaluation, we removed target words from the dataset if their synsets have either relation in the concept hierarchy of WordNet. Besides, to ensure that only the concepts in Wikipedia are included in the dataset, we removed target words if they have a synset that appear in WordNet, but not in BabelNet.

3.3   Evaluation Metric on the Proposed Dataset

One way often used to evaluate whether word vectors that are learned taking into account semantic polysemy properly represent multisense words is checking words that appear around each sense vector of a multisense word in the multidimensional space. This is because it is expected that those surrounding or neighboring words specify the context or meaning of the target word. On the other hand, it is desirable to exhaustively and quantitatively evaluate word vectors. Thus, it is necessary to investigate as many multisense words as possible by using neighboring words of their sense vectors. To this end, we propose an evaluation metric that utilizes the precision calculated with respect to the *relation words* T_{w_s}. T_{w_s} is a set of words that appear in the union of a set of synonyms of word w that appear in a synset s including w and hypernym synsets of s. Let N_{w_s} be a set of N neighboring words for a sense vector v_{w_s} that corresponds to the sense defined by the synset s of word w. Then, we consider the precision, $Precision@N(N_{w_s}, T_{w_s})$, defined in $|N_{w_s} \cap T_{w_s}|/N$. Note that when learning word vectors for multisense words, different sense vectors of word w are expected to correspond to different synonym synsets in the dataset according to their meanings, but which sense vector corresponds to which synonym synset is actually unknown. Thus, we consider every possible combination and determine the one that achieve the highest precision as the proper combination. Based on these definitions, we give a score to each word, which is defined by Eq. (5), and define the entire score for the learning result as shown in Eq. (6).

$$score_w = \frac{\sum_{1 \le s \le S_w} \max_{1 \le d \le S_{d_w}} Precision@N(N_{w_s}, T_d)}{\max(S_w, S_{d_w})} \tag{5}$$

$$score = \frac{1}{|W|} \sum_{w \in W} score_w, \tag{6}$$

where S_{d_w} is the number of synsets of word w in the proposed dataset, and S_w is the number of sense vectors learned for w. In this experiment, we set N, the number of neighbor words, to 1, 5, 10, and 100. Considering multisense words when learning word vectors, it may happen that the number of sense vectors learned for a word becomes greater than the number of correct meanings the word really has, if the learning method learned different vectors for an identical meaning or if it does not worked well. To impose penalties on such a case, in Eq. (5), the score is divided by the maximum value of S_{d_w} and S_w.

4   Experiments

4.1   Learning and Obtaining Word Vectors

In this work, we evaluated word vectors learned from Wikipedia by using word2vec, sense2vec, and MSSG. As for word2vec and sense2vec, we used their implementations provided through the gensim package [16] of Python. On the other hand, since the implementation of MSSG is not available, we used the word-vectors pre-trained for Wikipedia with MSSG that are publicly available[3]. To learn word vectors with word2vec and sense2vec, we constructed 2 types of corpora from Wikipedia: $wiki_{nl}$ and $wiki_{multi}$. $wiki_{nl}$ is the one that was constructed without applying lemmatization. Namely, it is a raw text corpus. Whereas, in $wiki_{multi}$, words are lemmatized by WordNetLemmatizer function of nltk [3], and then tokenized by MWETokenizer of nltk to deal with compound words. When learning with sense2vec, we further added the PoS information into each corpus by means of the Universal PoS tagset and nltk. In our experiments, we set a window size to 5, the minimum frequency count to 10, the number of negative samples to 5, and the size (dimension) of a word vector to 300. Besides, we evaluated word vectors pre-trained for the Google News dataset by word2vec[4] and DeConf[5] that are publicly available.

4.2   Evaluation with Proposed Dataset

We first evaluated the word vectors that are aforementioned above with our proposed dataset and metric. In this experiment, we set N, the number of neighboring words, to 1, 5, 10, and 100, when calculating $Precision@N$ in Eq. (5) as mentioned previously. Table 5 summarizes the resulting scores for each set of word vectors, in which scores indicated by boldface denote the best score for the corresponding corpus. Note that, in every row of this table, the smaller the value of N, the better the score. This is because when calculating $Precision@N$ for word w, in many cases, only the nearest vector to v_{w_s}, a sense vector of w, is included in w's related words T_{w_s}. Thus, in such a case, even if N is increased, $Precision@N$ does not get larger as its denominator N becomes larger while its numerator does not. But, this is not always the case for word vectors learned from the corpus $wiki_{nl}$ because words in $wiki_{nl}$ are not lemmatized. One word may have some variants in $wiki_{nl}$, whose vectors would appear around the word in the multidimensional space if they are used in the identical context in $wiki_{nl}$. Although this does not affect our evaluation so much if N is set to a value that is larger than 1, say 5, it seems important to lemmatize words in order to properly learn and evaluate word vectors.

As for the results for $wiki_{nl}$, it is found that MSSG achieves better scores compared to word2vec except for the case of $N = 1$. Although it is difficult to directly compare these results as we used pre-trained word vectors for MSSG in this experiment, this result shows that our dataset and evaluation metric can properly evaluate sense vectors of multisense words. It is noted that the performance of sense2vec was worse than that of word2vec in this experiment. This is due to PoS tagging errors. To investigate how the errors affect the resulting score of sense2vec, we evaluated only sense vectors whose PoS tag corresponds to the

---

[3]   http://iesl.cs.umass.edu/downloads/vectors/release.tar.gz.

[4]   https://code.google.com/archive/p/word2vec/.

[5]   https://pilehvar.github.io/deconf/.

Table 5. Evaluation of word vectors based on the proposed metric

Word vectors	# of words	$N = 1$	$N = 5$	$N = 10$	$N = 100$
word2vec(wiki_{nl})	1000	**0.182**	0.085	0.058	0.011
sense2vec(wiki_{nl})	1000	0.109	0.053	0.036	0.008
sense2vec*(wiki_{nl})	1000	0.146	0.074	0.050	0.011
MSSG(wiki)	501	0.172	**0.092**	**0.063**	**0.016**
word2vec(wiki_{multi})	988	**0.200**	**0.106**	**0.076**	**0.017**
sense2vec(wiki_{multi})	1000	0.114	0.061	0.044	0.011
word2vec(google)	748	0.191	0.102	0.070	0.015
DeConf(google)	882	**0.381**	**0.234**	**0.159**	**0.032**

one of a synset of the targeted word in the proposed dataset. The resulting scores are shown in the row of sense2vec* in Table 5, from which it is observed that the scores are improved for every value of N. This result suggests that wrong PoS tags that do not correspond to any of correct tags in a given corpus could degrade the score of our proposed metric, which implies that the denominator of Eq. (5) works correctly as we expected. Note that the scores of sense2vec* are still worse than those of word2vec. Theoretically, it is expected that sense2vec outperforms word2vec by assigning correct PoS tags to each word. But, actually, perfect PoS tagging is a challenging task at present.

Next, focusing on the difference between wiki_{nl} and wiki_{multi} in terms of scores in Table 5, we can find that the best score for wiki_{multi} is always better than that for wiki_{nl} regardless of the value of N. This means that it is important for properly learning sense vectors to lemmatize and tokenize words in a learning corpus. Besides, from these results, we can say that word2vec does work well even if a learning corpus involves compound words.

As for the results for the pre-trained word vectors learned from the Google News dataset, we can see that DeConf outperforms word2vec. Actually, the score of DeConf is the best for every value of N. This is because DeConf learns vectors based on WordNet, which allows to obtain sense vectors that well reflect the relationship between synsets in the proposed dataset.

4.3 Comparison with SimLex-999

Next, we compared the proposed dataset and evaluation metric with SimLex-999 and its evaluation metrics based on $avgSim$ and $maxSim$. In this experiment, when calculating scores of each metric, we used 50 words that commonly appear in SimLex-999 and the proposed dataset, out of which 47 words are multisense. More specifically, in the evaluation based on $avgSim$ and $maxSim$, we used 77 word pairs in SimLex-999 such that they consist of two of the 50 common words. As for the proposed metric, we adopted $N = 5$ in this experiment because the results in Sect. 4.2 show that $N = 1$ is too restrictive to evaluate sense vectors

Table 6. Comparison of scores in the proposed metric with those of *avgSim* and *maxSim* with respect to 50 words common in both the proposed dataset and SimLex-999

word	SimLex-999		proposed dataset
vectors	*avgSim*	*maxSim*	$(N = 5)$
word2vec(wiki$_{nl}$)	**0.379**	**0.375**	0.098
MSSG(wiki)	0.275	0.271	**0.103**
word2vec(wiki$_{multi}$)	**0.366**	**0.366**	**0.104**
word2vec(google)	0.490	0.490	0.084
DeConf(google)	**0.539**	**0.580**	**0.149**

learned for multisense words. In addition, since sense2vec could not properly learn word vectors due to PoS tagging errors as shown in the previous section, we did not take sense2vec into account in this experiment.

The resulting scores are shown in Table 6. From these results, we can observe that the proposed metric exhibits different tendencies from those of *avgSim* and *maxSim*. In the cases of *avgSim* and *maxSim*, word2vec(wiki$_{nl}$) outperforms both MSSG(wiki) and word2vec(wiki$_{multi}$), and DeConf(google) achieves the best score. On the other hand, in the case of the proposed metric, MSSG(wiki) outperforms wiki$_{nl}$, and wiki$_{multi}$ achieves better performance than MSSG(wiki). DeConf(google) is the best also in this case. To investigate these differences more in depth, we picked up some multisense words and examined the meaning of their sense vectors by checking the 5 nearest words of each sense vector of the selected words in each set of word vectors in terms of the similarity between vectors. We show the nearest words of "accomplish" and "announce" in Tables 7 and 8, respectively. These tables do not include the results of word2vec(wiki$_{multi}$) because compound words did not have any impact on the scores of these two words. Additionally, to confirm whether these nearest words are correct or not, for each synset of "accomplish" and "announce", we show words that appear in its related words, that is, words included in either its synset or its hypernym synsets up to the 3 upper level in the proposed dataset in Table 9. Due to the space limitation, in Table 9, we only show words that appear in Tables 7 and 8 except for the last synset of "announce" whose sense vector was not learned by any method. For that synset, we show some representative words in its related words in parentheses. In Tables 7 and 8, words indicated by boldface stand for the ones that appear in Table 9.

In Table 7, it is found that word2vec learned a single vector for "accomplish" and the vector learned from wiki$_{nl}$ involves two related words "achieve" and "fulfill" in its top 5 nearest words. However, these words belong to different synsets in Table 9, which means two different meanings of "accomplish" are mixed into a single vector. The same thing is observed for MSSG. On the other hand, DeConf succeeds in learning two sense vectors corresponding to the two meanings of "accomplish", each of which has appropriate related words that

Table 7. The 5 nearest words of "accomplish" in terms of the similarity between sense vectors.

word vectors	5 neighbor words
word2vec(wiki$_{nl}$)	accompishing, **achieve**, **fulfill**, accomplishes, ninestrikethreestrikeout
MSSG(wiki)	**achieve**, accompishingm accomplished, **fulfill**, accomplishes
word2vec(google)	accomplishing, accomplished, **attain** accomplishes, Accomplisihing
DeConf(google)	accomplish, **carry_out**, **fulfil**, **carry_through**, myrmidon
	accomplish, **achieve**, by_luck, haply, by_chance

Table 8. The 5 nearest words of "announce" in terms of the similarity between sense vectors.

word vectors	5 neighbor words
word2vec(wiki$_{nl}$)	announcing, announces, announced, **proclaim**, announcement
	announces, informed, **declare**, tearful, announcing
	ask, **inform**, listen, **declare**, predict
	announced, announcing, announcement, announce, announced
word2vec(google)	accnounced, announces, annouce, announcing, unveil
	announce, announce, announce, announced, blazon_out
DeConf	announce, announce, announced, **declare**, announcement
	announce, announce, announce, announced, blazon_out
	herald, announce, announce, announce, **foretell**

Table 9. The related words of each synset of "accomplish" and "announce" in the proposed dataset

word	related words
accomplish	carry_out, carry_through, fulfil, fulfill
	achieve, attain
	proclaim, inform
announce	declare
	foretell, herald, inform
	(identify, name, denote, refer, intend)

belong to different synsets in Table 9. In Table 8, we can see that MSSG and DeConf succeeded in learning multiple sense vectors. But, one of sense vectors learned by MSSG has two related words "inform" and "declare" in its top 5 nearest words that belong to different synsets in Table 9. Again, this means two different meanings are mixed into a single vector.

From the overall results, it seems reasonable that the set of word vectors learned by DeConf can always get the best score. However, the evaluation that the set of word vectors learned by word2vec outperforms the one by MSSG does not because word2vec always mixes multiple meanings of a multisense word into a single vector as mentioned above. It is better to distinguish sense vectors according to the meanings of a word as MSSG does. But, in the way of evaluation based on SimLex-999, even if multiple sense vectors are learned, only either summarized or representative similarities derived from the vectors are used to calculate the rank correlation. When using $avgSim$, the average of similarities of all possible combinations of sense vectors for a word pair is used, while the maximum value among them is used in the case of $maxSim$. In other words, the evaluations of individual sense vectors are mixed into a single value. Furthermore, it should be noted that the combinations may include inappropriate ones consisting of two vectors corresponding to completely different meanings. Unlike such a way of evaluation on SimLex-999, the proposed metric evaluates each sense vector independently. In that sense, the proposed metric seems more suitable for evaluating sense vectors of multisense words.

Finally, it is noted that words in Tables 7 and 8 are sorted in order of the similarity to the sense vector of a targeted word. Considering this order, we can say that the examples shown in these tables justify setting N to 1 is too restrictive because the related words in boldface do not always appear at the top of each ordered list. Rather, considering the fact that some sense vectors do not involve any related word in its top 5 nearest words such as the last sense vector of "announce" learned by MSSG, either setting N to a larger value or extending the range of related words up to a higher hypernym synset in the concept hierarchy may allow us to evaluate sense vectors more appropriately. In addition, in the top 5 nearest words for sense vectors learned by DeConf, the targeted words occur multiple times, which means the sense vectors are close to each other. To make the difference between them more clearly, it is necessary to increase sentences associated with each meaning of words in the learning corpus.

5   Conclusion

In this paper, to properly evaluate word vectors that reflect multiple meanings of multisense words, we proposed a method of constructing a novel dataset based on concept hierarchies in WordNet and BabelNet and the evaluation metric for the dataset. We experimentally demonstrated that the proposed dataset and evaluation metric can evaluate word vectors for multisense words more properly than the existing dataset does. The proposed method constructs a dataset in a systematic way only from existing language resources, which means we can easily construct another dataset from various corpora written in various languages in the same manner. As our future work, we are planning to extend the proposed evaluation metric so that it can reflect the structure of the concept hierarchy from which the dataset is generated. This is necessary to alleviate the problem that the evaluation score of the proposed metric depends on the vocabulary size of a given corpus. To this end, we will try to use metrics such as Label Ranking Average Precision (LRAP) and mean Average Precision (mAP) used in ImageNet [17]. Besides, through further experiments on various datasets using various learning models, we will investigate the characteristics of the proposed dataset more in depth.

References

1. Agirre, E., Alfonseca, E., Hall, K., Kravalova, J., Paşca, M., Soroa, A.: A study on similarity and relatedness using distributional and wordnet-based approaches. In: Proceedings of Human Language Technologies: The 2009 Annual Conference of the North American Chapter of the Association for Computational Linguistics. Association for Computational Linguistics, pp. 19–27 (2009)
2. Bakarov, A.: A survey of word embeddings evaluation methods. arXiv preprint arXiv:1801.09536 (2018)
3. Bird, S., Klein, E., Loper, E.: Natural language Processing with Python: Analyzing Text with the Natural Language Toolkit. O'Reilly Media Inc., Sebastopol (2009)
4. Fellbaum, C.: Wordnet and wordnets. In: Barber, A. (ed.) Encyclopedia of Language and Linguistics, pp. 2–665. Elsevier, Amsterdam (2005)
5. Finkelstein, L., et al.: Placing search in context: the concept revisited. ACM Trans. Inf. Syst. **20**(1), 116–131 (2002)
6. Grave, E., Mikolov, T., Joulin, A., Bojanowski, P.: Bag of tricks for efficient text classification. In: Proceedings of the 15th Conference of the European Chapter of the Association for Computational Linguistics, pp. 3–7 (2017)
7. Harris, Z.S.: Distributional structure. Word **10**(2–3), 146–162 (1954)
8. Hill, F., Reichart, R., Korhonen, A.: Simlex-999: evaluating semantic models with (genuine) similarity estimation. Comput. Linguist. **41**(4), 665–695 (2015)
9. Mikolov, T., Chen, K., Corrado, G., Dean, J.: Efficient estimation of word representations in vector space. arXiv preprint arXiv:1301.3781 (2013)
10. Mikolov, T., Sutskever, I., Chen, K., Corrado, G.S., Dean, J.: Distributed representations of words and phrases and their compositionality. In: Advances in Neural Information Processing Systems, pp. 3111–3119 (2013)
11. Navigli, R.: Babelnet and friends: a manifesto for multilingual semantic processing. Intelligenza Artificiale **7**(2), 165–181 (2013)
12. Navigli, R., Jurgens, D., Vannella, D.: Semeval-2013 task 12: multilingual word sense disambiguation. In: Second Joint Conference on Lexical and Computational Semantics (* SEM), Volume 2: Proceedings of the Seventh International Workshop on Semantic Evaluation (SemEval 2013), vol. 2, pp. 222–231 (2013)
13. Navigli, R., Ponzetto, S.P.: Babelnet: the automatic construction, evaluation and application of a wide-coverage multilingual semantic network. Artif. Intell. **193**, 217–250 (2012)
14. Neelakantan, A., Shankar, J., Passos, A., McCallum, A.: Efficient non-parametric estimation of multiple embeddings per word in vector space. In: Proceedings of the 2014 Conference on Empirical Methods in Natural Language Processing (EMNLP), pp. 1059–1069. Association for Computational Linguistics (2014). https://doi.org/10.3115/v1/D14-1113. http://aclweb.org/anthology/D14-1113
15. Pilehvar, M.T., Collier, N.: De-conflated semantic representations. In: Proceedings of the 2016 Conference on Empirical Methods in Natural Language Processing, pp. 1680–1690. Association for Computational Linguistics (2016). https://doi.org/10.18653/v1/D16-1174. http://aclweb.org/anthology/D16-1174

16. Řehůřek, R., Sojka, P.: Software framework for topic modelling with large corpora. In: Proceedings of the LREC 2010 Workshop on New Challenges for NLP Frameworks, ELRA, Valletta, Malta, pp. 45–50, May 2010
17. Russakovsky, O., et al.: Imagenet large scale visual recognition challenge. Int. J. Comput. Vis. **115**(3), 211–252 (2015)
18. Trask, A., Michalak, P., Liu, J.: sense2vec-a fast and accurate method for word sense disambiguation in neural word embeddings. arXiv e-prints arXiv:1511.06388 (2015)

Adaptive Database's Performance Tuning Based on Reinforcement Learning

Chee Keong Wee[(✉)] and Richi Nayak[(✉)]

Science and Engineering Faculty, Queensland University of Technology,
Brisbane, QLD 4001, Australia
ckwee@outlook.com, r.nayak@qut.edu.au

Abstract. Database (DB) performance tuning is a difficult task that requires a vast amount of skill, experience and efforts in tweaking a DB for optimum results. With the hundreds of parameters to be considered under the diverse application configurations, business logic and software technology, getting a true global optimum setting is difficult for a DB administrator. We propose a novel approach based on Reinforcement Learning to tune a DB adaptively with minimum risk to the production setup. It results in a new set of parameters tailored to the production DB. Empirical results show that there is a significant gain in performance for the DB in its overall efficiency while reducing the IO overheads, based on a set of key performance statistics collected before and after the optimization process.

1 Introduction

Database (DB) tuning is complex and tedious where an alteration to its configuration can have a big impact on its performance, especially for a large-scale database. The tuning task is undertaken by a DB administrator (DBA) that has the skills, experience, and knowledge on database tuning [1]. A DBA tunes the DB parameters in accordance with the operation that is posed by depending applications to get the right balance. Getting the balance between control and performance is difficult and it requires numerous iterations of trials before it can be balanced. However, it is very time-consuming to perform this through trials and errors. Moreover, it is risk sensitive if the underlying database supports a mission-critical system as the system cannot tolerate any downtime nor degradation in its performance and functionality.

We propose a novel approach of DB performance tuning based on Reinforcement Learning (RL), named as Adaptive DB Performance Tuning (ADPT). The conjecture is that ADPT will follow the process what a sentient being will do in performing tasks in the real world. We propose a customized process that presents a workload duplication process between production and test environment to mitigate the risk in the tuning process. Several Oracle's features are used in ADPT, primarily to simulate actual production workload in the test environment. The guiding principle of RL is to learn what actions work and what's not for the underlying DB environment, then build up the agent experience until it can work positively with the environment with minimum penalty or faults. The length of training is dependent on the duration of the DB workload replay and the number of iterations required [2]. In our experiments with the

© Springer Nature Switzerland AG 2019
K. Ohara and Q. Bai (Eds.): PKAW 2019, LNAI 11669, pp. 97–114, 2019.
https://doi.org/10.1007/978-3-030-30639-7_9

374 MB size of replay, the RL agent managed to achieve an expert level in the test environment within 2 days. The experimental results show that ADPT can improve the DB's IO performance by a factor of 25%.

This RL-based tuning can be regarded as self-learning and correcting while performing the tuning process which sets ADPT apart from prior methods [3]. One major distinction from existing works [4–9] is that the tuning is adaptive and able to incorporate higher realism into the processes instead of relying on artificially simulated loads from the load test tools.

2   Related Works

Database tuning is considered as a challenging task for a DBA [10]. The DB vendors support the customers with training, knowledge, and software [11] that can assist the DBAs in monitoring and identify bottlenecks in the DB. But these tools require manual interventions to extract and initiate the diagnostic process [12]. The recommendations provided by these tools are up to the DBA's discretion including the risk involved in implementing them on the production systems.

In recent times, there has been a surge in the interest of automating the database tuning process with a variety of methods that are statistical, heuristic, rule-based or machine learning based [4–9]. A common statistical tuning method is to use cost-benefit analysis [13] to locate cost savings for DB's components using estimates from the correlation of the accumulated processing time to the parameters' values. However, the results are reported not to be optimum as the parameters alteration is dependent on the window period setting; the size of the window's time has an impact on the possibility of excessively tuned parameters [13]. A genetic algorithm was used as part of the DB performance predicting model's configuration search strategy in conjunction with a neural network to find the optimum setting for a system that runs on a NoSQL database [7]. The concept is to build a subset of the data derived from the main system and the tuning system will loop through the configuration search, invoking performance prediction checks in a hill climbing approach to find the best parameter settings.

A series of machine learning algorithms were used to tune an MYSQL database that supports a complex protein synthesizing system [8]. Starting with the use of clustering, it finds the most significant parameters against the captured data from different workloads that have been executed with different settings. Next, the lasso regression is used to identify the important parameters, or knobs, based on their changes against the variation encountered in the DB's statistics. They are then passed to the next tuning process. Several iterations of the DB workloads are acquired to calculate each knob measurement, followed by the application of Gaussian regression to locate the best configuration. This entire process is repeated until an optimal DB performance outcome is achieved.

We summarised a list of DB tuning methods that span from the manual techniques to artificial intelligence approach in Table 1. Delphi technique [14] is used to gather the information from a group of DBAs that are currently working for a power utility company. These methods are ranked in term of their complexity, capability, scalability and time requirement based on their collective feedback. Each one of them come with their own strength and weakness, starting with the manual methods that are the most tedious to use, to the most effective methods that use machine learning and DB supplied tools.

Existing works display the following shortcoming; (1) Existing methods assume a consistent, stable and well-defined DB in operation that doesn't vary in workload behaviour. They rely on this DB to collect statistics and data to support their models' training dataset, but they ignore the level of uncertainties. (2) Existing methods focus on achieving the optimum parameters settings for a consistent and stable DB that operated under the simulated workload which is not a clear reflection of the real-world DB scenario. (3) Majority of these works handle DBs with Online Transaction Processing (OLTP) operation and do not emphasize on another form of data operations such as Online Analytical Processing (OLAP) or Decision Support System (DSS). (4) These works operate against a small set of workloads and cover a small subset of the vast number of DB initialization parameters. The optimum parameters may not yield the same result when it is applied in the production environment due to different workload and operations. (5) Some methods depend on hand-crafted fuzzy rules or machine generated guidelines which are inflexible and narrowly scoped, that constraint them to adapt with the constant changing conditions that will occur in real-world DBs.

Table 1. Database's performance tuning techniques (low 1 to high 10)

Method	Complexity	Effort	Remark
Manual [15]	9	9	Require in-depth knowledge and skill. Passive, very time consuming, error-prone and may not get optimum result. Most economical of all. Not scalable
DB tuning tool [15]	4	3	Require average/good DBA knowledge and skill, less error-prone and faster than manual. Passive and require DBA to operate. Tools may be costly. Limited scalability
Rule-Based [15]	7	6	Passive to semi-proactive. Only as good as its knowledge rule-based. Built into monitoring tool. Scalability is low
Heuristic fuzzy based [6, 16]	8	8	Semi-active. Need a lot of prior statistics data. May not achieve the global optimum. May need a reset if schema changes. Use benchmark workloads. Scalability is low
Statistical-based [5]	5	7	Semi-active. Need a lot of prior statistics data. May not achieve the global optimum. May need a reset if schema changes. Scalability is medium
Other ML models [7, 8]	4	6	Semi-active. Need a lot of prior statistics data. May not achieve global optimum, adaptive to schema changes. Scalability is medium

The best way to tune a mission-critical DB is to learn and adapt the changes in its parameters that are suited for the real production workload. We propose the ADPT method to perform adaptive database tuning focusing on the IO that is based on deep reinforcement learning on a sandpit setup that we can replicate and replay the production workload on it. To our knowledge, ADPT is one of the first method using RL in DB tuning.

3 Adaptive DB Performance Tuning (ADPT)

Since the major DB performance relies strongly on the underlying IO throughput, ADPT focuses predominantly on DB's IO tuning. As shown in Fig. 1, the main component is the reinforcement learning (RL) agent that interacts directly with the test DB setup. It iterates through a series of activities that can be described as phases of learning and tuning in its course of DB optimization. The RL agent starts off as a "young model" with no knowledge and learns through a series of trial-and-error. As it gets more experienced in interacting with the test DB on parameter settings versus performance achieved, it will start to predict the outcome and choose the best outcome. However, being a "young apprentice", the RL agent has much to learn so its prediction will not be accurate and needs correction. Towards the end of the tuning iteration, it will achieve the "adult" experience of the system and will be able to know precisely what action it should take for certain states in order to achieve optimum results.

3.1 Process of ADPT

The process of ADPT starts by setting the length of a workload period that should be used. This period should represent the time when meaningful activities are present in the DB that can form a substitute model for the test environment. A backup is taken via Recovery Manager (RMAN) and is used to clone the test DB. When the DB-Replay has captured enough workload, its files are transferred to the test environment. DB Flashback is enabled on the test DB so that it can revert the DB back to the original state once the workload is replayed. This keeps the test DB in its pristine state before any changes were made.

The copied workload files are pre-processed to set them ready for replay. The first DB-Replay's run sets the baselines. Both the AWR statistics and parameters are obtained and used for later reference. Scoring of the DB is done by a process that summarizes the eight major fields as shown in Table 3 in the DB's statistics report to produce a final score. These fields have been identified as the key anchors that determine each aspect of the DB's individual subsystem performances such as memory, IO, SQL and overall efficiency [15]. In the next iteration, new parameters' values are applied to the DB and the workload is replayed. It is followed by scoring and the results are recorded by the RL agent in its knowledge-base. The process is repeated until the output of the DB's score has reached an optimum value or the iteration count set at the beginning has been reached (Fig. 2).

This process is outlined in Algorithm 1 and Fig. 1.

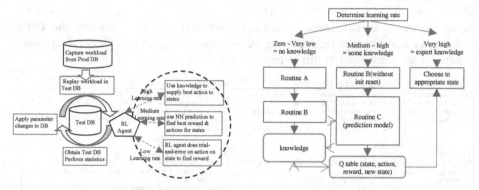

Fig. 1. Adaptive DB Tuning model overview   **Fig. 2.** Different phases of RL agent learning

3.2   Database's Tools

Oracle database is selected to support the implementation of the method. The following describes the various Oracle's features that have been used in ADPT;

Flashback DB: This feature enables the DB to be restored back to a point in time by rolling back all the changes that have occurred since then [17].

Automatic Workload Repository (AWR): AWR is commonly used to report on the DB's performance statistics which covers wait events, time model statistics, active session, object user and expensive SQL statements. The outputs that AWR produces identify the bottleneck, waits, and other performance issues that are associated with them. We use a subset of the results that have been aggregated from different groups of statistics as listed in Table 2 [18].

DB Replay: This is one of the components of Oracle's Real Application Testing suite [2]. It captures the workloads from a source DB and then replays it on a target DB. [18].

Automatic Big table Caching: This feature enables Oracle to reserve part of the buffer cache to cache data for table scans by using temperature and object-based Algorithm to track medium to large tables. It is to allow queries to be made against memory which is much faster [19].

In-Memory Column Store: This feature enables the DB to allows the user to store tables and other objects in a columnar-format instead of the common row format [19].

3.3   Subroutines for the RL Agent

There are activities that need to be executed sequentially between the DB and the RL agent. For the test environment preparation, we duplicate the production workload onto the test DB by using DB-Replay to capture the workload in the production system during the busy period for a certain duration. A suitable period is chosen for the scale of the anticipating tuning process. The DB-Replay's captured files are copied over to the test environment. The test DB is cloned from the production DB's backup using the recovery tool called RMAN [20]. The DB is configured for the flashback, followed by setting the baseline initialization parameter. The next step is to capture the DB's performance statistics with the first replayed workload, as a baseline. Only the dynamic parameters are considered in this tuning process scope.

Algorithm 1: Main DB optimizing Algorithm	Algorithm 2 - Routine A
Input: The state of DB from the AWR report and computed rewards	Input: baseline init file, captured replay log files.
Output: The action of new parameters' value for the database	Output: statistics report for baseline, s_0.
Initialization1: set value for learning, reward preference and exploration rate, for exploration, learning, and exploitation, decay_rate	Initialization 1: create flashback restore point.
Initialization2: initialize memory, Q-table collection and respective counters	Initialization 2: reset init parameter, a flush memory, clear old snapshots.
Get a baseline of DB from routine A	Create "before" snapshot.
Acquire the state from the AWR report	Run DB Replay to play the workload.
Set the learning rate to zero, med_learning to 30%, high_learning to 90%	Create "after" snapshot.
Loop the iteration process	Run awrreport.sql for the statistics report as the baseline state, s_0.
Check the learning rate.	Flashback DB
If learning <= med_learning, do the exploration phase	Execute command to flush memory
/* exploration phase */	Reset the DB's init parameter
Generate random initialization configuration.	Drop and clear all snapshots.
Run Routines A and B	
/*reset DB environment. Run Action against Environment and get a new	
state. find the score as a reward. Store knowledge of	
state, action, reward, and new_state to knowledgebase */	
If learning is > med_learning and < high_learning, then do	
/* learning phase */	
Run Routine C	
/* reset the DB by flashback and flush memory.	
Predict new action for state and potential reward.	
Apply Action to Environment and get new state plus reward.	
Correct the reward and store information into knowledgebase */	
If learning > high_learning,	
/*refer to the knowledgebase for action to state. */	
If exploration_rate < exploration_limit then	
Exploits the knowledgebase to find optimum action for given state that	
Gives best rewards	
Else	
Go to exploration phase – Routine A	
learning rate +=1	
exploration rate= exploration_rate *=decay_rate	

There are three DB-based routines that will be performed throughout the different learning phases in the tuning process, and they alter the DB' settings for the RL support. Routine A sets the DB to baseline through flashback and parameter reset. It replays the workload and acquires its stats score at baseline, s_0. Routine B scores the DB statistics difference between the previous state and the current one, Δs, after applying the parameters change. The results are kept in the knowledgebase. Routine C predicts the scores based on parameters change and state, followed by self-correction. The results are added into the knowledgebase. At the end of routine C, we conjecture that the prediction model in the RL agent will achieve a high degree of accuracy, due to the acquisition of a large knowledgebase including information on various states, actions, and rewards. When the process reaches the high learning phase, the RL agent is assumed to achieve an expert level where it can refer to this knowledgebase to find the best global actions. For a single state of the test DB, the RL agent can traverse down the relationship of a sequence that leads from one state to another. It will result in finding the optimum choice of an action that yields the best rewards and the RL agent will use that action to apply to the test DB which eventually will achieve the best-performing state.

The routines A, B, and C are described in Algorithms 2, 3 and 4, respectively.

Algorithm 3 – Routine B	Algorithm 4 – Routine C
Input: Captured replay log files, baseline statistics reports Output: statistics report new state, *s'*, reward, *r'*, update knowledgebase Initialization 1: randomize configuration file. Flush memory, flashback DB, reset init. Perform Routine A. Create "before" snapshot. Select one of the parameters' set values from the config file. Apply the action with parameter set. Run DB Replay to play the workload. Create "after" snapshot. Run awrreport.sql for statistics report for the state, *s'*. Consolidate and differentiate both old and new states, *s* and *s'*. Score the changes. Record the result into the knowledgebase.	Input: Captured replay log files, statistics reports, knowledgebase Output: statistics report new state, *s'*, reward, *r'*, Update knowledgebase. Initialization 1: randomize configuration file. Flush memory, flashback DB, reset init. Initialization 2: NN predicting model. Perform Routine A but without init reset. Train NN and then use it to predict action and reward. Create "before" snapshot. Apply the action. Run DB Replay to play the workload. Create "after" snapshot. Run awrreport.sql for statistics report for the state, s'. Consolidate and differentiate both old and new states, s and s'. Score the changes and correct the reward, *r*. Record the result of the new state, old state, action, predicted reward, actual reward into the knowledgebase.

3.4   RL for DB Tuning: Q Learning

For a typical RL model, the agent interacts with the environment and perceives the state of the environment to take actions and receive rewards [3]. The goal is to choose actions to maximize rewards. As seen in Fig. 3, at time t, the agent observes the environment which gives the state, s_t, and the agent executes an action, a_t, and receives a reward, r_t, from the environment. The environment then changes and reaches a new state, s_{t+1}. This cycle repeats until the goal is achieved. The optimal behaviour π is based on past actions and the agent tries to maximize the expected cumulative rewards over time [3]. In this method, the environment refers to the DB, a state refers to the DB's performance in response to the workload replayed after experiencing the DB parameters' values, and an action refers to the process of changing the DB's initialization parameters.

As the test DB environment has a big combination of parameters versus workloads, there is no true model that the agent can rely on. Therefore, it relies on trial-and-error to find the action. For the proposed self-tuning approach, the agent learns by interacting with the DB. Action, a_t, will be performed by applying the parameter change for an epoch t then receive reward or penalty r_t, that is derived by the scoring of the DB performance after the workload is replayed and the AWR report is generated. The agent will be able to judge whether the last change made is for the better or worse. However, it is not able to reason about the long-term effects of the actions it takes. Delay to feedback is acceptable in this case as there is no need for immediate response.

The agent's objective is to learn about its current situation and try to maximize the chance to score more rewards through trial-and-error by the exploration of other actions as well as exploitations. This ensures that all variation of parameters-changing actions and the rewards that they will get from the environments' state. Once the optimum actions have been identified, the agent will exploit them. It also finds a balance by choosing between the exploring and exploiting actions using a ε-greedy action selection algorithm with a random number between 0 and 1 [3].

Table 2. Selected Oracle's initialization parameters

Parameters	Description
Memory_target	It enables automatic memory management (AMM) which allocate memory dynamically as required by the DB for all the main important memory parameters such as DB_CACHE_SIZE, SHARED_POOL_SIZE, PGA_AGGREGATE_TARGET, LARGE_POOL_SIZE, and JAVA_POOL_SIZE
Optimizer_mode	Set the optimization approach for the instance to the option of FIRST_ROWS, FIRST_ROWS_n, or ALL_ROWS
Optimizer_index_cost_adj	Set the relative costs of full scan versus index operations. OLTP queries gain better performance with lower settings
Optmizer_index_caching	Set the amount of an index will reside in the data buffer which also determines the cost of an index probe in a nested loop join
Db_file_multi_block_read_count	Sets the value of blocks to read in a single IO which determines the efficiency of a full table scan
Log_buffer	Set the buffers for the uncommitted transaction in memory. It affects DB performance when there are high updates but less on queries
Db_keep_cache_ size	Set the size of the KEEP buffer pool which retains data in the memory so that the queries read from memory and less from disk
Db_recycle_cache_size	Set the size of the RECYCLE buffer pool and keep data in the memory for a longer period instead of ageing out
Db_big_table_cache_percent_target	Set the percentage of the buffer cache for automatic big table caching. This is only activated from a DB restart
Inmemory_size	Set the size of the in-memory column store to keep tables that use this feature

Table 3. Performance statistics report from AWR.

Statistics	Description
Cache sizes	Information on the system global area (SGA)
Load profile	Information about the data workload for the selected period between the snapshots
Instance efficiency percentage	Information about the memory usage ratio for the buffer, library, sorting, redo, latch and parsing
Shared pool statistics	information on the system's memory usage for shared pool and SQL execution
Top ten foreground event	information on the top wait events that cover details such as DB CPU, amount of IO used by SQL, type of reading (sequential or parallel), log synchronization
Top SQL ordered by elapsed time	information on those SQL queries that took a long time to run
Top SQL ordered by CPU time	Information on those expensive SQL queries that consume the most CPU time
IO statistics	information on the tablespaces' IO activities

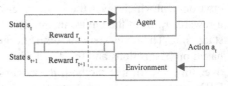

Fig. 3. RL agent's processes

In this paper, we propose to use Q-learning, a model-free learning algorithm [3], that explores the environment and exploits the current knowledge simultaneously via trial-and-error to find both good and bad actions. At each step, it looks forward to the next state and observes the best possible reward for all available actions in that state. It uses the knowledge to update the action-value of the corresponding action in the current state with the learning rate α $(0 \leqslant \alpha \leqslant 1)$. The $Q(s,a)$ value becomes a combination of immediate reward and discounted future reward. It is expressed [3] as:

$$Q(s, a) \leftarrow Q(s, a) + \alpha \{r + \gamma \, max'_a \, Q(s', a') - Q(s, a)\} \tag{1}$$

Where α is the learning rate, γ is the discount factor, r is the reward, s is the state of the DB performance result, a is the action on the parameter changes, a' is the new action, s' is the new state. $Max_{a'} \, Q(s',a')$ is the expected optimal value, $Q(s,a)$ is the old value. Equation (1) begins using random conditions at the start and iterates to converge to the optimum function, $Q^*(s,a)$. The entire process is iterative and is driven by the optimal policy as in Eq. (2):

$$\Pi* = argmax_a Q^*(s, a) \tag{2}$$

The Q-learning Algorithm starts with the initialization of Q table *(Q(s,a))* to zero for all state-action pairs *(s, a)*. It will observe the state, *s*, of the DB at the beginning followed by iterating actions until it converges. The agent will need to choose between exploration and exploitation as some changes can achieve local maxima. We propose to use the ε greedy algorithm [3] that randomly chooses the action whether to explore or to exploit. The ε value can decrease over time when the agent becomes more confident with its estimate of Q-values using a value of range 0.8–0.9. This is to minimize the agent's chance of getting skewed toward a single set of action for a given Q-value and persistently reusing the actions for a given state. The state is ambiguous and can only relate to the performance statistics produced by the AWR report.

Approximation of States and Actions. Both the optimum value and optimal policy can be used if the states and actions are small in numbers. However, a DB has many possible states and actions which cannot simply be determine by Eqs. (1) and (2). For example, if we consider the state of DB's statistics (as listed in Table 4), the combination can range up to $5n$ and the combination of the actions' parameters (as listed in Table 5) can exceed $10m$ where n and m are the possible combinations of permutation that can possibly exist. The sheer number, of the parameter's permutation and combination reaching into hundreds of thousands, exhibits the typical problem of curse dimensionality. To mitigate this problem, we use a neural network model [21] as illustrated in Fig. 4, which uses inputs as states s which are aggregated sums of DB statistics n, a scalar reward r as a target value, and the possible m number of parameter values of actions, a, of that attribute to the final Q-value derivation in Eq. (3). s_n refers to the state of the DB comprising of n statistics, a_m is the action that applies parameter change of the m combinations and i is the iteration. Figure;

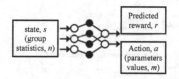

$$\begin{aligned} \text{Predicted reward}, r &= f^1(s_1, \ldots s_n)_t \\ \text{Predicted action}, a &= f^2(s_1, \ldots s_n)_t \end{aligned} \tag{3}$$

Fig. 4. NN function approxmiation of states vs rewars and actions

The data set used for NN training is from the knowledge-base that the RL agent builds up at the start with its trial-and-error testing. To simplify our approach, we focus on the current reward and equate reward to Q-value. The predicted reward from the NN versus the actual reward will form the mean square error function for the NN for optimization in Eq. (4). Within the NN model, there are several predictions of the score and actions required for the state. The maximum sets that give the best scores are selected, followed by a discount from the previous score. The calibrate reward function uses the action, $a_{predict}$, and find the real reward, $r_{predict}$ against the state, s.

$$MSE = r_{predict} - calibrate\_reward(s', a_{predict}) \tag{4}$$

In the proposed implementation, the Q-value is a normalized and calculated value of reward r for an action between two states. Normalization is done in order to bring all AWR statistics in the same range, as some measurements generate values in percentage and some in millions. The NN training process, to produce the predicted optimum reward, continues until the reward (or Q-value) meets the requirement of $max_a\ Q(s',a')$. The predicted action at each iteration in the medium learning phase is re-validated by the agent against the environment to derive the real reward. The validated information of $Q(s,a,r,s')$, which refers to the normalized Q value of the reward for the action applied to the existing state and bring it to a new state, s', is then added to the knowledge base for the next iteration of NN training. Figure 5 shows the flow of the RL agent in finding the optimum route along with the DB's states and best actions that yield the optimum reward. The Q value is the computed normalized value that takes into consideration the current and future rewards. γ is set to 0.1 for consideration of future states-actions but the emphasis is still on the current states.

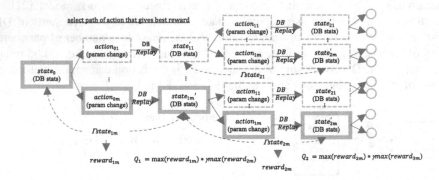

Fig. 5. RL process of discovering optimum DB's state-action-reward path

Scoring the Environment's State. The AWR report will generate and consolidate the statistics which are used to calculate the overall score for the DB's performance as shown in Table 4;

Table 4. DB's consolidated main statistics

Statistics	Description
Oracle instance efficiency	Contained the statistics on the memory components in the SGA such as buffer, sort, library, and execution ratio
Shared pool stats	contained the summary of the percentage of memory usage of the shared pool for executing SQL
Timed events stats	Showed the most significant waits contributing to the DB Time. Waits such as DB or log file read/write, CPU time, latch, sort
SQL stats	A summary of a list of top expensive SQL that occurred and their values in term of elapsed time read and write. For the intent of this score calculation, only the category of top SQL that consumed the most CPU time will be considered
Disk IO stats	Listed the IO values for all the tablespaces in the DB

Table 5. Actions' configuration parameters spec

Var	Initialization parameters	Range
p1	Memory_target (mt)	$1000 \leq MT \leq 3000$
p2	Optimizer_mode (om)	{first_rows_N| first_rows| all_rows}
p3	Log_buffer (lb)	$100 \leq lb \leq 500$
p4	Optimizer_index_cost_adj (oica)	$0 \leq oica \leq 100$
p5	Optimizer_index_caching (oic)	$0 \leq oic \leq 100$
p6	Db_file_multiblock_read_count (dfmrc)	$4 \leq dfmrc \leq 128$
p7	Db_keep_cache_size (dkcs)	$0 \leq dkcs \leq 1000$
p8	Db_recycle_cache_size (drcs)	$0 \leq drcs \leq 1000$
p9	Db_big_table_cache_percent_target (btcpt)	0–40% of p1
p10	Inmemory_size (inms)	0–40% of p1

The value among the group statistics varies widely, some are in percentage, milliseconds, counts, etc. We propose to normalize the accumulated statistics from the new state s_{t+1}, after the parameter change in relation to the previous state s_t. A weight is associated with the statistics' ratio if further tuning is required to emphasize a difference among them as shown in Eq. (5). A score for the new state is calculated as follows,

$$s_{t+1} = \frac{1}{ks}\sum_{i=1}^{k}\left(\frac{E_i}{E_0}w_E + \frac{P_i}{P_0}w_P + \frac{T_i}{T_0}w_T + \frac{Q_i}{Q_0}w_Q + \frac{D_i}{D_0}w_D\right) \qquad (5)$$

where k is the number of statistics considered, i is the instance in the loop that the agent uses to learn the optimum configuration, E is the summation of the Oracle instance efficiency percentage on all the memory components in the System Global Area (SGA), P is the summed value of the shared pool statistics of memory usage for the SQL execution, T is the summed value of the top 5 wait event statistics that occurred, Q is the summed value of the top expensive SQL's execution statistics and D is the summed value of the disk IO statistics of the tablespaces. W is the weight that emphasizes the importance of the individual statistics group. E_0, P_0, T_0, Q_0, and D_0 refers to the initializing values which are used as the baseline reference.

We also introduce another scaling factor against the statistics group to mitigate the basis of excessive value increment versus diminishing performance returns. For example, a choice is needed to be made between +60% increase in memory to get 20% DB performance returns and +20% increase for 12% return. Therefore, the scaling factor is presented as followed,

$$\textit{Scaling factor, } di = \frac{s_{i+1} - s_i}{s_i}/(\frac{1}{n}\sum_{i=1}^{m}\left(\frac{p_{i+1} - p_i}{p_i}\right)) \qquad (6)$$

where s is the state, i is the iteration of the environment instances, m is the number of parameters that will be modified, p is the parameter of change. So, the new value for s_{t+1} will be $s_{t+1} * d_i$.

Action for the Environment. Table 2 lists the top important initialization parameters that have a major impact on DB performance [22]. In this paper, we propose to use them to form the actions of change that the presented RL agent will employ against the database environment. The action for the environment is a compound configuration set of DB's initialization parameters as shown in Table 5. For action, $A_i = \{p1_i, p2_i, p3_i, p4_i, p5_i, p6_i, p7_i, p8_i, p9_i, p10_i\}$ where $p1..10$ are the parameters and i is the iteration in the learning loop. Each parameter has its own unique value, limit, and literals that cannot be inter-exchanged. An extra routine of parameters generation must be created to ensure that each one of them not only has to abide within the value limits but also ensures that it has sufficient interval block ranges to avoid unnecessary iterations within the training loop. It is not feasible to test all permutation and combination of the parameters due to exponential computation efforts involved. To reduce the range of testing, we use a series of parameters values combination as a single set of action instead adjusting the parameter value one by one individually.

4   Empirical Analysis

The purpose of experiments is to determine the effectiveness of ADPT for tuning the DB for optimum performance. The experiment starts by capturing workloads from a DB that supports transactional processing for a period of several hours during office hours. The files are then transferred to the test environment which is in turn processed and primed for replay. As for the test DB, it was cloned from the source DB and configured with the exact configuration like memory setting, tablespaces block allocation, and other parameters. The source DB has 2 schemas and there are over 50+ objects such as tables, views, and procedures which reside in two tablespaces. It has a peak of 18 users during peak hours, all of which use dedicated connections. The volume of transaction is estimated to be around 10 GB+ per week. As modern DBs are complex in design with hundreds of parameters and a wide range of features plus option, we must narrow the scope of test down to a manageable size; the 380+ initialization parameters of a typical Oracle 12c DB has been scaled to the top ten most influential ones as shown in Table 2 [22]. In the test environment, ADPT goes through the tuning process, iterating through and writing the results of each iteration out to the display and log files. By the end of the experiment, we expect the RL agent to find new parameters' values that can improve the DB efficiency and balance other performance statistics.

The main difference between the proposed test setting versus existing works [5, 6, 16, 23–25] is that (1) ADPT derives the results from the AWR outputs which contain detailed information on the performance statistics, and (2) ADPT uses a production workload to replay against the target database which keeps the test environment very close to the production. Whereas the common practice in existing works [5, 6, 16, 23–25] is to use a set of SQL samples to simulate the DB load which does not reflect the types of SQL executed in the production environment. They used readings from the database's dynamic views such as library or buffer hit ratio which may not have the capacity to capture the statistics for the entire test duration. Other statistics from the CPU, IO or memory utilization from the OS are also commonly used. ADPT finds the best combination of parameter values that suit the source DB. We do not stress the DB setup to the limit which is not practical.

The experiment runs on a Linux virtual machine which runs the production standard Oracle DB with 2 CPUs each with 2 cores, has 12 Gb of RAM and 500 GB of storage with 100 GB that is managed by Oracle's ASM. The Oracle version used is 12cR2 enterprise edition. As for the RL agent's predicting model, ADPT uses a neural network that comprised of 3 hidden layers of 100 nodes. It is trained with data in 50 batches and 100 epochs. Different configurations and combinations of neural networks have been tested, but, this setup was selected based on the better results with the least fluctuations.

4.1   ADPT Performance and Results

This section details the outcome of the tuned DB. Figures 6, 7, 8, 9, 10, 11 and 12 showed the results of the DB's performance statistics between two types of tunings made against the same DB and the workload. For one DB tuning, the big table in-memory caching initialization parameter is turned on that allows the DB to make more use of onboard memory to cache all of its tables. Without this parameter, the DB operates on the basis of caching only those rows of data that have been most recently used. The graphs values in Figs. 6, 7, 8, 9 and 11 have been normalized to bring all variables in a common range. Figure 6 shows that the overall efficiency improvement in the Oracle instance efficiency ratio, timed event statistics and disk IO statistics. The shared pool and SQL statistics showed incurring extra loads in their performance as compared to before. There is high probability that the contest of buffer cache for both in-memory and big table caching demand more from the overall instance's memory pool. But, as shown by the improvement in the overall instance efficiency, the overall results were improved.

Figures 6, 7, 8, 9, 10, 11 and 12 showed that the three phases of the RL learning process start with the number of iterations below 40 as the exploration phase and followed by the iteration of 90+ onwards as expert learning. Those that are in between is regarded as the learning-predicting phase where the RL agent learns to adjust its prediction. Figure 7 showed the difference between the actual versus the predicted rewards between 30th and 90th iteration band. For the Oracle instance efficiency ratio, shared pool statistics, timed event statistics and SQL statistics in Figs. 8, 9, 10 and 11 respectively, a strong fluctuation is shown in the parameters' values assigned by the RL agent. The degree of change was evident in the middle phase until the final state, where the RL has to rely primarily on its knowledge for assigning the actions to the state. Disk IO statistics in Fig. 12 takes a more volatile fluctuation especially for the DB that is tuned without the big table caching. However, the DB's disk IO statistics were reduced to the lowest readings toward the final.

Figures 13 and 14 showed the trends in the changes of the ten parameters throughout the tuning iterations for the DB's when the big table caching was turned on and off. The balancing process toward the latter state of the middle phase is leading toward a lower set of values that the RL agent has regarded to be the best. The final values were decided by the agent at the last phase.

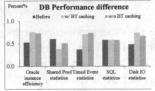

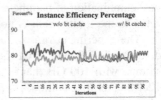

Fig. 6. DB Performance difference (with and without Automatic Big table Caching).

Fig. 7. Tuning runs' reward prediction deviations

Fig. 8. Instance efficiency ratio trend

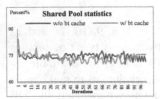

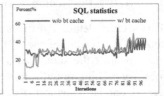

Fig. 9. Shared pool statistics

Fig. 10. Timed event statistics

Fig. 11. SQL statistics

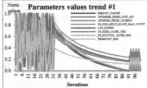

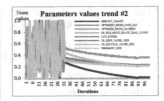

Fig. 12. Disk IO statistics

Fig. 13. Parameters values trend for DB without big table caching setting

Fig. 14. Parameters values trend for DB with big table caching setting

4.2   ADPT's Comparative Performance on OLTP, DSS and Hybrid DBs

Another set of tests were conducted to validate the ADPT efficacy in tuning DBs with different types of usage like DSS which has more select queries and experience more IO or, Hybrid DB which has a combination of OLTP and DSS operation. The experiments are repeated by capturing workloads from the DBs of three other IT systems each with a different workload. Figure 15 showed the DBs' performance in accordance with the captured statistics before and after they have been tuned with the ADPT. OLTP DB#1 and #2 serve the different applications and both have their unique set of user-base, schemas and transaction operations. DB#1 has a higher workload with more inserts transactions and DB#2 has a mixed of insert-updates. Improvement in performance of OLTP DB#2 is significant when the ADPT tuned the parameters in accordance to suit the current operation of OLTP particularly in the reduction of IO stats. The hits on shard pool stats metric has improved with an optimum sized SGA, which attributes to higher SQL stats and gives overall DB's efficiency.

Same results can be seen in the DB's results with the DSS load. Overall DB's efficiency has seen improvement with an increase in memory hit, reduction in IO while working increasing the cost of the SQL execution. The DB with the mixed workload has experienced lesser improvement as compared to the others. Mainly parameters set for OLTP are usually not optimum for DSS and vice versa. This resulted in a compromise in the operation improvement when ADPT tried to bring a common configuration setting to meet the hybrid operation. It is then settled for less optimal.

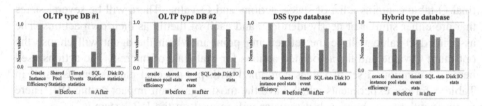

Fig. 15. ADPT test against DBs with OLTP DB#1, OLTP DB#2, DSS and mixed workloads

Table 6. Benchmarking RL tuning with other methods

Method	Complex/skill needed	Effort/labour	The risk to Prod DB	Adaptive to changes	Tuning coverage	Achieve opt result	Duplicate to other DBs
Manual tuning method [15]	High	Very high	High	No	limited	Low	Very slow
Use DB tuning packages [15]	High	High-v high	High	No	limited	Med	Slow
Performance tuning software [15]	Med	Med	Med	No	Med	High	Med
Rule-based tuning [15]	Low-Med	low	Med-high	limited	high	Med-high	Fast
Heuristic-based tuning [6, 16]	Med-high	Low-Med	Med-high	limited	Med-high	High	Fast
NN based tuning(need large dataset) [7, 8]	Med	Low-Med	Med-high	limited	High	High	Fast
RL tuning	**Low-Med**	**Low-Med**	**Very low**	**Yes**	**High**	**High**	**Fast**

4.3   Discussion

One observation made during experiments was that the state produced by the DB environment may not generate a consistent reaction to the actions as there are numerous other Oracle's background processes running which may impact on the final score. The current way to mitigate this is to run the learning process with a large number of iterations so that the variation of states' value will be reduced to a point where the magnitude is small and acceptable. Another observation, on the future reward and action predicted from the Q-learning's NN model, is that the reward has a higher error rate as compared to the realistic environment state's rewards. The MSE function is managed by another routine that verifies the real reward that the predicted action will produce, then add them back incrementally into the knowledge-base to enrich it. As more information about the actual state versus the action of the DB including the actual reward is made available to the NN model, the better the prediction it will make. The final Q-table contains a list of states, actions and Q-value. There will be several states that are either similar or nearly identical, and each of them has their own actions. The associated Q-value will be the referencing point in which the agent will choose the optimum Q-value and the associated actions for that state of interest. The actions used here is a compound set of values combined with pre-selected parameters as listed in Table 5 for our experiments which have the most significant impact on the DB. There is no granularity or how each parameter will impact on the DB's state.

Existing methods require the effort of collecting large workloads under different configurations setting before they engage their tuning process [8]. Whereas ADPT operates on the assumption that there is no prior knowledge or datasets to learn from. It must learn from scratch by interacting with the DB adaptively of what works and what not. The goal is not to do testing for extreme high one-dimensional load variation, but multi-dimensional that include changes in application structure too. The space of complexities in DB tuning is high; there are over 380+ major and minor parameters in a DB, over 500+ readings that are related to a DB's performance statistics plus DB's usage that has additional features. It becomes impossible to factor all these in academic experiments. Therefore, we narrow down the problem's scale to a manageable size.

From a common DBA's perspective, the transactional output and latency are a one-dimensional measure of DB and SQL performance. We need to cater for a wider variety of DB usage instead of confining the measurement to just pure transactional which are always in demand in OLTP systems. How can one tune a DB that has a combination of order processing, geospatial, reporting and ETL combined? Modern DB's landscapes are complex and ADPT proves to be effective in finding a matching set of parameters that is topical to a real system and not some simulated fictitious load. Table 6 gives a qualitative evaluation of the ADPT with other methods. As shown by experiments, ADPT can help the organization to optimize its DBs.

5 Conclusion

We present a novel machine learning-based approach, ADPT, using RL to optimize DB performance under a changing workload throughout the period. ADPT safeguards the stability and privacy of the DB by conducting the regressive tuning process onto a test environment that has duplicate setup with production workload activities replayed there. The RL agent learns what works and what does not on the parameters versus the outcome of the DB's statistics after workload replay in an iterative way. The reward is calculated from the difference between the DB's statistics before and after the parameter changes. Upon the completion of the performance tuning process, each state instances have multiple different actions and rewards associated with it. The RL agent uses the neural network model which learns to predict the rewards-actions. It recognizes the error gap between its predictions versus the actual rewards from the environment and it recalibrates through error correction. It then adds these instances to the training dataset cumulatively, thereby re-train and improves on its overall prediction accuracy. The empirical analysis was conducted using ADPT to learn and adapt to the workload replayed from the production DB's image. The results showed improvement in the performance results in the five DB statistics group areas while reducing unnecessary excessive value increases on the initialization parameters.

This paper uses the top significant initialization parameters to develop the prototype. There are over 650+ parameters initialization parameters that have other minor influences on the DB's performance, but they should be included in the future works. Another area to incorporate is the SQL tuning part which has a large impact on the DB's throughput, especially on the IO part. There are many other types of relational databases and each has its own unique set of configuration and administration. The work to adapt ADPT into another DB platform will require some effort to learn and understand their mode of operation first. Any IT systems' requirement changes throughout its lifespan and having an adaptive and intelligent tuning system to optimize them is the best approach to gain the best return of investment and performance from it.

References

1. Hoffer, J., Ramesh, V., Topi, H.: Modern Database Management. Prentice Hall, New Jersey (2015)
2. Colle, R., et al.: Oracle database replay. Proc. VLDB Endow. **2**(2), 1542–1545 (2009)
3. Mellouk, A.: Advances in Reinforcement Learning. InTech, London (2011)
4. Ding, Z., Wei, Z., Chen, H.: A software cybernetics approach to self-tuning performance of on-line transaction processing systems. J. Syst. Softw. **124**, 247–259 (2017)
5. Rabinovitch, G., Wiese, D.: Non-linear optimization of performance functions for autonomic database performance tuning. In: Third International Conference on Autonomic and Autonomous Systems, ICAS 2007. IEEE (2007)
6. Rodd, S., Kulkarni, U.P.: Adaptive self-tuning techniques for performance tuning of database systems: a fuzzy-based approach with tuning moderation. Soft. Comput. **19**(7), 2039–2045 (2015)

7. Mahgoub, A., et al.: Rafiki: a middleware for parameter tuning of NoSQL datastores for dynamic metagenomics workloads. In: Proceedings of the 18th ACM/IFIP/USENIX Middleware Conference. ACM (2017)
8. Van Aken, D., et al.: Automatic database management system tuning through large-scale machine learning. In: Proceedings of the 2017 ACM International Conference on Management of Data. ACM (2017)
9. Oracle Corporation: Master Note: Database Performance Overview (Doc ID 402983.1) (2018)
10. Antognini, C.: Troubleshooting Oracle Performance. Apress, New York (2014)
11. Coronel, C., Morris, S.: Database Systems: Design, Implementation, & Management. Cengage Learning, Boston (2016)
12. Alapati, S.R., et al.: Oracle Database 12c Performance Tuning Recipes: A Problem-Solution Approach. The Expert's Voice in Oracle. 1 online resource (li, 581 p.)
13. Kans, M., Ingwald, A.: Common database for cost-effective improvement of maintenance performance. Int. J. Prod. Econ. **113**(2), 734–747 (2008)
14. Habibi, A., Sarafrazi, A., Izadyar, S.: Delphi technique theoretical framework in qualitative research. Int. J. Eng. Sci. **3**(4), 8–13 (2014)
15. Alapati, S., Kuhn, D., Padfield, B.: Oracle Database 12c Performance Tuning Recipes: A Problem-Solution Approach. Apress, New York (2014)
16. Wei, Z., Ding, Z., Hu, J.: Self-tuning performance of database systems based on fuzzy rules. In: 2014 11th International Conference on Fuzzy Systems and Knowledge Discovery (FSKD). IEEE (2014)
17. Kuhn, D., Alapati, S., Nanda, A.: Performing flashback recovery. In: Kuhn, D., Alapati, S., Nanda, A. (eds.) RMAN Recipes for Oracle Database 12c, pp. 395–442. Apress, Bereley (2013). https://doi.org/10.1007/978-1-4302-4837-8_13
18. Ngai, G., et al.: Automatic workload repository battery of performance statistics. Google Patents (2009)
19. Oracle Corporation: Oracle Database 12c Release 2 (12.2) New Features (2018)
20. Kuhn, D., et al.: RMAN Recipes for Oracle Database 12c: A Problem-Solution Approach. The Expert's Voice in Oracle, 2nd edn. Apress, Berkeley (2013). 1 online resource (730 p.)
21. Van Hasselt, H., Guez, A., Silver, D.: Deep Reinforcement Learning with Double Q-Learning. In: AAAI (2016)
22. Gryglewicz-Kacerka, W., Kacerka, J.: Analysis of the effect of chosen initialization parameters on database performance. In: Kozielski, S., Mrozek, D., Kasprowski, P., Małysiak-Mrozek, B., Kostrzewa, D. (eds.) BDAS 2015. CCIS, vol. 521, pp. 60–68. Springer, Cham (2015). https://doi.org/10.1007/978-3-319-18422-7_5
23. Sharma, H.K., Nelson, S.: Performance enhancement using SQL statement tuning approach. Database Syst. J. **8**(1), 12–21 (2017)
24. Wiese, D., Rabinovitch, G.: Knowledge management in autonomic database performance tuning. In: Fifth International Conference on Autonomic and Autonomous Systems (ICAS 2009). IEEE (2009)
25. Zhou, J., et al.: Improving database performance on simultaneous multithreading processors. In: Proceedings of the 31st International Conference on Very Large Data Bases. VLDB Endowment (2005)

Prior-Knowledge-Embedded LDA with Word2vec – for Detecting Specific Topics in Documents

Hiroshi Uehara[1(✉)], Akihiro Ito[1], Yutaka Saito[1], and Kenichi Yoshida[2]

[1] Akita Prefectural University, Akita, Japan
{uehara,m20d001,yutakasai}@akita-pu.ac.jp
[2] University of Tsukuba, Tokyo, Japan
yoshida@gssm.otsuka.tsukuba.ac.jp

Abstract. This paper proposes a method to apply prior knowledge about topics of interest to Latent Dirichlet Allocation (LDA). The conventional LDA sometimes fails to detect specific topics of interest. Therefore, our approach uses word2vec to acquire linkages between words related to specific topics. The extracted linkages are used as prior knowledge about the topics in the subsequent LDA process. The extracted linkages can also be used to annotate words in a consistent manner. Such consistent annotations cannot be realized using conventional LDA, which relies on bag-of-words–based clustering. We examine our approach by applying it to travelers' reviews, to detect topics related to Japanese shrines. The experimental results show that our approach is effective in the following three aspects: (1) The average coherence of our approach, i.e., the semantic consistencies among words, outperforms that of the conventional LDA. (2) Words in each sentence are annotated such that the annotations reflect the topic of the sentence. The conventional LDA sometimes makes confusing/mixed annotations to the words in a single sentence. Our approach, on the contrary, can make annotations that reflect the topic of the sentence in a consistent manner. (3) Our approach enables to detect very specific topics complying with users' interests.

Keywords: Latent Dirichlet Allocation · Word2vec · Topic model · Prior knowledge

1 Introduction

Latent Dirichlet allocation (LDA, a.k.a. topic model) is widely used for classifying documents according to topic, in research and in other practical applications. LDA classifies topics based on the estimation of topic distributions in each document and word distribution in each topic. Once the number of topics is fixed, the word distributions of the topics are estimated so that the distribution of each topic is optimally distinctive from that of the other topics. However, such

© Springer Nature Switzerland AG 2019
K. Ohara and Q. Bai (Eds.): PKAW 2019, LNAI 11669, pp. 115–126, 2019.
https://doi.org/10.1007/978-3-030-30639-7_10

a classification of topics may not be satisfactory in terms of the semantic consistency of each topic [7] or the correlation to users' specific interests [4]. To overcome this issue, various researches have been applied prior knowledge to LDA. Recently, several researches [2,4,6] have adopted word2vec [5], a method to detect semantic similarities among words, to acquire such prior knowledge.

As a trial of LDA combined with word2vec, this paper tries to acquire specific topics of interest from a large volume of travelers' reviews, based on the semantic consistency of word distributions in a topic. When compared with the previous works on this topic, our approach is distinctive in two aspects, which are mentioned below.

1. Adoption of word2vec for maintaining not only the semantic consistency of words in a topic but also consistency of topic alignment in each sentence.
2. Enables LDA to detect specific topics of sentences, which conventional LDA is unable to recognize.

Even if the bags-of-words in each topic are semantically consistent, the topics annotated to words in each sentence may not be aligned with the context of the sentence. Rather, LDA based on bag-of-words sometimes assigns mixed topics to the words, even within a single sentence. Here after, "alignment" is used to refer to the process of making topics annotated to adjacent words in a sentence consistent. Our proposal intends to improve the topic alignment, and use an information entropy index to evaluate the performance of the alignment. As mentioned above, word2vec is also used to highlight specific topics which tend to buried in more general topics detected by conventional LDA.

Although these advantages above seem to be unrelated with each other, they are realized based on our single method of LDA combined with word2vec. Here after, we elaborate our proposal and clarify how our proposal realizes both of these advantages.

Section 2 reviews the previous researches on LDA with prior knowledge, to highlight the characteristics of our approach. Section 3 explains our approach that combines LDA with word2vec. Section 4 introduces the data used in the examinations, i.e., travelers' reviews, as well as the complimentary texts, for acquiring prior knowledge. Section 5 presents the evaluations and results, followed by the conclusion.

2   Related Work

LDA [1] has been applied in various researches, including empirical data analysis and modeling. Among them, several researches tried to make LDA apply prior knowledge for extracting specific topics of interest. One of these approaches used the bag-of-phrases approach, which recognizes patterns of continuous words as phrases. [3] made use of a phrase-recognition tool for medical terms and proposed the "Topical Phrase Model," which was an LDA with prior probability of n-gram phrases.

Incorporating semantic word networks into LDA was another type of prior knowledge. [7] embedded knowledge graphs into LDA (KGE–LDA), and quantitatively demonstrated higher coherence over conventional LDA. Additionally, qualitative analyses performed by [7] indicated that KGE–LDA classified words in a consistent manner, in terms of semantic interpretation.

As in the case of knowledge graph embedding, word2vec, which is known to produce good performance in capturing semantic similarities of words, can be used to provide prior knowledge to LDA. In this respect, several different ways of combining LDA with word2vec were proposed recently. LDA2vec [6] extended the skip-gram, one of the algorithms of word2vec, such that the similarities among words could reflect the topics classified by LDA. PW–LDA [4] demonstrated the advantage of topic clustering. Especially, when a set of short documents contained narrow topic domains, PW–LDA could find appropriate topic classifications, which were difficult for conventional LDA to find. PW–LDA applied LDA's topic probabilities to classify documents. Here, the topic probabilities were weighted by the similarities found by word2vec. [2] proposed another hybrid method combining LDA and word2vec, for document classification.

This paper proposes the use of word2vec to acquire prior knowledge for LDA. However, the purpose of this research is different from the above researches. We adopt prior knowledge based on word2vec for not only acquiring semantic consistency among topics but also zooming in specific topics with lower frequency of words. As stated in [4], LDA tends to fail in appropriate topic clustering if the frequencies of words are insufficient in documents. This issue exists even in the case of documents with large frequencies, if the words of a particular topic of interest are sporadic. LDA classifies words into topics based on distinctive patterns of word distributions. Therefore, if the topics of interest involve minor patterns of distribution, they tend to be buried among the major topics. In this paper, prior knowledge is used to zoom in on these types of topics.

3   Implementing Prior Knowledge in LDA

3.1   Issue of Topic Assignment to Each Word by LDA

In this work, we utilize a set of travelers' reviews of Kyoto, which is a famous place for traditional culture and food in Japan. One of the reviews describes the Japanese culture and is quoted below.

Example of traveler's review
    "I have been to Kyoto in Japan to try green tea ceremony held in famous temple. Whipped green tea in earthenware was fantastic! I enjoyed Japanese culture."

Because the words representing Japanese culture (i.e.,"ceremony," "temple," and "culture") are dominant, all the nouns, including "green tea," represent the topic of Japanese culture, in this sentence. However, LDA does not work as

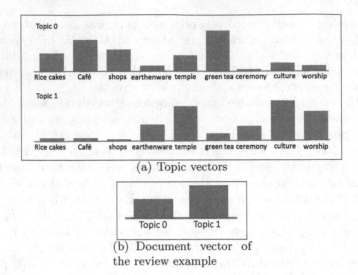

(a) Topic vectors

(b) Document vector of
the review example

Fig. 1. Examples of distributions estimated by latent Dirichlet allocation (LDA)

expected. Figure 1(a) shows an example of topic vectors, i.e., the distributions of words in each topic estimated by LDA. Topic 0 is a topic of Japanese food and beverages, while topic 1 is that of Japanese culture. In these topic vectors, "Green tea" has higher probability in topic 0 than in topic 1.

Figure 1(b) shows the example of a document vector of the review above. The document vector represents the distributions of topics in each document. Because the LDA determines the topic of each word based on the combinatorial probabilities of the topic vector and document vector, the topics of "ceremony," "temple," and "earthenware" in the review are likely to be annotated by topic 1, i.e., Japanese culture. On the other hand, "green tea" in the review is annotated by topic 0, i.e., food and beverages, because the combinatorial probabilities of topic vectors and document vectors might be larger in topic 0 than in topic 1. As such, simple LDA tends to produce semantically inconsistent alignments of topics, as follows (values in parenthesis are annotated topics).

Topic annotations with simple LDA
　　"I have been to Kyoto in Japan to try green tea(0) ceremony(1) held in famous temple(1). Whipped green tea(0) in earthenware(1) was fantastic! I enjoyed Japanese culture(1)."

3.2　Prior Knowledge to Overcome Inconsistent Alignments of Topics

One of the ideas to cope with the abovementioned issue is to acquire semantic linkages between "green tea" and a word representing Japanese culture, i.e., the words having high probability in the topic vector. For example, if "earthenware"

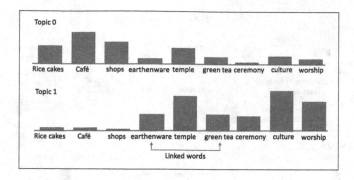

Fig. 2. Topic vectors

is found to be linked to "green tea," the probability can be biased by the value of "earthenware," leading to a large probability of the vector of topic 1 being described as in Fig. 2. As a result, the likelihood of topics in the annotations exhibits consistent alignment as below:

Topic annotations with appropriate topic alignment
  "I have been to Kyoto in Japan to try green tea(1) ceremony(1) held in famous temple(1). Whipped green tea(1) in earthenware(1) was fantastic! I enjoyed Japanese culture(1)."

We adopt word2vec to acquire such linkages as the form of words' semantic similarities. Additionally, we prepare domain-specific documents such as the ones concerning green tea ceremony to train word2vec. Such narrow domain documents enable word2vec to learn specific word linkages in a precise manner. That is, word2vec with domain-specific documents is expected to work as prior knowledge to create word linkages representing semantic similarities in specific contexts.

Prior knowledge produces linkages between multiple words, for example, "green tea," "earthenware," and "ceremony". If these words are distinctive within topic 1 of the topic vector, they might be dealt as an independent topic by the LDA when a larger number of topics is given. Such prior knowledge enables the LDA to zoom in on specific topics, which were buried by topics more general, in conventional LDA. The next subsection describes how prior knowledge can be applied in LDA.

3.3   Contextual LDA to Handle Prior Knowledge

Figure 3 illustrates the procedure for applying the prior knowledge. Based on domain-specific documents such as green-tea ceremony, word2vec provides semantic linkages for words (Fig. 3①). Then, the allocation dictionary is created, where unique IDs are assigned to all the vocabularies in the travelers' reviews. In this procedure, the same IDs are given to the words connected by

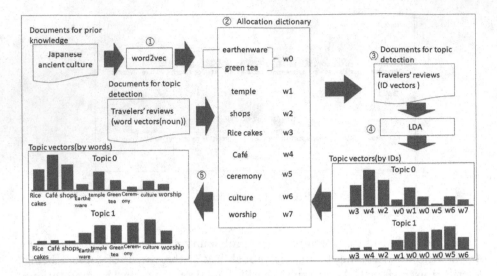

Fig. 3. Procedure applying prior knowledge to LDA

the same links, while IDs are assigned independently to each word without any link (Fig. 3②). Based on the dictionary, the word vectors in the travelers' reviews are converted to ID vectors (Fig. 3③).

LDA is applied to these IDs, instead of words. The IDs representing words under the same links are dealt with as if they are the same vocabulary (Fig. 3④), during the LDA process. Thus, the distributions are acquired in the form of IDs. Here, although Fig. 3 illustrates only the topic vectors, some document vectors may also be present.

Finally the IDs are converted back to the original words (Fig. 3⑤). With the distributions analyzed, words under the same ID have the same probabilities. Thus, "green tea" is more likely to be annotated by topic 1 rather than topic 0, in the review. As such, implementing prior knowledge as unique IDs to LDA is expected to realize more consistent alignment of topics in the same contexts of the document, than conventional LDA. We name this LDA with prior knowledge "Contextual LDA".

3.4   Examining Topic Alignments in Documents

We developed a system to evaluate the topic alignments by using contextual LDA. It uses the procedure shown in Fig. 3. When word vectors for topic detection are prepared in Fig. 3 (corresponding to ① in Fig. 4), the array of indices of the words are extracted as well (② in Fig. 4). The indices represent the locations of words in the original documents. For example, the index of cafe in Doc 2 is 6 as it is in the second row of the word index vectors. It is located at the sixth position, when counting from the beginning of the second document.

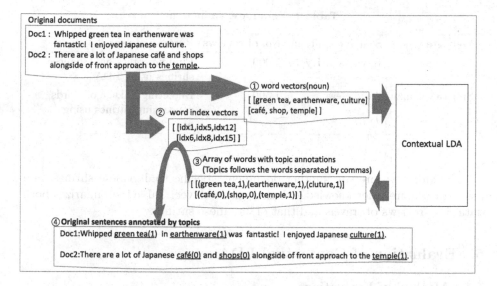

Fig. 4. Topic annotations to the words in the documents

The outcomes from contextual LDA include an array of words annotated with their topics in the documents (Fig. 4③), since the topics are determined by combinatorial values of topic vectors and document vectors, both of which are estimated by the LDA, as described in Subsect. 3.1. By referring to the word index vectors (② in Fig. 4), all the topics in Fig. 4③ are mapped to relevant words in the original documents, as in Fig. 4④.

If contextual LDA works effectively, the topic of each word reflecting the prior knowledge consistently aligns within the context, similar to Doc 1 in Fig. 4④. To compare the performance with conventional LDA, we prepared a similar system to show annotated topic alignment in the case of the conventional LDA.

4 Data for Examination

In our experiments, we used 5,000 traveler reviews concerning Kyoto, Japan. Kyoto has acquired global reputation as a place representing ancient Japanese culture. Currently, 17 Buddhist temples and Shinto shrines in Kyoto have been registered as World Heritage Sites. Because of this popularity, large amounts of traveler reviews can be found in various travel sites. Generally, the reviews of Kyoto present a mixture of interests such as construction of temples and shrines, traditional foods, and other cultural experiences such as tea ceremonies.

From among these miscellaneous contexts, we try to obtain a contextual LDA that detects specific topics concerning shrines. For example, the Japanese (traditionally) believe that shrines bring "Goriyaku,' good luck from Gods, to those who worship at the shrines. However, words concerning "Goriyaku" are less frequent, compared to general words concerning shrines. This situation is similar to the case of "green tea" in topic 1 in Fig. 1(a).

Table 1. Data for examination

Web site	Search condition	No. of reviews	Purpose of use
For travel	Reviews of Kyoto	5,000	Finding topics on Japanese shrines using LDA
Spiritual Japan	All reviews	1,500	Detecting linkage of words concerning shrines using word2vec

Therefore, we prepare another document specific to Japanese shrines, and use it to acquire prior knowledge, based on word2vec. Table 1 summarizes both data, i.e., reviews of travels and that of Japanese shrines.

5   Evaluation of Contextual LDA

5.1   Method of Evaluation

The performance of contextual LDA is examined quantitatively and qualitatively, and compared with that of conventional LDA. The following are the items to be evaluated.

(1) Quantitative Analysis
  - Comparison of coherence by topic
  - Comparison of topic alignment in each context
(2) Qualitative Analysis
  - Detection of topic vectors reflecting prior knowledge
  - Detection of sentences expressing the topic of interest in the original document

In the previous studies, coherence was used to evaluate the semantic consistencies of words in each topic. Although coherence is a bag-of-words–based measurement, it can be used to evaluate the overall semantic consistency of topics found by contextual LDA. We use the point-wise mutual information (PMI) coherence defined by the following formula (1) [7].

$$PMI(k) = \sum_{j=2}^{N} \sum_{i=1}^{j-1} \log \frac{p(w_i, w_j)}{p(w_i) p(w_j)} \tag{1}$$

Here,

k: Each topic
N: Number of top words of $k (N = 100)$
$p(w_i)$: Probability that the word w_i appears in a document
$p(w_i, w_j)$: Probability that words w_i and w_j co-occur
    in the same document

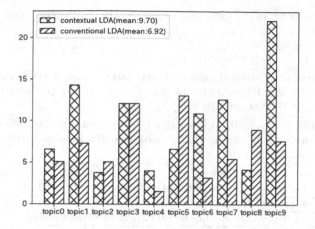

Fig. 5. Coherence for each topic

We make use of information entropy to evaluate the topic alignments in the documents. Assuming one sentence expresses only one context, the alignment of a topic in each sentence should be unique. This results in smaller information entropy for the topics within it. Therefore, if contextual LDA is successful in terms of topic alignment, a specific topic reflecting prior knowledge should show a smaller value of information entropy than the topics that do not reflect it. The following formula represents the information entropy for topic alignment.

$$I_H(k_{target}) = \frac{\sum_{i=1}^{D}(-\sum_{k=1}^{K} p(k|k_{target}) \log_2 p(k|k_{target}))}{D} \qquad (2)$$

$I_H(k_{target})$: Information entropy of the targeted topic
D: Number of sentences in the documents within which the targeted topic appears with the most frequency
K: Number of topics in each sentence
$p(k|k_{target})$: Probability that topic k appears in each sentence

5.2 Results of Quantitative Analysis

Figure 5 shows that the mean coherence of contextual LDA is much better than that of conventional LDA, i.e., our approach can classify words into topics in a more consistent manner than conventional LDA.

Table 2 shows the top 10 words (Fig. 5) of the topic vectors. The underlined words are the ones whose linkages were found by word2vec. Apparently, topic 9, showing the highest peak in Fig. 5 comprises many underlined words. Here, the words for topic 9 concern Japanese shrines.

Table 3 shows the information entropy of each topic. As shown in this table, the information entropy of contextual LDA is smaller than that of conventional LDA. For example, topic 9 of contextual LDA has less entropy. This indicates that topic 9 is annotated in sentences, with purity.

Table 2. Top 10 words in the topic vectors with peaks of coherence (contextual LDA)

Topic no	Top 10 words (probability)
1	autumn color(0.05), Japanese cherry(0.04), season(0.03), beauty(0.02), tourist(0.02), Kiyomizu temple(0.02), garden(0.02), picture(0.01), sight(0.01), visitor(0.01)
7	room(0.04), hotel(0.04), usage(0.03), convenience(0.03), station(0.02), sightseeing(0.02), cuisine(0.02), book-in(0.01), breakfast(0.01), reservation(0.01)
9	shrine(0.11), car parking(0.05), female(0.04), shrine ground(0.04), Shimogamo shrine(0.04), Shrine gate(0.04), easy birth(0.04), main shrine(0.02), worship hall(0.02), Inari shrine(0.02)

Table 3. Information entropy of topics

	Information entropy of each topic										Average
	0	1	2	3	4	5	6	7	8	9	
Contextual LDA	0.86	0.68	0.69	0.70	0.65	0.46	0.49	0.36	0.45	0.37	0.57
Conventional LDA	0.86	0.83	0.73	0.50	0.68	0.41	0.59	0.51	0.45	0.47	0.60

In summary, contextual LDA demonstrates superior word coherence as well as the advantage in information entropy analysis. This superiority is clear when the topic is strongly affected by prior knowledge.

5.3   Results of Qualitative Analysis

Interpretation of Detected Topics with High Coherence. Table 4 shows the topics concerning Japanese shrines. The first row shows topic 9, according to the contextual LDA described above. The second row shows topic 7, according to the conventional LDA. Although the latter is characterized by the words, "shrine," "shrine gate," and "shrine ground," topic 7 represents more general interests than topic 9, owing to words such as "tourist," "sight," and "season". Additionally, topic 7 includes Kiyomizu temple, which is one of the world heritage temples. Generally, the vocabularies of shrine reviews and temple reviews are quite similar. Topic 7 shows that conventional LDA recognizes the vocabularies of shrines and temples as the same topic, i.e., conventional LDA cannot distinguish between shrine and temple.

Meanwhile, topic 9 consists of specific words concerning shrines only. As shown in Table 4, topic 9 is specific. For example, the words "easy birth" is related to the legendary good luck brought by the Gods of Japanese shrines.

Table 4. Top 10 words in the topic vectors concerning shrines

	Topic No	Top 10 words (probability)
Contextual LDA	9	shrine(0.11), car parking(0.05), female(0.04), shrine ground(0.04), Shimogamo shrine(0.04), Shrine gate(0.04), easy birth(0.04), main shrine(0.02), worship hall(0.02), Inari shrine(0.02)
Conventional LDA	7	autumn color(0.05), shrine(0.04), shrine ground(0.03), tourist(0.03), stroll(0.018), sight(0.018), Kiyomizu temple(0.017), season(0.016), shrine gate(0.016), atmosphere(0.013)

Table 5. Comparison of topic alignments concerning Japanese shrines

Contextual LDA(Topic No.)	Conventional LDA(topic No.)
This shrine is said to bring about fortune(9) of marriage tie(9)	This shrine is said to bring about fortune(8) of marriage tie(7)
This shrine brings about fortune(9) of easy birth(9)	This shrine brings about fortune(7) of easy birth(9)
Ladies(9) should go circles(9) around the sacred tree(9)	Ladies(7) should go circles(6) around the sacred tree(7)
I enjoyed to worship at god(9) of marriage tie(9) and god(9) of beauty(9)	I enjoyed to worship at god(7) of marriage tie(7) and god(7) of beauty(0)
Construction(9) of this shrine(9) dates back to the 766 year of Tenpyou, ancient era	Construction(8) of this shrine(9) dates back to the 766 year of Tenpyou, ancient era

Topic Alignment in Each Sentence. As described in the previous subsection, the notably small information entropy of topic 9 in contextual LDA indicates that topics tend to be annotated uniquely within the sentence. In other words, the coherence value is high and entropy is low.

The followings are examples of annotated topics. (a) is the result of contextual LDA. All nouns are annotated by topic 9 with high probabilities (the terms in parenthesis are the topic number, followed by the probability). (b) is the result of conventional LDA, where "sake" is annotated by topic 3, which is not a topic concerning shrines. In fact, the origin of Sake comes from the ancient mythology of shrines. Matsuo shrine is known as the God of Sake, similar to Bacchus of Greek mythology. Although Sake does not appear among the top words in the first row of Table 4, it does appear as the 37th word from the top, in the vector, which is quite high among the total of 2106 vocabularies. Meanwhile, it appears as the 429th word in the vector of the second row of Table 4, which fails to recognize the word as belonging to topic 7.

(a) "Matsuo shrine(9,1.0) is very unique shrine(9,1.0) that it enshrines god(9,1.0) of Sake(9,0.9), Japanese rice wine."

(b) "Matsuo shrine(7,0.9) is very unique shrine(7,1.0) that it enshrines god(7,1.0) of Sake(3,0.9), Japanese rice wine."

More examples are provided in Table 5, all of which exhibit specific topics including "Goriyaku," with fine alignments of topics, similar to the results above.

6   Conclusion

This paper tried to detect specific topics from miscellaneous documents. For this purpose, we proposed a method to apply prior knowledge in LDA. Word2vec was used for this purpose. Our approach was different from the previous researches on LDA combined with word2vec in that our approach could annotate topics aligned with the context of each sentence.

The effectiveness of our approach was supported by the following evaluation results:

- Coherence of our approach was superior to that of conventional LDA
- Information entropy reduced following the use of prior knowledge. This guaranteed that the annotation for a single sentence would focus on its topic.
- The topic vector given by the proposed approach could use prior knowledge to distinguish similar topics, which conventional LDA could not distinguish.
- Annotated topics were aligned to comply with the context of each sentence.

Although, the examined data were limited to travelers' reviews, in this paper, our approach is expected to be effective, irrespective of the type of document. The evaluation of performance under general conditions has been left as a future research topic.

References

1. Blei, D.M., Ng, A.Y., Jordan, M.I.: Latent Dirichlet allocation. J. Mach. Learn. Res. **3**(Jan), 993–1022 (2003)
2. Budhkar, A., Rudzicz, F.: Augmenting word2vec with latent Dirichlet allocation within a clinical application. arXiv preprint arXiv:1808.03967 (2018)
3. He, Y.: Extracting topical phrases from clinical documents. In: Thirtieth AAAI Conference on Artificial Intelligence, pp. 2957–2963 (2016)
4. Li, C., et al.: LDA meets word2vec: A novel model for academic abstract clustering. In: Companion Proceedings of the The Web Conference 2018, pp. 1699–1706. International World Wide Web Conferences Steering Committee (2018)
5. Mikolov, T., Sutskever, I., Chen, K., Corrado, G.S., Dean, J.: Distributed representations of words and phrases and their compositionality. In: Advances In Neural Information Processing Systems, pp. 3111–3119 (2013)
6. Moody, C.E.: Mixing Dirichlet topic models and word embeddings to make lda2vec. arXiv preprint arXiv:1605.02019 (2016)
7. Yao, L., et al.: Incorporating knowledge graph embeddings into topic modeling. In: Thirty-First AAAI Conference on Artificial Intelligence, pp. 3119–3126 (2017)

Comparative Analysis of Intelligent Personal Agent Performance

David Herbert(✉)⬤ and Byeong Kang⬤

University of Tasmania, Hobart, Australia
{david.herbert,byeong.kang}@utas.edu.au

Abstract. Intelligent Personal Assistant (IPA) devices such as *Google Home* and *Amazon Echo* have become commodity hardware and are well-known in the public domain. Leveraging these devices as speech-based interfaces to bespoke conversation agent (CA) systems in vocabulary-specific domains exposes their underlying Automatic Speech Recognition (ASR) transcription error rates, which are usually hidden behind a probability matching of utterance to intent (*slot filling*). We present an evaluation of the two aforementioned IPA's isolated word and phrasal recognition rates together with an improvement scheme associated with a Contextual Multiple Classification Ripple Down Rules (C-MCRDR) CA knowledge-base system (KBS). When measuring isolated-word word error rates (WER) for a human speaker, Google Home achieved an average WER of 0.082 compared to 0.276 for Amazon Echo. Computer-generated utterances unsurprisingly had much poorer recognition rates, with WER for Google Home and Amazon Echo of 0.155 and 0.502 respectively. For phrasal tests, Google Home had an average WER of 0.066 in comparison to the Amazon Echo WER of 0.242 when processing human-sourced sentences. We applied a rule-based transcription error-correcting scheme for isolated words and achieved correct recognition rates of 100% for the Google Home in five of the isolated word data sets, and across all isolated words datasets we improved the initial average WER of 0.082 to 0.0153, a significant decrease of 81.34%.

Keywords: MCRDR · Intelligent Personal Assistant ·
Knowledge-base systems · Conversational agent

1 Introduction

In a separate study [13], we modified and applied MCRDR [17] to create a contextually-aware conversational system, initially in a pedagogical domain. When coupled to a speech interface (via an in-browser speech API) it was quickly determined ASR transcription errors were an issue when domain-specific utterances where not correctly recognised. Simple correction rules to replace misinterpreted expressions (either isolated words or phrases) were implemented as pre- and post-processing phases (with post-processing to correct mispronounced

© Springer Nature Switzerland AG 2019
K. Ohara and Q. Bai (Eds.): PKAW 2019, LNAI 11669, pp. 127–141, 2019.
https://doi.org/10.1007/978-3-030-30639-7_11

text-to-speech). Common corrections included replacing one-to-one terms, for example, *unicorn* with *unitcode*, but non-English, atypical utterances such as individual undergraduate unit-code identifiers (consisting of letters and numbers) are more difficult to recognise. The rule-based correction mechanism was expanded to include general regular-expression pattern-matching, together with the concept of having a contextual proximity to the rule(s) in an C-MCRDR knowledge-base where such replacement is referenced.

To improve the speech interface to our system, it was determined that the web speech API (that relied on poor laptop/desktop microphone support) should be replaced by a commodity IPA device. An evaluation of the "best" device (in terms of isolated-word ASR transcription performance) is needed which, when coupled to a correction system, can be used as the primary speech interface to our conversation system. This present study includes the initial evaluation.

1.1 IPA Workflow

Contemporary IPA devices follow the same general workflow (see Fig. 1) when processing a user's spoken utterance:

1. A user's utterance audio is compressed and sent to the vendor's cloud-based servers;
2. The vendor's cloud-based server performs ASR and the transcription result is sent as structured data (text) to the client's end-point;
3. The client endpoint returns a structured data reply;
4. The vendor's cloud-based server renders the reply as Text-To-Speech (TTS) audio, which is sent to the IPA.

Ordinarily in the client's endpoint, an appropriate response is returned for the specific slot-matched intent (step 3 above). All intents (or *skills*) however are statically predefined in the vendor's development environment, and significant effort is required to modify these intents. Using a knowledge-based system (KBS) approach as detailed below, we can overcome this static, unnecessary and time-consuming undertaking when defining conversational knowledge within the vendor's development environment, and instead move the definition (or *knowledge capture*) to a more rigorous and efficient KBS.

1.2 C-MCRDR Conversational Agent

MCRDR [17], which is an extension of Ripple Down Rules (RDR) [6] to allow for concurrent, multiple classifications for a case, has a knowledge acquisition technique that allows a domain expert to classify cases in the local context in which they arise – a case's classification is simply a refinement or justification of how it differs to the previous case that caused its current (incorrect) classification. Our modification of MCRDR, called Contextual MCRDR (C-MCRDR) [13] alters the inference mechanism to retain topical context between cases. Here we define cases to be individual utterances that are classified by conversational responses.

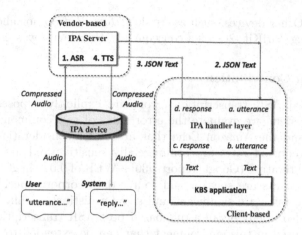

Fig. 1. IPA workflow architecture

With other modifications not detailed here, we have created a conversational agent (CA) based on C-MCRDR.

KBS CA systems retain all "conversational knowledge" in the knowledge-base itself, and when our C-MCRDR system is used, rules can be maintained dynamically, allowing an expert to add new rules at any time. This is problematic when using an IPA vendor's normal intent workflow, as to add new rules (or utterance matching slots), the entire vendor-based application needs to be redefined and compiled [1,11], and we have an unnecessary duplication in equivalent conversational rules. The solution is to capture the original raw utterance (bypassing intent matching) and pass it to the client KBS for inference, using the knowledge maintained in the KBS. The workflow is thus enhanced by the following, starting with the input from Step 2 in Fig. 1:

a. The custom device-specific IPA handler extracts the raw utterance from the structured data input;
b. The utterance is transformed based on rule-based corrections (correcting known transcription errors) and it is then passed for inference to the C-MCRDR KBS conversation system;
c. Result(s) from inference are transformed (for pronunciation) by rule-based corrections where known mispronunciations occur;
d. Responses are encoded by the custom IPA handler for return to the vendor IPA server.

Actual utterances received at Step 2 in Fig. 1 are subject to ASR transcription errors. At step (a) above the utterance is logged and tagged to be associated with the original user utterance. It is here we can now compare the transcription error rates of the IPA devices (or more specifically, the associated agents – *Google Assistant* and *Amazon Alexa*). These agent's device software development interfaces have provisions for the capture of the intermediate raw Speech-To-Text

(STT) results. Other devices, such as Apple's *HomePod* do not allow the same level of access e.g. SiriKit [2] – as a consequence, this device was not evaluated.

1.3   Research Contribution

As isolated word ASR transcription errors are explicitly exposed in our C-MCRDR CA system, we evaluate the error rates of two common devices, the Google Home and the Amazon Echo that are under consideration for speech input. Vendor-reported rates are commercially sensitive and are not reliably reported in the literature (Google reports [30] a WER of 0.049 in 2017), although the evaluation results are speaker and source-data corpora specific. However, the comparative rates are significant and show a distinctive difference in performance. We also briefly detail a rule-based post-ASR transcription error correction scheme used in this environment that can be extended to a contextual replacement scheme. Although the correction rules are added in a supervised mode, we differ to the statistical (for example, phonetic similarity) approaches for contextual replacement such as [3,34] by the use of incremental knowledge acquisition (KA) and maintenance of said rules via the MCRDR KA methodology.

2   Related Work

2.1   IPA Performance Evaluation

Intelligent Personal Assistants (IPA) are coupled speaker-and-microphone devices designed for mass-market use. With the ever-growing market of "smart" devices and the Internet of Things (IoT), the list of capabilities IPA devices gain to control and assist with aspects of modern life is considerable [20]. Evaluation typically compares psychological issues, such as cognitive load (e.g. how easy are the devices to use) [36], social engagement (elderly sociability) [31], user satisfaction [16], privacy concerns [14,15,23], learning languages [8], and a comparison of services [15]. These studies do not evaluate the actual ASR transcription error rates, possibly due to the device's performance achieving a level where they are not usually perceptible to the end users.

2.2   IPA Error Detection and Correction

Errors resulting from ASR transcription typically occur either as substitutions (S), insertions (I) and deletions (D) [37] that occur for a given source of words, N. This leads to the definition of the Word Error Rate (WER, Eq. 1):

$$WER = \frac{S + D + I}{N} \tag{1}$$

Schemes using confidence scores and intermediate probabilistic matches [4, 28] to detect transcription errors require that information to be available i.e.

inside the STT pipeline, but without access to the internal processes (a blackbox approach) this is not possible. Other schemes process signal-level acoustics and filtering for both detection and improvement [19,25], but these are acoustical and electrical engineering approaches and are beyond the scope of our research – we are limited to transcription results from the hardware "as-is" and consequently we take the approach to accept that errors occur and to manually measure the rates under standard, repeatable conditions. Recognition rates will change based on speaker vocalisation variability (for a single speaker and across different speakers) and spoken corpus [27], however for simplicity and repeatability we adopt the WER as our evaluation criteria, and measure it for two voices, the primary author and a computer-generated voice.

Generally ASR transcription correction is conducted through a manual process, selection between alternative probabilistic (most-likely) hypotheses, post-transcription editing [33] or pattern-based learning [22]. Unsupervised methods for correction basically take statistical approaches [3,34], for example, looking at phonetic similarity with region-based subsets of the target vocabulary.

2.3 Ripple down Rules (RDR)

The underlying KBS CA system that has been coupled to IPA devices uses a derivation of RDR. A considerable problem with a KBS is how to extract knowledge from a local domain expert. Typically they are highly specialised in their field, and are hard to engage and maintain access to for sufficient periods of time [6]. Compton et al. devised RDR, a derivation of case-based reasoning, to allow the expert to build a KB incrementally (when they have time) without the need of a knowledge engineer. The expert is presented with new cases as they arise and they then determine whether the existing classifications are correct. If they are not, they only need to justify a new classification (or reclassification) of a case based on differences between attributes of the case and the previous case that caused the incorrect classification.

MCRDR [17] extended RDR (now termed *Single Classification Ripple Down Rules*) with an n-ary tree structure to allow for multiple, concurrent classifications by allowing the inference mechanism to support multiple paths ending in satisfied rules with no children (leaf nodes), or satisfied rules with no satisfied children (intermediate nodes). RDR-based systems have had considerable academic and commercial success [32] in diverse areas such as health diagnosis and pathology systems [5,12,24], vision systems [29], and legal text citation [9].

We extended MCRDR (which we term Contextual MCRDR, C-MCRDR [13]) with conversational, natural language features by: altering the inference mechanism further to stack frames consisting of inference results (supporting *topical* context) [10,21]; incorporating post-inference query references (supporting Natural Language Interfaces to Databases (NLIDB)); retention of inter-inference request context (variables, supporting limited reasoning) and brittleness reduction by forward-rule lookahead and lexical and phrasal paraphrasing. Evaluation of a prototype system's viability in a pedagogical domain with a relatively shallow semantic range found the system responded appropriately for 80.3% of participant inference requests, and it responded inappropriately for 19.7% of requests (due to incorrect dialog classifications (4.4%) or out of scope requests (15.3%)).

3   Method

We measure the isolated-word and sentence ASR transcription error rates of Google Home and Amazon Echo by comparing the pre-selected spoken user utterances with expected speech-to-text (STT) results. This is achieved by configuring the vendor-based "skill" application *in the cloud* (see Fig. 1) to pass through the raw utterance without the selection of a preconfigured skill slot (this raw utterance is the final vendor-based ASR transcription). Each STT result from the vendor is then passed to a locally-based handler application (*IPA handler layer* in Fig. 1) that simply requests inference from our C-MCRDR system. Here the received utterance is logged for analysis and then potentially corrected based on a *regional* rule-based approach mentioned below (Sect. 3.1). The C-MCRDR KB for the error rate evaluation in this study is very simple, with one rule that is always satisfied – the rule's conclusion simply repeats the utterance text in response. Utterance corrections in the test system are applied in a preprocessing stage prior to inference, and for this base-line ASR transcription error measurement we chose non-contextual utterance correction, leading to a software implementation that defaults to a global region replacement policy. In actual production domains, regional-based replacement policies may be required – we note here the main aim of this particular evaluation is to measure the performance of IPAs, not correct them, however correction is required in real domains so simple rule-based corrections are performed.

3.1   WER Reduction by Correction

Our measurement and correction scheme is a supervised, rule-based, contextual, pre-processing method, where correction is determined by, in essence, out-of-vocabulary (OOV) terms, with context (based on satisfied rules' locations in the KB decision tree) used to pick candidate corrections. Correction rules (currently pattern-matching regular expressions) are associated and applied depending on the current context (a KB region based on the previous inference request), and we define two types of region: *global* (i.e. corrections applied irrespective of context) and *local* (a region extending from the last satisfied rule(s) to all children). Local regions allow utterance corrections to occur that would otherwise replace terms that satisfy rules elsewhere in the decision tree. For our transcription error rate evaluation, the size of the KB (one rule) is insufficient for anything other than a global correction policy, meaning we correct all errors, except when such corrections replace utterances that are not incorrectly transcribed. In this study simple (direct) word replacements by word-matching via regular expression patterns were performed. The developed application provides a GUI interface for the conversation author to enter such patterns (without knowledge of regular

Table 1. Example of regular expressions for correction

Rule	Replacement	Example
kicks (/d)	KIT$1	*kicks 123→KIT123*
unicorn	unitcode	*unicorn→unitcode*
item for	item 4	*item for→ item 4*
one	1	*one→ 1*
.*[i][t] (/d)	KIT$1	*crit 123→KIT123*

expression syntax), however more general regular expression are possible and examples as used in [13] are shown in Table 1. Future work will abstract common regular expression patterns via the GUI interface.

3.2 Environment

Two data corpora were used in IPA performance evaluation:

1. Isolated word evaluation: 1096 words in total were tested from the British National Corpus (BNC), [18, 26], which consists of 6318 words. Twelve groups of data were used, based on letter count (2 to 13 letters) from the BNC, and in each group the first 100 words were chosen (although the 2 and 13-word groups were limited to 25 and 71 words respectively in the corpora).
2. Phrasal evaluation: 700 sentences sourced from the text corpora"*A Christmas Carol*" [7] – a Markov chain [35] was used to generate seven groups of sentences ranging from 4 to 10 words, with 100 sentences per group.

We chose BNC as it seems a reasonable assumption high-frequency English words would be likely to be recognised by the ASR models used by the vendor's service when language settings are set to English. Letter count, manually annotated syllable count and sentence word count were used to establish if there is any direct relationship between length and recognition status – increasing letter count (with a general correspondence in syllable count) possibly leads to a increased spoken duration in the utterance which may influence the quantity of data subsequently captured for processing by the IPA's microphones. As opposed to just simply testing the top number (for example, the first 1000) of highly-frequency words, segregating the test data by letter count allows for further interesting analysis. For the phrasal evaluation, some pre-processing of small amounts of highly anachronistic words or proper nouns in the generated sentences from [7] were manually conducted to adopt a more contemporary vocabulary.

The room acoustics, device proximity and speaker were not altered between tests. Isolated word utterances were spoken by the primary author (with English as their native language), and *Karen*, a high-quality computer voice included in the Apple macOS X High Sierra 10.13 operating system, was included for comparison. No other human speakers were tested, so spoken variations in voice caused by differences in gender, pitch and timbre, accent etcetera were not assessed. Such assessment will be part of future studies.

4   Results

We examine the effects of BNC word letter count vocalised by a human and *Karen*. The effect of the BNC word ranking is then analysed, followed by sentence length from sentences generated by a Markov chain. When then examine the application of our global replacement policy correction scheme to reduce the average WER for the isolated word data.

4.1   BNC Word Letter Count

When voiced by a human, there is an unsurprising, significant decrease in the WER for both devices (Figs. 2 and 3) when compared to the computer-generated utterances. Here we also see significant performance differences between both devices with Google Home achieving lower WER for all letter ranges and speaker. Table 2 shows the average WER across all letter counts for both devices and for both speakers. We see Amazon Echo fairs considerably worse in both categories, for example, the device was not able to reach a WER below 40% when the source was *Karen*.

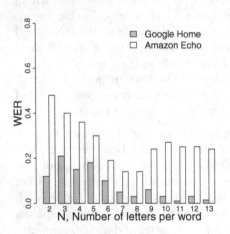

Fig. 2. Human – WER by letter count   **Fig. 3.** *Karen* – WER by letter count

Table 2. Mean device WER by letter count

Source	Google Home		Amazon Echo	
	$\mu(\times 10^{-2})$	$\sigma(\times 10^{-2})$	$\mu(\times 10^{-2})$	$\sigma(\times 10^{-2})$
Human	8.20	6.86	27.16	10.13
Karen	15.48	13.63	50.22	9.28

When voiced by a human, inspection of Fig. 2 seems to indicate a linear relationship between the WER and letter count, (N) for Amazon Echo, between

2 and 7 letters per word. A scatterplot (not shown) and linear regression analysis produces a model for this subset of the letter count (Eq. 2).

$$WER = 0.6190 - 0.06823N, R^2 = 0.9807, p = 9.017 \times 10^{-5} \qquad (2)$$

Amazon Echo performs worst at $N = 2$ ($WER = 0.48$) for a human speaker, and $N = 3$ ($WER = 0.77$) for *Karen*. This is perhaps of no surprise as low letter count words are phonetically short and thus possibly more difficult to recognise. Surprisingly performance worsens for $N > 8$, indicating in our evaluation, word counts of 7 and 8 letters are optimal for a human speaker.

In contrast, Google Home generally exhibits an increase in performance by increasing N, and shows the worst performance at $N = 2$ ($WER = 0.21$) for a human speaker and $N = 3$ ($WER = 0.38$) for *Karen*.

4.2   BNC Rank

We would expect the BNC word ranking to have an effect on recognition status – highly ranked words are very frequent in English and are then likely to be included in the ASR training models. However, two sample statistical t-tests indicated the mean BNC word rankings within each letter-count group had no effect on the recognition status of isolated words. When considering the overall mean rankings for the entire chosen isolated word corpora (i.e. independent of letter count), there was a significant difference in the rank means for *correctly recognised* (μ_{recog}) words and *recognition error* (μ_{error}) words for the Google Home – see Table 3. Although there was considerable variability in the data, in both human and *Karen* utterances, lower BNC frequency words (which corresponds to higher numerical rank) were recognised more consistently than higher-frequency words. Scrutinisation and a histogram (not shown here) of the source corpora indicated lower frequency words tended to have longer lengths (in terms of syllable count and thus more phonetic terms).

Table 3. Effect of BNC word rank on Google Home recognition status

	Human	Karen
t	$t(178.13) = -4.42$	$t(318.48) = -5.74$
p	1.69×10^{-5}	2.24×10^{-8}
μ_{recog}	1278.37	1319.05
σ_{recog}	1345.56	1345.84
μ_{error}	785.28	770.11
σ_{error}	1171.37	1188.84

4.3 Sentence Word Count

Sentences were vocalised by a human only as we have already established there is a considerable increase in WER when *Karen* vocalises words.

Referring to Figs. 4 and 5, the performance comparison between the two devices is very pronounced – the mean WER for both devices is shown in Table 4, and it is also shown as the dotted horizontal line in both figures. There does not appear to be any statistical significance with the WER based on sentence word count, however the lower average WER values compared to isolated word evaluations show the addition of more context (more words in a sentence) improves the recognition performance. Table 5 provides the percentage improvement in WER for both devices, and although small in actual magnitude, Google Home had approximately a 20% WER improvement when comparing the average isolated word mean to the sentence mean.

Table 4. Mean device WER by word count

Source	Google Home		Amazon Echo	
	$\mu(\times 10^{-2})$	$\sigma(\times 10^{-2})$	$\mu(\times 10^{-2})$	$\sigma(\times 10^{-2})$
Human	6.58	1.34	24.16	5.53

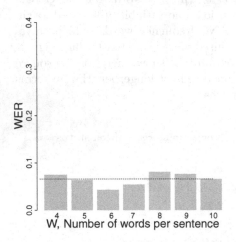

Fig. 4. Google Home WER

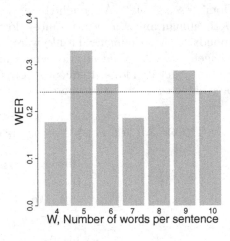

Fig. 5. Amazon Echo WER

Table 5. WER improvement for the human speaker between isolated words and sentences

Source	Google Home $\mu(\times 10^{-2})$	Amazon Echo $\mu(\times 10^{-2})$
Isolated words	8.20	27.16
Sentences	6.58	24.16
WER improvement	19.76%	11.05%

4.4 C-MCRDR WER Improvement

The final figure, Fig. 6, provides a visual summary of the global C-MCRDR correction method applied to the source BNC data grouped by letter count for the Google Home with a human speaker. A maximum of five correction rounds were required to minimise the WER across all letter count groups (66.67%, eight out of twelve groups, were minimised after only two correction rounds). A round consists of identifying all transcription errors and defining corresponding global correction rules for remediation.

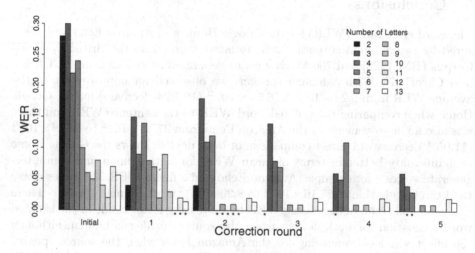

Fig. 6. Correction-based WER improvement. * – *indicates the round where the WER was first minimised for each specific letter count*

It can be seen in Fig. 6 that the WER was initially highest for the 2–5 letter count words – these contributed the most to the grouped average WER in each round. The WER was not reduced to zero in all letter-length groups as seven of the groups contained words from the source corpora that could not be corrected (the ASR transcription errors produced words that are also present in the corpora, so they cannot be globally replaced). As previously mentioned, due to the simplicity of the evaluation one-rule C-MCRDR KB, a regional (contextual)

Table 6. C-MCRDR WER improvement by correction round

Correction round	Google Home	
	$\mu(\times 10^{-2})$	$\sigma(\times 10^{-2})$
0 (no correction)	8.20	6.86
1	6.60	4.95
2	4.20	6.04
3	2.87	4.46
4	2.28	3.40
5	1.53	1.92
WER improvement (0 to 5)	81.34%	

correction policy could not be applied – in a production system, in theory the WER can be reduced to zero in all cases where regional context is incorporated. Table 6 shows the final, average improvement of the WER for the Google Home after five correction rounds.

5   Conclusions

The word error rates (WER) for the Google Home and Amazon Echo were measured by two different corpora – 1096 isolated words from the British National Corpus (BNC) [26] and 700 Markov chain-generated sentences from "A Christmas Carol" [7]. With a human speaker, we observed an improvement in the average WER from 8.20×10^{-2} to 6.58×10^{-2} (19.76% decrease) for the Google Home when comparing the isolated word WER to the sentence WER and there was also an improvement for the Amazon Echo from 27.16×10^{-2} to 24.16×10^{-2} (11.05% decrease). A direct comparison of both devices shows the Google Home is significantly better in terms of mean WER for both human and computer-generate voices – for example, Amazon Echo had a mean WER 3.31 times worse than the Google Home (27.16×10^{-2} to 8.20×10^{-2}) for a human speaker. There was a general trend of decreasing WER by increasing letter count in the isolated word evaluation for both devices when the source speaker is human, although the effect was less convincing for the Amazon Echo when the source speaker is computer-generated. Evaluation also showed a significant effect of the BNC word rank for the Google Home isolated word performance, with lower-frequency words achieving a higher recognition rate – this appears to be due to such words having longer average lengths.

Finally, there was no apparent relationship between WER and the sentence length for either device (the minimum and maximum sentence word counts evaluated were four and ten respectively). When coupled to a global rule-based ASR transcription correction scheme associated with our C-MCRDR conversation system, we reduced Google Home's average WER for the BNC isolated word category from 8.20×10^{-2} to 1.53×10^{-2}, a reduction of 81.34% after five rounds of correction rule definitions and their application.

5.1   Future Work

We will be selecting an IPA device as the primary speech input source for the control of semi-autonomous systems in other research. Based on our findings the Google Home has better ASR performance in our testing environment, however other factors such as the differences in the acoustic and signal processing electronic components in each device obscures the actual ASR performance of the vendor's cloud-based services themselves (i.e. Google Assistant and Amazon Alexa). An ideal comparison environment would present each service the same pre-processed, compressed audio, but this is beyond the scope of this work. Further evaluation will consider multiple speakers to assess the variability of vocalisations between speakers, as well as within the same speaker's session. Our C-MCRDR WER improvement scheme in this scenario may also consider the addition of individual speaker context when selecting correction rules. Finally, the widening of comparison to include other IPA devices such as the Apple HomePod (and variations of existing IPAs, such as Google Home Mini, Amazon Echo Plus etcetera) will be considered.

Acknowledgments. This research has been supported by financial support via a grant from the Asian Office of Aerospace Research and Development (AOARD). The research is also supported by an *Australian Government Research Training Program Scholarship*, and it has University of Tasmania Ethics Approval, number H0016281.

Data cited herein has been extracted from the British National Corpus Online service, managed by Oxford University Computing Services on behalf of the BNC Consortium. All rights in the texts cited are reserved.

References

1. Amazon: Alexa Skills Kit (2018). https://developer.amazon.com/alexa-skills-kit. Accessed 1 Feb 2019
2. Apple: SiriKit   (2019).   https://developer.apple.com/documentation/sirikit. Accessed 1 Feb 2019
3. Bassil, Y., Semaan, P.: ASR context-sensitive error correction based on Microsoft N-gram dataset. arXiv preprint arXiv:1203.5262 (2012)
4. Chen, W., Ananthakrishnan, S., Kumar, R., Prasad, R., Natarajan, P.: ASR error detection in a conversational spoken language translation system. In: 2013 IEEE International Conference on Acoustics, Speech and Signal Processing, pp. 7418–7422, May 2013. https://doi.org/10.1109/ICASSP.2013.6639104
5. Compton, P.: Pacific knowledge systems - challenges with rules. Report, University of New South Wales. http://pks.com.au/wp-content/uploads/2015/03/WhitePaperChallengesWithRulesPKS.pdf
6. Compton, P., Jansen, R.: Knowledge in context: a strategy for expert system maintenance. In: AI 1988, pp. 292–306 (1990)
7. Dickens, C.: A Christmas Carol. Project Gutenberg (1843). https://www.gutenberg.org/ebooks/46. Accessed 15 Dec 2018
8. Dizon, G.: Using intelligent personal assistants for second language learning: a case study of Alexa. TESOL J. 8(4), 811–830 (2017)

9. Galgani, F., Compton, P., Hoffmann, A.: LEXA: building knowledge bases for automatic legal citation classification. Expert Syst. Appl. **42**(17), 6391–6407 (2015). https://doi.org/10.1016/j.eswa.2015.04.022

10. Glina, E.M., Kang, B.H.: Conversation system with state information. J. Adv. Comput. Intell. **14**(6), 741–745 (2010)

11. Google: Google Actions SDK (2019). https://developers.google.com/actions/. Accessed 1 Feb 2019

12. Han, S.C., Mirowski, L., Jeon, S.H., Lee, G.S., Kang, B.H., Turner, P.: Expert systems and home-based telehealth: exploring a role for MCRDR in enhancing diagnostics. In: International Conference, UCMA, SIA, CCSC, ACIT-2013, vol. 22, pp. 121–127 (2013)

13. Herbert, D., Kang, B.H.: Intelligent conversation system using multiple classification ripple down rules and conversational context. Expert Syst. Appl. **112**, 342–352 (2018). https://doi.org/10.1016/j.eswa.2018.06.049

14. Horwitz, J.: Siri, Alexa, and Google Assistant can be controlled by inaudible commands. Venture Beat, May 2018. https://venturebeat.com/2018/05/10. Accessed 15 Dec 2019

15. Hoy, M.B.: Alexa, Siri, Cortana, and more: an introduction to voice assistants. Med. Ref. Serv. Q. **37**(1), 81–88 (2018)

16. Jiang, J., et al.: Automatic online evaluation of intelligent assistants. In: Proceedings of the 24th International Conference on World Wide Web, pp. 506–516. International World Wide Web Conferences Steering Committee (2015)

17. Kang, B.H.: Validating knowledge acquisition: multiple classification ripple down rules. Ph.D. thesis, University of New South Wales Sydney (1995)

18. Kilgarriff, A.: BNC database and word frequency lists (2006). http://www.kilgarriff.co.uk/bnc-readme.html. Accessed 1 Feb 2019

19. Li, B., et al.: Acoustic modeling for Google Home. In: INTERSPEECH-2017, pp. 399–403 (2017)

20. Lopatovska, I., et al.: Talk to me: exploring user interactions with the Amazon Alexa. J. Libr. Inf. Sci. (2018). https://doi.org/10.1177/0961000618759414

21. Mak, P., Kang, B.H., Sammut, C., Kadous, W.: Knowledge acquisition module for conversation agent. School of Computing, University of Tasmania, Technical report (2004)

22. Mangu, L., Padmanabhan, M.: Error corrective mechanisms for speech recognition. In: Proceedings of 2001 IEEE International Conference on Acoustics, Speech, and Signal Processing (Cat. No.01CH37221), vol. 1, pp. 29–32 (2001). https://doi.org/10.1109/ICASSP.2001.940759

23. Manikonda, L., Deotale, A., Kambhampati, S.: What's up with privacy? User preferences and privacy concerns in intelligent personal assistants. arXiv preprint arXiv:1711.07543 (2017)

24. Miranda-Mena, T.G., Ochoa, J.L., Martínez-Béjar, R., Fernández-Breis, J.T., Salinas, J.: A knowledge-based approach to assign breast cancer treatments in oncology units. Expert Syst. Appl. **31**(3), 451–457 (2006). https://doi.org/10.1016/j.eswa.2005.09.076

25. Moore, A., Parada, P.P., Naylor, P.: Speech enhancement for robust automatic speech recognition: evaluation using a baseline system and instrumental measures. Comput. Speech Lang. **46**, 574–584 (2017)

26. Natcorp: British National Corpus [BNC]. University of Oxford (2018). http://www.natcorp.ox.ac.uk. Accessed 15 Dec 2018

27. O'Shaughnessy, D.: Invited paper: automatic speech recognition: history, methods and challenges. Pattern Recognit. **41**(10), 2965–2979 (2008). https://doi.org/10.1016/j.patcog.2008.05.008
28. Pellegrini, T., Trancoso, I.: Improving ASR error detection with non-decoder based features. In: Eleventh Annual Conference of the International Speech Communication Association, pp. 1950–1953 (2010)
29. Pham, K.C., Sammut, C.: RDRvision-learning vision recognition with ripple down rules. In: Proceedings of Australasian Conference on Robotics and Automation, p. 7 (2005)
30. Protalinski, E.: Google's speech recognition technology now has a 4.9% word error rate. Venture Beat, May 2017. https://venturebeat.com/2017/05/17. Accessed 1 Feb 2019
31. Reis, A., Paulino, D., Paredes, H., Barroso, J.: Using intelligent personal assistants to strengthen the elderlies' social bonds. In: Antona, M., Stephanidis, C. (eds.) UAHCI 2017. LNCS, vol. 10279, pp. 593–602. Springer, Cham (2017). https://doi.org/10.1007/978-3-319-58700-4_48
32. Richards, D.: Two decades of ripple down rules research. Knowl. Eng. Rev. **24**(2), 159–184 (2009). https://doi.org/10.1017/S0269888909000241
33. Ringger, E.K., Allen, J.F.: Error correction via a post-processor for continuous speech recognition. In: 1996 IEEE International Conference on Acoustics, Speech, and Signal Processing Conference Proceedings, vol. 1, pp. 427–430, May 1996. https://doi.org/10.1109/ICASSP.1996.541124
34. Sarma, A., Palmer, D.D.: Context-based speech recognition error detection and correction. In: Proceedings of HLT-NAACL 2004: Short Papers, pp. 85–88. Association for Computational Linguistics (2004)
35. Singer-Vine, J.: Markovify (2014). https://github.com/jsvine/markovify. Accessed 15 Dec 2018
36. Strayer, D.L., Cooper, J.M., Turrill, J., Coleman, J.R., Hopman, R.J.: The smartphone and the driver's cognitive workload: a comparison of Apple, Google, and Microsoft's intelligent personal assistants. Can. J. Exp. Psychol./Rev. Can. Psychol. expérimentale **71**(2), 93 (2017)
37. Zhou, L., Shi, Y., Feng, J., Sears, A.: Data mining for detecting errors in dictation speech recognition. IEEE Trans. Speech Audio Process. **13**(5), 681–688 (2005). https://doi.org/10.1109/TSA.2005.851874

Toxicity Prediction by Multimodal Deep Learning

Abdul Karim[1]([✉]), Jaspreet Singh[1], Avinash Mishra[2], Abdollah Dehzangi[3],
M. A. Hakim Newton[4], and Abdul Sattar[4]

[1] School of Information Communication Technology, Griffith University,
Brisbane, Australia
{Abdul.karim,jaspreetsingh2}@griffithuni.edu.au
[2] Department of Chemical Engineering, Indian Institute of Technology Hauz Khas,
New Delhi 110016, India
avish2k@gmail.com
[3] Department of Computer Science, Morgan State University, Baltimore, USA
abdollah.dehzangi@moegan.edu
[4] Institute of Integrated and Intelligent Systems, Griffith University,
Brisbane, Australia
{mahakim.newton,a.sattar}@griffith.edu.au

Abstract. Prediction of toxicity levels of chemical compounds is an
important issue in Quantitative Structure-Activity Relationship (QSAR)
modeling. Although toxicity prediction has achieved significant progress
in recent times through deep learning, prediction accuracy levels obtained
by even very recent methods are not yet very high. We propose a multimodal deep learning method using multiple heterogeneous neural network types and data representations. We represent chemical compounds
by strings, images, and numerical features. We train fully connected,
convolutional, and recurrent neural networks and their ensembles. Each
data representation or neural network type has its own strengths and
weaknesses. Our motivation is to obtain a collective performance that
could go beyond individual performance of each data representation or
each neural network type. On a standard toxicity benchmark, our proposed method obtains significantly better accuracy levels than that by
the state-of-the-art toxicity prediction methods.

Keywords: Molecular activities · Toxicity prediction · Deep learning

1 Introduction

Every year a broad spectrum of chemical compounds are produced in various
laboratories all over the world. A large number of these chemical compounds
are suspected to be toxic or hazardous for human life, and at the end, many
of them are proven so. As a result, *toxicity prediction* has become one of the
most important issues in Quantitative Structure-Activity Relationship (QSAR)
modeling [10,21]. Various functional groups and their specific three dimensional

© Springer Nature Switzerland AG 2019
K. Ohara and Q. Bai (Eds.): PKAW 2019, LNAI 11669, pp. 142–152, 2019.
https://doi.org/10.1007/978-3-030-30639-7_12

orientations make chemical compounds toxic in nature. The principal metric used for the measurement of toxicity is the concentration of compounds and the time of exposure to humans [15]. The concentration of compounds that cause toxic or hazardous effect on human health are measured by experiments and are considered as *endpoints*. The exposure of toxic compounds to humans can take place through oral or intravenous uptake or inhalation. There exist several toxicity metrics but the most popular one is IGC50 [24]. IGC50 measures the concentration of the compounds that inhibit 50% of growth on test population.

QSAR modelling has made significant progress in recent years through deep learning [11]. To predict molecular activities via computational models, molecules are usually represented as strings of a given textual language such as Simplified Molecular-Input Line-Entry System (SMILES) [1]. Such SMILES strings can then be used to compute various types of numerical features (e.g. physicochemical descriptors) and molecular images [23]. Numerical features have been used in various traditional machine learning approaches such as K-Nearest Neighbours (KNN), Support Vector Machines (SVM), Random Forest (RF), and Fully Connected Neural Networks (FCNN) [14]. On the other hand, molecular images have been used in Convolutional Neural Networks (CNN) [6]. Computation of molecular images needs relatively less domain specific expertise than that of numerical features, but CNN models using them still achieve reasonable performance levels [6] compared to the other models using numerical features. SMILES strings can also be transformed into a vector representation and used in Recurrent Neural Networks (RNN) for molecular activity prediction [5].

In recent work on toxicity prediction, physicochemical descriptors and fingerprints are used in deep neural networks and consensus models by TopTox [20] to predict regression activity such as Pearson correlation coefficient R^2 between the experimental and predicted toxicity levels. Another system named AdmetSAR [22] uses molecular fingerprints to predict R^2 values by RF, SVM, and KNN models. Yet another system referred to here by the name Hybrid2D [10] uses a hybridization of shallow neural networks and decision trees on 2D features only to predict R^2 values. TopTox, AdmetSAR, and Hybrid2D use an IGC50-based benchmark dataset as one of their benchmarks and obtain accuracy levels 0.80–0.83 on that dataset. Clearly, these are not very high accuracy levels.

In this paper, we propose a *multimodal deep learning method* that uses multiple *heterogeneous* neural network types and data representations. We represent the formula of a chemical compound as a SMILES string and as a molecular image. We further represent the chemical compound using numerical features obtained from physicochemical descriptors. We train an RNN on vector representations of SMILES strings, FCNN on numerical feature values, and CNN on molecular images. We then build an ensemble from the RNN, the FCNN, and the CNN using an Ensemble Averaging (EA) method or a Meta Neural Network (MNN) to obtain the final output. Each data representation type or each neural network type has its own strengths and weaknesses. Our motivation is to obtain a collective performance that could go beyond the individual performance of each data representation or each neural network type. Our multimodal approach is different from a typical ensembling approach as the latter uses homogeneous neural networks and data representations. On the IGC50 toxicity benchmark dataset, our proposed method obtains significantly better accuracy levels (0.84–0.88) than that by the state-of-the-art toxicity prediction methods TopTox, AdmetSAR, and Hybrid2D.

In the rest of the paper, Sect. 2 covers preliminaries of toxicity prediction and neural networks, Sect. 3 describes our multimodal deep learning approach, Sect. 4 provides experimental results, and Sect. 5 presents conclusions.

2   Preliminaries

We give overviews of SMILES strings, the IGC50 dataset, and neural networks.

2.1   SMILES Strings

SMILES is a text-based chemical language that is used to describe the information about the structure of a molecule in a single line of characters [19]. SMILES strings obey a regular grammar or syntax. Various types of characters are used to denote atoms and bonds between them. For example, c is used for representing aromatic carbon whereas C represents aliphatic carbon. There are special characters like "=" and "-" to denote double and single bonds respectively. An example of a SMILE string is "CC1=CC(=O)C2=C(C=CC=C2O)C1=O".

2.2   IGC50 Dataset

Among several toxicity metrices, IGC50 is one of the most important endpoints [24]. IGC50 measures the concentration of compounds that inhibit 50% of growth on test population. The benchmark dataset, denoted henceforth by IGC50 dataset and used in this work, has IGC50 values and their test population is Tetrahymena Pyriformis [20]. Tetrahymena Pyriformis is an aquatic animal (Protozoa) that lives in fresh water. It is pear-shaped, 50×30 pm in length, multiplies in 3 h to 4 h and can be cultured in a single membered sterile culture [4,8]. Thus, IGC50 in the given dataset refers to acute aquatic toxicity of compound on Tetrahymena Pyriformis population. The time of exposure considered here is 40 h, which indicates that population of Tetrahymena Pyriformis are exposed to these compounds for 40 h and then reduction in growth was measured [20]. IGC50 values reported in the given dataset is measured in $-\log_{10}(C)$ where C is the concentration in mol/L [20]. There are 1792 compounds in the IGC50 dataset. These compounds are represented as SMILES strings with lengths ranging from 2 to 52 characters.

2.3   Neural Networks

A *deep neural network* (DNN) has multiple hidden layers while a *shallow neural network* (SNN) typically has only one hidden layer. We refer the reader to [17] for the concepts and mathematics of deep learning on DNNs. Below we briefly cover various types of neural networks based on their architectures.

1. **FCNN.** A neural network in which each unit of one layer is connected to all units of the next layer is termed as a *fully connected neural network* (FCNN). FCNNs take numerical features as an input to predict the output.
2. **CNN.** A *convolutional neural network* is a special type of neural network for the image data. CNNs can extract low level features from images and compute more complex features as we go deeper in the networks [18]. Variants of CNN like Inception, Alexnet and Resnet have been developed and employed as highly accurate image classification models [7].
3. **RNN.** A *recurrent neural network* is a specialized neural network for sequential data. RNNs can learn features directly from the sequence data without explicitly computing features. RNNs use their internal state (memory) to process the sequence of data. They have shown great success in natural language processing and machine translation [16]. RNNs usually are prone to short term memory problem [9]. The information flows from one cell to another sequentially and might be corrupted later in the network for longer sequences. Long short-term memory (LSTM) units or gated recurrent units (GRU) in RNN offer solutions to the short term memory problem [2].
4. **Ensembles.** An *ensemble* is a collection of multiple *component neural networks. Ensemble averaging* (EA) is a method to average out the outputs of multiple component neural networks in an ensemble. A *meta neural network* (MNN) may also be used for averaging out. Ensembles of neural networks often perform better than individual neural networks. Usually the data representations and the network types (e.g. FCNN or CNN or RNN) of all the neural networks in an ensemble are the same. An MNN if used is normally a shallow FCNN. We assume the FCNN, CNN, or RNN component neural networks used in ensembles are deep neural networks.

3   Methodologies

Our multimodal deep learning method uses multiple heterogeneous neural network types and data representations within an ensemble of neural networks. Figure 1 shows the proposed multimodal deep learning architecture. SMILES

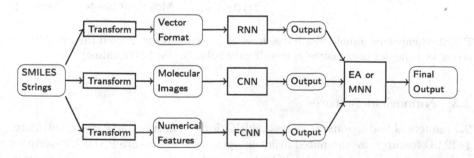

Fig. 1. Our proposed multimodal deep learning architecture for toxicity prediction

strings of chemical compounds are first transformed into a vector format, or a molecular image format, or a set of numerical features. Then, an RNN, a CNN, and an FCNN are trained respectively on the vector format, image format, and the numerical features. The coupling between the data representations and the neural network types are because the respective neural networks are the best suited ones for the respective data representations. The outputs of the component RNN, CNN, and FCNN are the averaged out through an EA method or using an MNN to obtain the final output. We further describe each part of the architecture.

3.1 Vector Representation

Each character of a SMILES string is represented by a 50 component one-hot vector, where only one bit is high and all other bits are low.

3.2 Molecular Images

SMILES strings are used to generate 2D molecular images [6]; see Fig. 2. An open source python library rdkit is used to generate 2D drawings of the SMILES strings in the IGC50 dataset [13]. The 2D coordinates are mapped onto a grid of size 100×100 with a pixel resolution of 0.2 A. Depending upon the presence of bonds or atoms, the gray scale images are color coded with 4 channels. Each channel encode different information about the molecule. Layer zero is used for the information about the bonds and the other three layers are for atomic numbers, gasteiger charges, and hybridization.

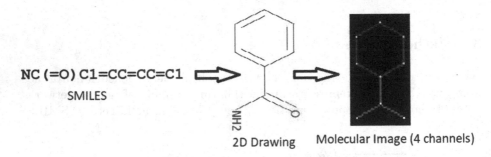

Fig. 2. Computing a molecular image from 2D coordinates generated from a SMILES string by using an open source python library rdkit (Color figure online)

3.3 Numerical Features

2D numerical features used are less multifarious in nature and easy to calculate. 1422 2D features are computed using an open source software PADEL descriptor [23]. The main reason for using 2D features is that these descriptors have shown promising prediction power in a previous study [10].

3.4   Input Output

All the three types of input data generated from the SMILES strings in the IGC50 dataset are fed into three types of suitable deep learning approaches to predict Pearson correlation coefficient R^2 values.

3.5   FCNN

We use a neural network with two hidden layers, each consisting of 100 units. The training data size is 1792 molecules with 1422 2D numerical features as described before. A random optimization technique **REF** is used to obtain the optimized values of the neural network parameters as shown in Table 1. Adam optimization with default learning rate is used as the back propagation gradient descent [12]. The drop out is used after first hidden layer only.

Table 1. Optimized parameters for FCNN

Parameter name	Parameter value	Parameter name	Parameter value
Epochs	400	Initialization function	Glorot-normal
DropOut	0.1	Activation (1st layer)	Sigmoid
Mini-batch	1024	Activation (2nd layer)	Relu

3.6   CNN

We use a three stage Resnet as shown in Fig. 3a. The Resnet consists of residual connections (skip connections), which make it prone to the vanishing gradient problem [7]. It allows the gradient to propagate to the early layer without vanishing. This type of skip connection is inherited in convolutional block and identity blocks in the network as shown in Fig. 3b and c. Adam optimizer with default learning rate and 128 batch size are used. The number of epochs is 150 with an early stopping criterion. The implementation detail of each layer is given below.

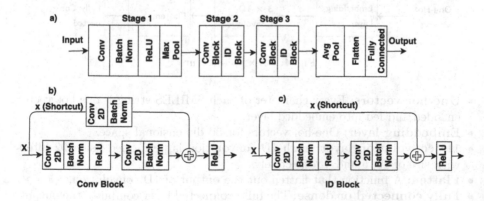

Fig. 3. Resnet architecture used in CNN

- **Input:** Input image is of the shape (100 × 100) with 4 channels.
- **Stage 1:** The 2D convolution has 64 filters of shape (7, 7) and uses a stride of (2, 2). BatchNorm is applied to the channels axis of the input. MaxPooling uses a (3, 3) window and a (2, 2) stride.
- **Stage 2:** The convolutional block uses three set of filters of size [64, 256, 256] each with a shape (1, 1) and stride (1, 1). The identity block use two sets of filters of size [64, 256] each with a shape (1, 1) and stride (1, 1).
- **Stage 3:** The convolutional block uses three set of filters of size [128, 512, 512] each with a shape (1, 1) and stride (1, 1). The identity block use two sets of filters of size [128, 512] each with a shape (1, 1) and stride (1, 1)
- **Average pooling:** The 2D average pooling uses a window of shape (2, 2).
- **Flatten:** It is a function that converts the pooled features from the max pooling layer into a single column feature vector.
- **Fully connected:** A dense layer which is fully connected to the previous single column vector generated by flatten. For a regression problem like in case of IGC50 molecular images, it consists of single neuron or unit.

3.7   RNN

We developed a variant of RNN which involves 1D convolutions instead of LSTM or GRU as shown in Fig. 4. The reason of using 1D convolution instead of GRU or LSTM is because IGC50 molecules are shorter in length. All the unique SMILES characters in the sequence are mapped to integer numbers using a dictionary. One-hot vector encoded characters are fed into a network. An embedding layer is used to compute an embedded vector representation of SMILES sequence. It should be noted that ReLu activation function is used with convolution layers while linear activation function is used with fully connected or dense layer. Adam optimizer with default learning rate and 128 batch size is used. The number of epochs is 150 with an early stopping criterion. The implementation detail of the RNN architecture in Fig. 4 is given below.

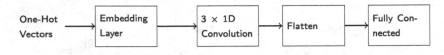

Fig. 4. RNN architecture

- **One-hot vectors:** Every character of each SMILES string is one hot vector encoded and fed into embedded layer.
- **Embedding layer:** One-hot vectors for 50 dimensional space.
- **1D convolution layer:** Each 1D convolution is performed using 92 filters with size of 10, 5 and 3 respectively.
- **Flatten:** A function that flatten out the output of 1D convolution.
- **Fully connected or dense:** The fully connected layer computes the output. It is densely connected all neurons from the previous layer.

3.8   EA or MNN

Each of the component FCNN, CNN, and RNN is trained independently. When the EA method is used, the final output is the average of the output of the component neural networks. When an MNN is used, we consider the outputs of the FCNN, CNN, and RNN as three input features to the MNN and then train the MNN. The MNN has only one hidden layer with 10 neurons. We use Adam optimizer with the default learning rate to optimise the MNN. Also, we use 400 epochs and an early stopping criterion. After performing hyper-parameter random search, we use mini-batch size of 512, drop-out of 0.4, glorot-normal initialization function and sigmoid activation.

3.9   Implementation

All the neural network models are built using a Keras deep learning framework on a system with NVidia Tesla K40 GPU.

4   Results

We split the data into train (70%) and test (30%) sets randomly in the beginning of modeling. The test set is kept aside (blind) for the final testing after finalizing the hyper-parameters like epoch, drop-out, activation function, mini-batch size and initialization function using 5 fold cross-validation (CV) on the train set. Table 2 presents the R^2 values obtained by component neural works, their ensembles, and the existing state-of-the-art methods.

Table 2. Performance comparison on (R^2) values using IGC50 dataset

	FCNN	CNN	RNN	EA	MNN	TopTox	AdmetSAR	Hybrid2D
CV	0.82	0.80	0.78	0.85	**0.88**	NA	0.82	0.83
Test	0.81	0.78	0.79	0.84	**0.86**	0.80	NA	0.81

4.1   Component Neural Networks

FCNN achieves better performance than CNN and RNN on test and CV. For CV, FCNN achieves 2% better accuracy than CNN and 4% better than RNN. For test, FCNN outperforms CNN and RNN base model by 3% and 2% respectively.

4.2   Ensemble Performance

For CV, the EA method improves the (R^2) value to 0.85 whereas the MNN approach improves it to 0.88. For test, the EA method improves the (R^2) value to 0.84 whereas the MNN approach improves it to 0.86.

4.3   Existing Methods

We compare the performance of our proposed methods with three state-of-the-art toxicity prediction methods. These three methods are described below.

1. **TopTox** [20] uses various types of approaches such as single task deep neural network, multi-task deep neural network and consensus models to verify the predictive power of element specific topological descriptors, auxiliary molecular descriptors (AUX), and a combination of both.
2. **AdmetSAR** [22] represents molecules by fingerprints such as MACCS, Morgan and AtomParis implemented with RDKit. Machine learning algorithms including RF, SVM, and KNN are used to build the models.
3. **Hybrid2D** [10] is using hybrid optimization of shallow neural network and decision trees to predict R^2 values using only 2D Features.

As we see from Table 2, performance of our ensembled approaches are better than that of all the three existing methods both on CV and test.

4.4   Analyses and Discussions

From the results in Table 2, it appears interesting that RNN with the vector representation of just SMILES strings and CNN with molecular images obtain similar performances on IGC50 datasets. It raises the question as to the usefulness of the CNN with molecular images. We leave this for future study. While ensembles improve performance over component neural networks, the MNN approach appears to be better than the EA approach.

We selected the IGC50 dataset which has relatively small compounds compared to the other datasets. This is because large molecules are difficult to encode in fixed sized 2D molecular images. We leave it for future study to use some other datasets or using some other data representations.

5   Conclusions

Multimodal data representations and network types best suited to the data representations can capture various aspects of a machine learning task. In this paper, we propose a multimodal deep learning method that uses multiple heterogeneous neural network types and data representations. We represent the formula of a chemical compound in a textual language, in an image format and also in terms of numerical features. We then build an ensemble from various types of deep neural networks suitable for the data representations. Our multimodal approach is different from a typical ensembling approach as the latter uses homogeneous neural networks and data representations. On the IGC50 toxicity benchmark dataset, our proposed method obtains significantly better accuracy levels (0.84–0.88) than that (0.80–0.83) by the state-of-the-art toxicity prediction methods.

Acknowledgment. We gratefully acknowledge the support of NVIDIA Corporation with the donation of the Titan XP GPU used for this research.

References

1. Bjerrum, E.J.: Smiles enumeration as data augmentation for neural network modeling of molecules. arXiv preprint arXiv:1703.07076 (2017)
2. Cho, K., et al.: Learning phrase representations using RNN encoder-decoder for statistical machine translation. arXiv preprint arXiv:1406.1078 (2014)
3. Dietterich, T.G., et al.: Ensemble learning. In: The Handbook of Brain Theory and Neural Networks, vol. 2, pp. 110–125 (2002)
4. Frankel, J.: Cell biology of Tetrahymena thermophila. In: Methods in Cell Biology, vol. 62, pp. 27–125. Elsevier (1999)
5. Goh, G.B., Hodas, N., Siegel, C., Vishnu, A.: Smiles2vec: predicting chemical properties from text representations. In: Workshop Track, International Conference on Learning Representations (2018)
6. Goh, G.B., Siegel, C., Vishnu, A., Hodas, N., Baker, N.: How much chemistry does a deep neural network need to know to make accurate predictions? In: 2018 IEEE Winter Conference on Applications of Computer Vision (WACV), pp. 1340–1349. IEEE (2018)
7. He, K., Zhang, X., Ren, S., Sun, J.: Deep residual learning for image recognition. In: Proceedings of the IEEE Conference on Computer Vision and Pattern Recognition, pp. 770–778 (2016)
8. Hill, D.G.: The Biochemistry and Physiology of Tetrahymena. Elsevier, Amsterdam (2012)
9. Hochreiter, S., Schmidhuber, J.: Long short-term memory. Neural Comput. $9(8)$, 1735–1780 (1997)
10. Karim, A., Mishra, A., Newton, M.H., Sattar, A.: Efficient toxicity prediction via simple features using shallow neural networks and decision trees. ACS Omega $4(1)$, 1874–1888 (2019)
11. Kato, Y., Hamada, S., Goto, H.: Molecular activity prediction using deep learning software library. In: 2016 International Conference on Advanced Informatics: Concepts, Theory and Application (ICAICTA), pp. 1–6. IEEE (2016)
12. Kingma, D.P., Ba, J.: Adam: a method for stochastic optimization. arXiv preprint arXiv:1412.6980 (2014)
13. Landrum, G.: Rdkit documentation. Release 1, 1–79 (2013)
14. Lima, A.N., Philot, E.A., Trossini, G.H.G., Scott, L.P.B., Maltarollo, V.G., Honorio, K.M.: Use of machine learning approaches for novel drug discovery. Expert Opin. Drug Discov. $11(3)$, 225–239 (2016)
15. McFarland, J.W.: Parabolic relation between drug potency and hydrophobicity. J. Med. Chem. $13(6)$, 1192–1196 (1970)
16. Mikolov, T., Chen, K., Corrado, G., Dean, J.: Efficient estimation of word representations in vector space. arXiv preprint arXiv:1301.3781 (2013)
17. Schmidhuber, J.: Deep learning in neural networks: an overview. Neural Netw. 61, 85–117 (2015)
18. Szegedy, C., et al.: Going deeper with convolutions. In: Proceedings of the IEEE Conference on Computer Vision and Pattern Recognition, pp. 1–9 (2015)
19. Weininger, D.: SMILES, a chemical language and information system. 1. Introduction to methodology and encoding rules. J. Chem. Inf. Comput. Sci. $28(1)$, 31–36 (1988)
20. Wu, K., Wei, G.W.: Quantitative toxicity prediction using topology based multi-task deep neural networks. J. Chem. Inf. Model. $58(2)$, 520–531 (2018)

21. Wu, Z., et al.: MoleculeNet: a benchmark for molecular machine learning. Chem. Sci. **9**(2), 513–530 (2018)
22. Yang, H., et al.: admetSAR 2.0: web-service for prediction and optimization of chemical ADMET properties. Bioinformatics **35**, 1067–1069 (2018)
23. Yap, C.W.: PaDEL-descriptor: an open source software to calculate molecular descriptors and fingerprints. J. Comput. Chem. **32**(7), 1466–1474 (2011)
24. Zhu, H., et al.: Combinatorial QSAR modeling of chemical toxicants tested against Tetrahymena pyriformis. J. Chem. Inf. Model. **48**(4), 766–784 (2008)

Context-Aware Influence Diffusion in Online Social Networks

Yuxuan Hu[1(✉)], Quan Bai[2(✉)], and Weihua Li[1(✉)]

[1] Auckland University of Technology, Auckland, New Zealand
{yuxuan.hu,weihua.li}@aut.ac.nz
[2] University of Tasmania, Hobart, Australia
quan.bai@utas.edu.au

Abstract. In recent years, online social network becomes an important channel for people to communicate and spread innovations. Most studies reveal that the diffusion of influence messages significantly relies on the network topological structure. However, an individual context, referring to a set of beliefs towards various topics based on past experiences, impacts the influence adoption to a large extent. Moreover, the broadcasting approaches from various channels, e.g., advertisements from TV, policies deployed by a country, a piece of breaking news, famous scandals, etc., also drive the network evolutionary pattern. In this study, we model the influence diffusion in online social networks by considering individuals' contexts and compare the influence propagation patterns under different scenarios. The results show that context-aware influence diffusion turns out to be an experienced model, where beliefs formed through users' past experiences affect the adoption of influences.

Keywords: Context awareness · Influence diffusion · Social network

1 Introduction

With the popularization of online social networks, the influence diffusion and decision-making behaviours of individuals are extensively studied since many real-world applications, e.g., personalised advertisement recommendation and influence maximisation, cannot survive without the investigation of the individual adoption behaviours [5].

Most studies reveal that the influence diffusion relies on users' interpersonal context. To be specific, influence spreads based on the links among users where implicit factors are considered comprehensively. However, interpersonal context is not enough to handle the complexity of influence diffusion in complex social networks, as well as modelling individuals' influence acceptance comprehensively, since the individual context formed over long term user experiences impact the influence adoption to a large extent.

© Springer Nature Switzerland AG 2019
K. Ohara and Q. Bai (Eds.): PKAW 2019, LNAI 11669, pp. 153–162, 2019.
https://doi.org/10.1007/978-3-030-30639-7_13

Individual context plays a vital role in determining the acceptance of an influence message. Researchers proved that an individual's adoption behaviour is a cognitive process, where individuals tend to make decisions according to the perceived beliefs derived from their past experiences. In turn, an adoption behaviour deepens these beliefs in individual context [2]. In other words, as individuals' decision-making is an experienced process, the influences like breaking news and public events which have higher importance affect individual contexts last for a long-time. Moreover, different from other ordinary influences, such impact lasts for long-time and is not supposed to be fading out of the public attention. However, in almost all the study, this critical factor is neglected.

Other than peer-to-peer influence, the broadcast, e.g., commercial advertisements in social networks, a newly deployed policy, etc., is acknowledged to be a practical approach to disseminate influences. The influence diffusion using broadcast is not restricted by the network topological structure but is probabilistic-based. For instance, there are many channels for users to perceive innovations, such as TV, internet, newspapers, etc., and each user has a certain chance to access the broadcast influence. Many studies explore how to maximize the positive impact by identifying a limited set of users from an online social network [5], but ignore the approaches via broadcast.

Agent-based Modellings (ABM) is an appropriate tool to model individuals' personalised heterogeneity and behaviours from a microscopic perspective [6]. Comparing with traditional mathematical influence diffusion models, ABM performs better in handling complex interactions among users and modelling influence diffusion in dynamic and large-scale networks [13]. Existing approaches based on ABM model context at a specific level, regarding individual features like preference and personalised behaviours like interpersonal interactions as contextual factors [4]. Therefore, in this research, ABM approach is utilised to model the influence diffusion by considering both interpersonal context and individual context.

The key contributions of this paper are summarized as: (1) we proposed a novel agent-based influence-diffusion model, Context-Aware Influence Diffusion (CAID) model, which takes interpersonal context and individual context into account to explore the influence diffusion patterns. (2) To solve the diverse performance of attenuation in influence diffusion process, we consider the importance of topics. By assigning importance weight of topics, the time decay function varied to different topics. An influence which is related to a topic like a sensational event with higher importance lasts for a longer time. (3) To model individual context which revised by experienced influences at a general level, we consider two possible channels for individuals to receive influences, i.e., peer-to-peer influence from online social networks and broadcasting influences out of the online social networks. Experiments are implemented to analyse the impact of individual context on influence diffusion process. We also examine how broadcasting influences revise individual context and therefore impact individuals' accepting influences. We believe this research can shed light on the individual context in terms of effective influence propagation in online social networks.

The rest of this paper is organized as follows: Sect. 2 reviews related literatures. In Sect. 3, we elaborate the proposed CAID model with the preliminaries and formal definitions. Section 4 shows the conducted experiments and results. Conclusion and future works are given in Sect. 5.

2 Related Works

In this section, we review the related literatures from two perspectives, namely influence diffusion models and context-aware influence diffusion models. The investigation of influence diffusion attracts the attention of many researchers. Enormous studies are dedicated to developing influence-diffusion models and exploring the propagation processes [5,6,8]. Many studies are conducted based on the two fundamental influence diffusion models, i.e., IC model and LT model. In both models, two significant features are explicitly presented, i.e., propagation and attenuation. To be specific, influence is initiated from a set of activated users and travels through the correlation graph. Whereas, the power of this effect decreases when hopping further and further away from the activated nodes [8].

With the novel features provided by social network platforms, context-aware influence diffusion models have been developed based on the traditional IC and LT models to investigate how contextual features impact individual adoption behaviours [10]. Liu et al. [12] propose a social context-aware trust network extraction model by taking social positions into consideration. Contextual features extracted from historical records are analysed to develop the effectiveness of influence diffusion and therefore to solve the influence maximization problem [1,9]. However, broadcasting influences like public event which have been proved to revise the individuals' adoption behaviours [11] to some extent are ignored by almost all of the existing context-aware influence diffusion frameworks when modelling context. Different from the studies mentioned above, the proposed model not only considers the interpersonal context but also captures the beliefs of users.

3 Context-Aware Influence Diffusion Modelling in Social Networks

3.1 Preliminaries

Beliefs and Context. Studies from discourse illustrate that a vast majority of influence messages follow topic-comment structure, which is composed of the topic and corresponding comments of the topic [3]. In other words, when individuals access an potential influence message, the decision is carried out based on the subjectively understanding of the message topics. In this sense, individual context is presented as a set of topic-oriented beliefs with a limited size. Psychology researchers also find the bidirectional influences between subjective beliefs and individual decision-making behaviours [2]. Specifically, individuals adopt influences based on these personal beliefs, in turn, their beliefs can be updated by the influences they accessed.

Context-Aware Influence Diffusion. Figure 1 illustrates the process at a microscope level. To take v_2 as an example. Once v_2 accessed the influence with a weight of individual context, the accessing influence updates v_2's individual context with importance weight and arrived time. $C_{v_2}(t_i)$ is its belief oriented to topic t_i. $prob_{v_2}^t(msg_p)$ represents the probability of v_2 adopt the influence at current time t by comprehensively considering interpersonal context and individual context.

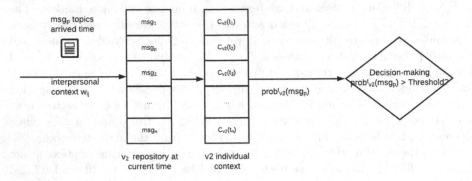

Fig. 1. Agent-based influence adoption process.

3.2 Formal Definition

Definition 1: A social network $G = (V, E)$ is a topological social network, where $V = \{v_1, ..., v_n\}$ is a set of users and $E = \{e_{ij}|1 \leq i, m \leq n\}, i, j \in N^+, \{v_i, v_j\} \subseteq V$, describes the interpersonal relationships among the users.

Definition 2: A user agent $v_i, v_i \in V$ represents an autonomous and interactive user in a social network G. User agent v_i has a set of neighbours $\Gamma(v_i) = \{v_j|e_{ij} \in E, v_i \neq v_j\}$. Each user agent proactively accesses the influence messages delivered from the neighbours and posts the existing messages over time.

Definition 3: An influence message $msg_p = (T, t)$ refers to a topic-related message delivered from one user to the reachable contacts, potentially affecting others' opinions and behaviours. Each influence message is associated with a number of topics $T = \{\tau_1, \tau_2, ..., \tau_n\}$ with different membership degrees $D = \{m(\tau_1), m(\tau_2), ..., m(\tau_n)\}$. Any topic τ_x comes with a different importance weight w_{τ_x}. The time step when msg_p arrived, i.e., t, appears to be a critical factor of msg_p, as users tend to access newly arrived messages and gradually forgetting those old ones. Therefore, a time decay applies to all the influence messages. As introduced previously, in the current setting, time decay does not significantly affect the topics with high importance degree but diminish those with average or low importance degree. The time decay function is described in Eq. 1.

$$f(t) = e^{-w_{\tau_x} \cdot \Delta t}, \tag{1}$$

with $\Delta t = t_{now} - t$, where t_{now} refers to the current time step and t denotes the time step when the influence message is received.

Definition 4: Broadcast influence is defined as an approach of injecting an influence message msg_p to an online social network $G = (V, E)$, where the initial infection does not rely on peer-to-peer influence. Specifically, for each user agent v_i, $v_i \in V$ receives a broadcast msg_p with a probability of p_{msg_p}.

Definition 5: An interpersonal context describes a user's influential relationships with the neighbour, considering various factoring affecting the effectiveness of influence propagation from one to another. $w(e_{ij})$, $w(e_{ij}) \in [0,1]$, refers to the influential degree of interpersonal context between user agent v_i and neighbour v_j, where $e_{ij} \in E$.

Definition 6: An individual context refers to a collection of limited topic-oriented beliefs, which is time-sensitive. Specifically, a user agent v_i's individual context at t derives from all the received influence messages, $M_{v_i}^t = \{msg_1, msg_2, ..., msg_n\}$, having topics with different belief degrees. Formally, the individual context of v_i at time step t is denoted by $C_{v_i}^t = \{C_{v_i}^t(\tau_1), C_{v_i}^t(\tau_2), ..., C_{v_i}^t(\tau_n)\}$, $\tau_k \in T$. $C_{v_i}^t(\tau_k)$ represents the degree of v_i's belief towards topic τ_k, which is formulated in Eq. 2.

$$C_{v_i}^t(\tau_k) = \sum_{msg_p \in M_{v_i}^t} msg_p(\tau_k) \cdot w_{\tau_k} \cdot f(t), \tag{2}$$

3.3 Individual Adoption Behaviour

Socio-psychology researches point out that the decision-making process as the stronger individuals' cognitive beliefs are, the more effort they devote to their adopting behaviours [2]. The probability for v_i adopt an influence message msg_p delivered from its neighbour v_j at the current time t can be formalised as:

$$prob_{v_i}^t(msg_p) = \begin{cases} \alpha \cdot w(e_{ij}) + (1-\alpha) \cdot f(C_{v_i}^t, msg_p), & \text{peer-to-peer} \\ \alpha \cdot p_{msg_p} + (1-\alpha) \cdot f(C_{v_i}^t, msg_p), & \text{broadcasting} \end{cases} \tag{3}$$

where $f(C_{v_i}^t, msg_p)$ is a function of individual context and received message msg_p, representing the degree of individual context affects influence acceptance. $w(e_{ij})$ denotes the influential degree between user agent v_i and message sender v_j. Comprehensive interpersonal contextual factors, e.g., trust degree, preference similarity and strength of ties contribute to this degree. α is a trade-off factor balancing the weight of two types of contexts, i.e., interpersonal context and individual context.

The impact of individual context $C_{v_i}^t$ on user agent v_i's adoption of msg_p at time t is formulated as:

$$f(C_{v_i}^t, msg_p) = \frac{\sum_{\tau_k \in T} C_{v_i}^t(\tau_k) * msg_p(\tau_k)}{\sum_{\tau_k \in T} C_{v_i}^t(\tau_k)} \quad (4)$$

Algorithm 1 illustrates the mechanism of user agents adopting an influence message. The input includes a user agent v_i and a desired influence message msg_p. The output is the acceptance probability for v_i to adopt msg_p at current time step t_{now}. Lines 2-7 calculate individual adoption probability by considering peer-to-peer influence. Lines 8-13 compute the individual adoption probability with the consideration of broadcasting diffusion.

Algorithm 1. Individual Adoption Behaviour

Input: A desired influence msg_p, a user agent v_i
Output: $prob_{v_i}^{t_{now}}(msg_p)$

1: **if** msg_p.sender is not None **then**
2:      v_i.repository.append(msg_p) with arrived time t and probability $w(e_{ij})$
3:      Calculate updated individual context with Equation 1 and 2
4:      Calculate the impact of $C_{v_i}^{t_{now}}$ on adopting msg_p with Equation 4
5:      Calculate accept probability $prob_{v_i}^{t_{now}}(msg_p)$ using Equation 3
6: **end if**
7: **if** msg_p.sender is None **then**
8:      v_i.repository.append(msg_p) with arrived time t and probability p_{msg_p}
9:      Calculate updated individual context with Equation 1 and 2
10:     Calculate impact of $C_{v_i}^{t_{now}}$ on adopting msg_p with Equation 4
11:     Calculate accept probability $prob_{v_i}^{t_{now}}(msg_p)$ using Equation 3
12: **end if**
13: return $prob_{v_i}^{t_{now}}(msg_p)$

---

4   Experiments and Discussion

4.1   Dataset and Experiment Settings

In the experiments, a real-world social network, i.e., Ego-Facebook[1], has been used. The dataset is clawed from Facebook, incorporating 4,039 users and 88,234 directed links [7]. For simplification, two sub-social networks are extracted from this dataset for the experiments, incorporating 899 users and 1000 users, respectively.

---

[1] http://snap.stanford.edu/data/ego-Facebook.html.

In this paper, two experiments are conducted to evaluate (1) the influence diffusion patterns under different individual contexts and (2) the impacts of broadcasting influences on influence diffusion. As the topic detection is out of the scope of this research, we make the following assumptions:

- For each network, there are five pre-defined topics $T = \{\tau_1, \tau_2, \ldots, \tau_5\}$ assigned. Influences and individual contexts are oriented to these topics with different membership degrees.
- Each user agent's interpersonal context represents a weight vector, i.e., the influential relationships with the neighbours, which is initialised using a Gaussian function.
- The probability of accessing a broadcasting influence is generated through a Gaussian function.
- In both experiments, the interpersonal context has an equivalent impact to that of the individual context, i.e., $\alpha = 0.5$.

Most research works in the field of influence-diffusion modelling utilise active coverage to evaluate the influence effectiveness. In both experiments, the same classic evaluation metrics are employed. Specifically, for a desired influence, active coverage represents the percentage of users who adopt the influence message in the entire network at time t.

4.2 Experimental Results

Experiment 1 is conducted in two social networks with different scenarios. As aforementioned, influence-diffusion patterns of the same influence can be varied in different social networks. In this experiment, assumptions are raised for both networks and topics. Network 1 is a social network of people from New Zealand; network 2 is a social network of people from Brazil. Two topics co-exist in these scenarios, i.e., the topic of "Rugby" as τ_1 and the topic of "Football" as τ_2. As the popularity of these two topics is different in these networks, the volumes of generated influences related to these topics are extremely different. For the public in New Zealand, rugby is more common in their daily life thus the volume of generated influences falls in the topic of "Rugby" is higher, similar for Brazilian to the topic of "Football". Therefore, individual contexts for users in these two networks, which are built up from their experienced influences, show a feature of diversity as well. We raised two scenarios to examine the variant property. Scenario 1 is to capture the diffusion pattern of an influence with the topic of "Rugby", the topic-related membership degree is therefore assigned as $D_{msg_1} = \{0.8, 0, 0, 0, 0\}$. Scenario 2 is to spread an influence falls in the topic of "Football" with assigned membership degree $D_{msg_2} = \{0, 0.8, 0, 0, 0\}$. Figures 2 and 3 illustrated the diffusion pattern under these two scenarios conducting with datasets of two networks. The experimental results support that CAID is an experienced model in which context places an impact on influence diffusion to a long extent. The higher beliefs the users have for a topic, the higher the probability for them to adopt the influences of the same topic. In turn, individual adoption behaviour strengthens their relevant individual context.

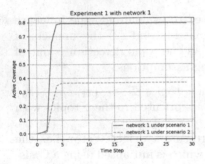
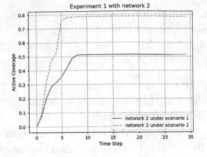

Fig. 2. CAID in network 1   **Fig. 3.** CAID in network 2

Experiment 2 examines how a broadcasting influence impacts individual context and influence diffusion. Two networks are used for the experiment. For user agents in both network, they are capable of receiving a broadcasting influence based on probabilistic. Figures 4 and 5 demonstrate the influence diffusion after the spreading of a broadcasting influence. As can be observed from both figures, the monitored influence diffusion performed more efficient after the spreading of a broadcasting influence. The reason may rely on the computation of $C_{v_i}^t(\tau_k)$ in Eq. 4 as the broadcasting influence is related to a high weight topic $w(\tau_k)$, while its topic membership degree is also high. This makes the broadcasting influence relatively takes a high weight in the contribution of individual context $C_{v_i}(\tau_k)$. When a desired influence which falls in the same topic is initialized in the network, $C_{v_i}^t(\tau_k) * msg_p(\tau_k)$ is big and therefore increase the probability of v_i to accept the desired influence. Conversely, when an influence is less irrelevant to the topic of broadcasting influence but related to another topic τ_j, $C_{v_i}^t(\tau_j) * msg_p(\tau_j)$ and $C_{v_i}^t(\tau_k) * msg_p(\tau_k)$ are both small, therefore v_i has a low probability of accepting the influence.

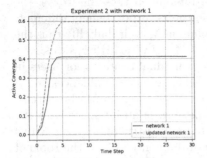

Fig. 4. Influence diffusion after broadcasting in network 1

Fig. 5. Influence diffusion after broadcasting in network 2

The experimental result and the above discussion demonstrate that individual context impacts influence diffusion. The higher beliefs an individual holds to a topic, the more likely for it to adopt influences falls in the same topic.

Moreover, a broadcasting influence spreading in the social network contributes to revising individual contexts. This finding sheds a light on the application of influence maximization leveraging by CAID.

5   Conclusion and Future Work

In this paper, we proposed CAID model, analysing context with the consideration of interpersonal context and individual context, to discover how context impacts individual adoption behaviour and influence diffusion. To model context-aware influence diffusion comprehensively, we generally defined context in two types, i.e., the interpersonal context and the individual context. Furthermore, considering the dynamic feature of context, a time-decay function is introduced to formulate how the timeliness of experienced influences building up an individual context. In Experiment 1, we demonstrated the use of CAID by measuring the active coverage under two scenarios. Experiment 2 proved that a broadcasting influence exerts an impact on individual context and therefore supports the prorogation of influences with the same topic. In the future, we will leverage this developed model by the following works:

- **Relationship of Individual Context.** Individual context is represented as a set of beliefs which are related to particular topics. It is intriguing to consider the relationships among beliefs for diffusion pattern explorations.
- **Analysing Influence Maximization Problem with the Developed Work.** With the development of social network platforms, contextual features have been explored with context-aware techniques to improve the effectiveness of influence maximization problem [10]. Our proposed CAID model could be extended to address the context-aware influence maximization problem.

References

1. Bai, Q., Li, W., Zhang, M.: A multi-agent system for modelling preference-based complex influence diffusion in social networks. Comput. J. **62**(3), 430–447 (2018)
2. Bandura, A.: Human agency in social cognitive theory. Am. Psychol. **44**, 1175–1184 (1989)
3. Hoeks, J.C., Vonk, W., Schriefers, H.: Processing coordinated structures in context: the effect of topic-structure on ambiguity resolution. J. Mem. Lang. **46**(1), 99–119 (2002)
4. Jiang, M., et al.: Social contextual recommendation. In: Proceedings of the 21st ACM International Conference on Information and Knowledge Management, CIKM 2012, pp. 45–54. ACM, New York (2012)
5. Kempe, D., Kleinberg, J., Tardos, É.: Maximizing the spread of influence through a social network. In: Proceedings of the Ninth ACM SIGKDD International Conference on Knowledge Discovery and Data Mining, pp. 137–146. ACM (2003)
6. Kiesling, E., Günther, M., Stummer, C., Wakolbinger, L.M.: Agent-based simulation of innovation diffusion: a review. Central Eur. J. Oper. **20**(2), 183–230 (2012)

7. Leskovec, J., Mcauley, J.J.: Learning to discover social circles in ego networks. In: Pereira, F., Burges, C.J.C., Bottou, L., Weinberger, K.Q. (eds.) Advances in Neural Information Processing Systems, vol. 25, pp. 539–547. Curran Associates, Inc. (2012)

8. Li, W., Bai, Q., Jiang, C., Zhang, M.: Stigmergy-based influence maximization in social networks. In: Booth, R., Zhang, M.-L. (eds.) PRICAI 2016. LNCS (LNAI), vol. 9810, pp. 750–762. Springer, Cham (2016). https://doi.org/10.1007/978-3-319-42911-3_63

9. Li, X., Cheng, X., Su, S., Sun, C.: Community-based seeds selection algorithm for location aware influence maximization. Neurocomputing **275**, 1601–1613 (2018)

10. Li, Y., Fan, J., Wang, Y., Tan, K.: Influence maximization on social graphs: a survey. IEEE Trans. Knowl. Data Eng. **30**(10), 1852–1872 (2018). https://doi.org/10.1109/TKDE.2018.2807843

11. Liu, C., Zhan, X.X., Zhang, Z.K., Sun, G.Q., Hui, P.M.: How events determine spreading patterns: information transmission via internal and external influences on social networks. New J. Phys. **17**(11), 113045 (2015)

12. Liu, G., et al.: Context-aware trust network extraction in large-scale trust-oriented social networks. World Wide Web **21**(3), 713–738 (2018)

13. van Maanen, P.P., van der Vecht, B.: An agent-based approach to modeling online social influence. In: Proceedings of the 2013 IEEE/ACM International Conference on Advances in Social Networks Analysis and Mining, ASONAM 2013, pp. 600–607. ACM, New York (2013)

Network Embedding via Link Strength Adjusted Random Walk

Chenliang Li[1], Donghai Guan[1,2], and Weiwei Yuan[1,2(✉)]

[1] Department of Computer Science and Technology,
Nanjing University of Aeronautics and Astronautics, Nanjing, China
{chenliangli,dhguan,yuanweiwei}@nuaa.edu.cn
[2] Corroborative Innovation Center of Novel Software Technology
and Industrialization, Nanjing 210093, China

Abstract. Network embedding is a useful tool to map graph structures into vector spaces, which facilitates graph analysis tasks including node classification, graph visualization, similarity calculation etc. Existing network embedding methods calculate embedding vectors based on node series generated by random walks. These methods treat all the links equally during the random walk procedure, which leads to the missing of structural information that is key to the embedding performance. We therefore propose in this paper a novel random walk-based network embedding method called Self-Adjusting Random Walk (SARW). SARW utilizes a self-adjusting strategy that makes the walking biased towards the links that are more strongly connected in order to better capture the structural information. Further more, the strengths of links are updated using the embedding output as feedback. Through experiments we have verified that our method out performs state-of-the-art network embedding methods, in node classification tasks and link prediction tasks.

Keywords: Network embedding · Network mining · Data mining

1 Introduction

Network embedding has become a hot research topic in network analysis nowadays. It maps vertices of a network into low-dimensional vector spaces. This can facilitate nearly every aspects of network analysis problems, such as node classification, graph visualization, similarity calculation. Random walk is one of the most popular algorithms used in embedding methods to extract structural similarity information between nodes. Existing random-walk-based network embedding methods [1–3] calculate embedding vectors based on the idea that two nodes appear in the original graph should remain such structural similarity in the vector space.

However, traditional random walk algorithm treats every link equally in the walking procedure. Links connected to a same node have the same probability to be included in the walking sequence. This kind of walking strategy ignores

© Springer Nature Switzerland AG 2019
K. Ohara and Q. Bai (Eds.): PKAW 2019, LNAI 11669, pp. 163–172, 2019.
https://doi.org/10.1007/978-3-030-30639-7_14

the fact that the links are not identical. According to the theory of Homophily [11], the structural environment of two nodes can reflect their similarity. Existing random walk based algorithms are unable to distinguish between links with different structural equivalence. To explicitly represent such latent feature of links, a new concept called link strength is introduced. Although classic similarity calculating methods such as common neighbors, are capable of representing implicit link strengths in local scales, such methods fail when the network is sparse. Higher-order similarity measurements such as 2-hop common neighbors, can depict link strengths more precisely, but it brings about high computation cost.

To solve the problems of the existing methods, we propose in this paper a novel random walk based network embedding method, called Self-Adjusting Random Walk (SARW). SARW utilizes self-adjusting scheme in the random walk procedure to better capture implicit link strengths in order to shed light on the latent structural information of networks, and eventually boost the embedding performances. The basic idea of the self-adjusting scheme is to use the embedding output to update the graph status, then again calculate embeddings based on the newly updated graph. The self-adjusting random walk algorithm inclines to walk through stronger links, and the strengths of links are calculated by the closeness of the embedding vectors. The embeddings can therefore reflect relationships between nodes more correctly. Moreover, using the embedding vectors as feedback does not require any other internal information, therefore it can save both time and space.

The main contributions of this paper are:

- We analyze the network structure and find that the embedding performance of the random walk algorithm with link strengths is better than traditional random walk network embedding algorithms.
- We propose a self-adjusting random walk network embedding algorithm adds link strengths in the walking procedure such that it inclines to walk through stronger links. The link strengths are calculated based on the closeness of embedding vectors.
- We conduct extensive experiments to verify that the proposed method has better performance than existing methods.

The rest of the paper is organized as follows: Sect. 2 introduces the related works; Sect. 3 describes the details of the SARW model; Sect. 4 shows the experiment results and the analysis of SARW; Sect. 5 is the conclusion and future works.

2   Related Works

Network embedding aims to map vertices into vector space, the embedding vectors can be used in various applications including node classification, graph visualization, link prediction and other network analysis tasks. In early 2000s, network embedding mainly focuses on reducing the high dimensionality of graph data. Since 2010, the trend of network embedding research has shifted to develop scalable, efficient embedding algorithms that facilitate graph mining researches in complex networks. Representative works include DeepWalk [1], LINE [2], and node2vec [3]. These algorithms utilizes the word2vec [7] algorithm of natural language processing that maps words into vector spaces according to the co-occurrence features of words.

Since 2017, there has been a surge of network embedding researches, including [4–6]. These works mainly improved the existing works to capture more structural information in the embedding process.

3   The Proposed Method

In this section, we mainly introduce the proposed network embedding algorithm SARW in detail. We will demonstrate how self-adjusting random walk embedding is performed and show how the objective is able to compute embeddings. First of all, we will define the network embedding problem in the mathematical way.

3.1   Definitions and Notations

We define a graph as $G = (V, E)$, where $V = \{v_1, v_2, ..., v_n\}$ is the set of vertives and E is the set of edges where e_{ij} represents the link between vertex i and vertex j. Let A denote the adjacency matrix of G, where $a_{ij} = 1$ if $e_{ij} \in E$, otherwise 0. Also, we have the link strength matrix S where S_{ij} indicates the link strength between vertex i and j. The network embedding problem is defined to find a mapping $\Phi : V \to \mathbb{R}^{|V| \times d, d \ll |V|}$. Let $\Phi(V) = B$, $B \in \mathbb{R}^{|V| \times d}$ defines the embedding matrix of G, and $\mathbf{b}_i$ defines an embedding vector of vertex i.

3.2   Framework

SARW is an iterative model. The model mainly consists of three steps, first of all a link strength adjusted random walker generates series of nodes. Then the embedding calculator maximizes the probabilities of nodes being close in the node series to obtain embedding vectors of all nodes. The key step is the link strength updating, the link weights between two nodes are determined by the embedding vectors. Then the random walker samples new node sequences and the calculation process starts over again. Next we will introduce the above mentioned steps in detail.

3.3   The Link Strength Adjusted Random Walker

Random walk is a popular way of extracting global similarity patterns in complex networks. Given a starting point i, and a target point j, the probability of walking from i to j is:

$$p_{ij} = \frac{a_{ij}}{\sum_{k \in V} a_{ik}}. \tag{1}$$

The Link Strength adjusted random walker just substitutes the adjacency matrix in (1) by the link strength matrix. The probability of the walker traveling from i to j is calculated by:

$$p_{ij} = \frac{s_{ij}}{\sum_{k \in V} s_{ik}}. \tag{2}$$

As is shown in the above equations, the link strength adjusted random walker inclines to walk towards points that are more strongly connected to the starting point. It's obviously a more precise way of extracting global similarity structures. In the walking phase of the embedding algorithm, the walker starts from every node for several times and cease walking when a certain length of node sequence is generated. Then the node sequences are passed to the embedding calculation phase.

3.4   The Embedding Calculation

The embedding calculation phase utilizes the Skip-gram [7] model, which is firstly used in natural language processing to learn word embeddings, and is then extended to compute graph embeddings. The basic idea is to maximize the likelihood of nodes appearing close in the node sequences. For a given node i, we call the nodes appearing close with i the context of i, denoted by C_i. C_i consists of nodes whose distance are no more than h steps from i in all the node sequences. It can be seen as a window of length $2h + 1$ sliding along the node sequence, and the nodes inside the window are the context of the node in the center. As mentioned above, the objective function seeks to maximize the appearance probability of C_i given i, that is $p(C_i|i)$. We assume that the probability of one single node existing in C_i is independent of the existence of any other nodes, then we have:

$$p(C_i|i) = \prod_{j \in C_i} p(j|i). \tag{3}$$

Since every node has two kinds of roles in the probability calculation, they can either be contextual nodes or central nodes. So we also assume that every node has two kinds of features, contextual features and central features, and both features work together to determine the co-appearance of contextual nodes and central nodes. In this manner, The chances of node j appearing in C_i is given by the softmax function:

$$p(j|i) = \frac{exp(\mathbf{b}_j'^T \cdot \mathbf{b}_i)}{\sum_{k \in V} exp(\mathbf{b}_k'^T \cdot \mathbf{b}_i)}, \tag{4}$$

where $\mathbf{b}_j'$ is the contextual feature vector of j, $\mathbf{b}_i$ is the central feature vector, also the embedding vector of i. Then (3) can be rewritten as:

$$p(C_i|i) = \prod_{j \in C_i} \frac{exp(\mathbf{b}_j'^T \cdot \mathbf{b}_i)}{\sum_{k \in V} exp(\mathbf{b}_k'^T \cdot \mathbf{b}_i)}. \tag{5}$$

By maximizing the log-likelihood of all nodes and contexts, we can get the objective function:

$$max_{B,B'} \sum_{i \in V} \left[\sum_{j \in C_i} \left(log \frac{exp(\mathbf{b}'^T \cdot \mathbf{b}_i)}{\sum_{k \in V} exp(\mathbf{b}_k'^T \cdot \mathbf{b}_i)} \right) \right], \tag{6}$$

where B and B' are embedding matrix and context feature matrix respectively. The calculation of (6) needs to visit all the nodes in the graph because of the existence of $\sum_{k \in V} exp(\mathbf{b}_k' \cdot \mathbf{b}_i)$. This problem can be solved by negative sampling [8]:

$$min_{B,B'} \sum_{i \in V} \left[\sum_{j \in C_i} \left(-log\sigma(\mathbf{b}_j'^T \cdot \mathbf{b}_i) + \sum_{k \in Ns(V)} log\sigma(-\mathbf{b}_k'^T \cdot \mathbf{b}_i) \right) \right], \tag{7}$$

where $\sigma(\cdot)$ denotes the sigmoid function, and $Ns(V)$ denotes the negative sampling function, which samples a set containing several noisy nodes from V. The probability of one node being included in is proportional to its degree.

Then The objective of the self-adjusting random walk embedding is optimized by stochastic gradient descent (SGD).

3.5   The Link Strength Updating

There are many ways of computing link strengths, but very few of them can compute link strengths both accurately and efficiently. Counting the numbers of common neighbors is a efficient way, but it can only reflect the two-hop neighborhood similarities, and fails to extract similarities with longer paths or larger scales. If we consider global similarity, time consuming will be exponential. So the most appropriate way is to update link strengths using the embedding vectors obtained at the embedding calculation phase, which is beneficial in two ways. First of all, it can reduce the time complexity, the strength between every two nodes can be calculated using merely one simple equation, e.g. Euclidean Distance, Cosine Similarity, etc. Secondly, the embedding vectors naturally contain the structural similarity information, since the objective minimizes the distances between nodes appearing together in random walks.

In this paper, Cosine Similarity is utilized to measure the link strengths based on the embedding vectors. For edge e_{ij}, the similarity between the node pair is calculated as:

$$sim_{ij} = \frac{\mathbf{b}_i^T \cdot \mathbf{b}_j}{\|\mathbf{b}_i\| \cdot \|\mathbf{b}_j\|}. \tag{8}$$

Generally, the link between two unsimilar nodes must have low strength. However, the comparison between two nodes with both high similarities are ambiguous, it's hard to say that whether a link e_{ij} with $sim_{ij} = 0.9$ is stronger than link e_{xy} with $sim_{xy} = 0.8$ or not. That is mainly because the links in graphs have different properties affecting the strength, similarity cannot represent all of them, moreover, the embedding matrix contains noise. The idea of strength adjusted random walk is to bias the walking towards strong links, the extent of strong is not important. So a threshold t is set to control the mapping from similarity to strength, any link with similarity above the threshold is considered to be strong equally. The strength of e_{ij} is calculated as:

$$s_{ij} = \begin{cases} 1, & \text{if } sim_{ij} > t \\ \dfrac{sim_{ij}}{t}, & \text{if } sim_{ij} < t. \end{cases} \qquad (9)$$

The updating of link strengths results in a graph with more precise reflection of how close vertices connect to each other. Therefore the algorithm starts again from the self-adjusting random walking phase, in order to get embeddings of the newly updated graph. The algorithm is self-adjusting in the way that paths generated by the random walker are adjusted by the closeness of the embedding vectors, and the embedding vectors are made to contain the structural information obtained by the random walker. The whole adjusting process is done without information from outside the circle.

4   Experiment Results

In this section we report the experiment of the proposed method on several real world networks. We not only compare the node classification performances of the self-adjusting random walk embedding to some state-of-the-art algorithms, but also analyse how the parameters would affect the performance. We start by introducing the datasets used in the experiments.

4.1   Datasets

The datasets used in the experiments are three real world complex networks, including the Citeseer [9] network, the Cora [10] network, and the Douban Movies network, which is crawled from the movie review website www.douban.com. Table 1 shows some important features of the three datasets.

4.2   Baseline Methods

To better demonstrate the performance of the proposed method, 5 state-of-the-art graph embedding algorithms are used as baselines.

- DeepWalk [1] (DW) is a random walk based network embedding algorithm. The random walker generates several node sequences for each node in the network. It utilizes the SkipGram [7] model to calculate embedding vectors out of node sequences. Nodes appearing close to each other in the sequences are embedded to be close in the vector space.

Table 1. The important features of the datasets.

Datasets	# of nodes	# of links	# of classes of nodes
Citeseer	3312	4732	6
Cora	2708	5429	7
Citeseer	4406	19727	19

- Line-1st [2] (Line-1). Line is a graph embedding algorithm that specializes in embedding large graphs. Line uses the SkipGram model to encode first-order or second-order proximity relationships of nodes into embedding vectors. Line-1 is the first-order proximity model.
- Line-2nd [2] (Line-2) is the second-order proximity Line model.
- Node2vec [3] (N2V) is similar to DW but uses a different random walk strategy. N2V uses a random walker that combines the depth-first searching strategy and the breadth-first searching strategy. It also uses a SkipGram model to calculate embeddings.
- Struct2vec [4] (S2V) is a network embedding algorithm that measures the structural similarity by using a hierarchy. At the bottom of the hierarchy, similarities of nodes are merely determined by degrees, while on top of the hierarchy, node similarities depend on the whole graph. S2V uses a weighted random walker that travels in different layers of the hierarchy to generate node sequences. A SkipGram model is used to learn embeddings out of the sequences.

4.3 Node Classification Performances

To validate the superiority of Self-Adjusting Random Walk (SARW), since the embedding quality cannot be measured directly, we perform node classification on the embedding matrices of the above mentioned datasets output by SARW as well as the baselines. For all methods, the random walking length is set to be 40, the number of walks per node is set to be 10, the window size is set to be 10, the embedding dimensions is set to be 100 and the negative sample numbers is set to be 5. For N2V, the hyper parameters $q = 0.9$, $p = 1.1$. For S2V, the all three optimization options are enabled. For SARW, the threshold is set to be 0.7, 0.6, 0.7 in Citeseer, Cora, Douban respectively. A Logistic Regression classifier is trained to classify nodes, using the embedding vectors as features. Every network dataset is separated into a training set and a testing set, the proportion of training set varies from 20% to 80%. The macro-f1 score and micro-f1 score are used as classification measurements.

The evaluation process runs 10 times and the average results are shown in Figs. 1, 2 and 3. As shown in the graphs, no matter what proportion does the training set take, the embedding matrix output by SARW has a clear advantage over the baselines. In Douban dataset, the macro- and micro-f1 of SARW are about 3% higher than N2V, in Cora, the f1 scores are about 2% higher and

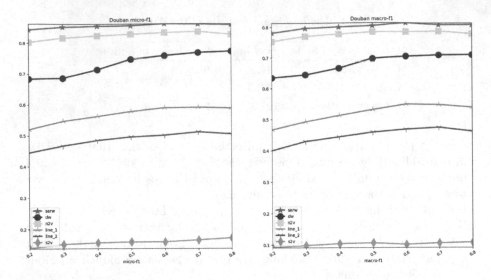

Fig. 1. The node classification performance on Citeseer

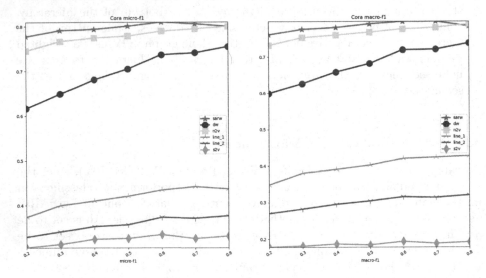

Fig. 2. The node classification performance on Cora

in Citeseer it's about 3%. This indicates that the embedding vectors of SARW are in a more separable status. Comparing to the baselines, SARW can embed nodes of the same class closer. This further illustrates that SARW can better capture the intrinsic connections between nodes and encode such information in the embedding vectors. The effectiveness of SARW on all three datasets also demonstrate its generalization ability. Furthermore, it is worth noticing that SARW achieves relatively higher f1 scores on unweighted graphs. This shows that link strengths, though implicit in some networks, exist extensively and can provide deeper insights into the network structure.

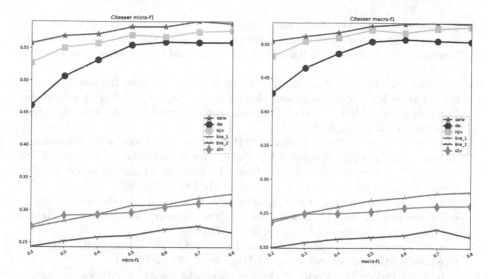

Fig. 3. The node classification performance on DoubanMovies

5   Conclusion

In this paper, we propose Self-Adjusting Random Walk (SARW), a random walk-based graph embedding algorithm adjusted by implicit link strengths. The core of the algorithm is that it updates link strengths based on the embedding matrix calculated by itself, and the newly updated links result in new node sequences generated by the random walker. The empirical study shows that SARW captures more structural information of networks and filters noise. Our future goal is to develop an embedding algorithm that efficiently extract large scale structural information in networks with more complex structure, like heterogeneous graphs.

Acknowledgement. This research was supported by Nature Science Foundation of China (Grant No. 61672284), Natural Science Foundation of Jiangsu Province (Grant No. BK20171418), China Postdoctoral Science Foundation (Grant No. 2016M591841), Jiangsu Planned Projects for Postdoctoral Research Funds (No. 1601225C)

References

1. Perozzi, B., Al-Rfou, R., Skiena, S.: Deepwalk: online learning of social representations. In: Proceedings of the 20th ACM SIGKDD International Conference on Knowledge Discovery and Data Mining, pp. 701–710. ACM (2014)
2. Tang, J., Qu, M., Wang, M., Zhang, M., Yan, J., Mei, Q.: Line: large-scale information network embedding. In: Proceedings of the 24th International Conference on World Wide Web, pp. 1067–1077. International World Wide Web Conferences Steering Committee (2015)
3. Grover, A., Leskovec, J.: node2vec: scalable feature learning for networks. In: Proceedings of the 22nd ACM SIGKDD International Conference on Knowledge Discovery and Data Mining, pp. 855–864. ACM (2016)

4. Ribeiro, L.F., Saverese, P.H., Figueiredo, D.R.: struc2vec: learning node representations from structural identity. In: Proceedings of the 23rd ACM SIGKDD International Conference on Knowledge Discovery and Data Mining, pp. 385–394. ACM (2017)
5. Cavallari, S., Zheng, V.W., Cai, H., Chang, K.C.C., Cambria, E.: Learning community embedding with community detection and node embedding on graphs. In: Proceedings of the 2017 ACM on Conference on Information and Knowledge Management, pp. 377–386. ACM (2017)
6. Chen, H., Perozzi, B., Hu, Y., Skiena, S.: Harp: hierarchical representation learning for networks. In: Thirty-Second AAAI Conference on Artificial Intelligence (2018)
7. Mikolov, T., Chen, K., Corrado, G., Dean, J.: Efficient estimation of word representations in vector space. arXiv preprint arXiv:1301.3781 (2013)
8. Mikolov, T., Sutskever, I., Chen, K., Corrado, G.S., Dean, J.: Distributed representations of words and phrases and their compositionality. In: Advances in Neural Information Processing Systems, pp. 3111–3119 (2013)
9. Sen, P., Namata, G., Bilgic, M., Getoor, L., Galligher, B., Eliassi-Rad, T.: Collective classification in network data. AI Mag. 29(3), 93–93 (2008)
10. Šubelj, L., Bajec, M.: Model of complex networks based on citation dynamics. In: Proceedings of the 22nd International Conference on World Wide Web, pp. 527–530. ACM (2013)
11. McPherson, M., Smith-Lovin, L., Cook, J.M.: Birds of a feather: homophily in social networks. Annu. Rev. Sociol. 27(1), 415–444 (2001)

Study on Influencers of Cryptocurrency Follow-Network on GitHub

Naoki Kobayakawa[1,2]($\boxtimes$) and Kenichi Yoshida[2]($\boxtimes$)

[1] Hewlett-Packard Japan, Ltd., Tokyo, Japan
naoki.koba.6@gmail.com
[2] Graduate School of Business Science, University of Tsukuba, Tokyo, Japan
yoshida.kenichi.ka@u.tsukuba.ac.jp

Abstract. Open-source software (OSS) is widely used and has become an essential infrastructure for our society today. Substantial research has been done to improve the success of OSS development. Of them, studies about influencers have gained attention in recent times. Influencers are regarded as an evangelist in a specific domain, and play an important role in persuading others. They are frequently analyzed on Twitter and other SNSs. With the advent of social coding platforms such as GitHub, research has started on OSS influencers who seem to affect the behavior of developers. However, there is not yet enough research on the method of identifying influencers and their effects on OSS. In this study, we analyzed the follow-network of cryptocurrency projects developed on GitHub quantitatively, and found (1) The HITS algorithm is more effective when compared with in-degree centrality and PageRank algorithm in identifying influencers of a specific domain. (2) The rate of contribution of a user correlates with their rate of influence, but the explanatory power is small. The amount of activity on GitHub is not as essential for OSS influencers as it is on Twitter, which requires a lot of activity to be an influencer. (3) The rate of influence of influencers on a project correlates with the number of contributors.

Keywords: Open Source Software · Mining software repositories · Cryptocurrency

1 Introduction

OSS (Open-Source Software) is now widely used not only by individuals, but also by companies and services. It is an important infrastructure for society. The development of OSS is supported by volunteers. In order for an OSS to succeed, it is essential that it acquires contributors such as developers and maintainers from outside of the project.

The presence of influencers is attracting attention in recent times. An influencer is regarded as an evangelist in a specialized field and is expected to play an important role in persuading others. Various analysis has been performed on SNSs such as Twitter. With the advent of social coding platforms, research has

© Springer Nature Switzerland AG 2019
K. Ohara and Q. Bai (Eds.): PKAW 2019, LNAI 11669, pp. 173–183, 2019.
https://doi.org/10.1007/978-3-030-30639-7_15

started on OSS influencers who seem to affect the behavior of developers. However, there is not yet enough research on the method of identifying influencers and their effects on OSS.

The representative of social coding platform is GitHub. Since GitHub launched in 2008, the number of projects that use GitHub have increased exponentially. As of April 2017, 57 million projects exist, and more than 20 million users are using the service [7]. One of the characteristics of GitHub is its transparency. Not only can anyone refer to the artifacts such as source code and documents but also he/she can acquire the user's activity records.

"Follow" is a function of GitHub. By following a user whom you are paying attention to, you can track his/her activities. A directed graph can represent this following relationship. This is called a follow-network. By analyzing a follow-network, it becomes possible to quantitatively reveal the features of GitHub.

As mentioned above, GitHub has large amounts of data. Because it is not easy to analyze all the data, many previous studies used subsets of this data. However, there are indications that the extraction method is biased [5], and the method of selecting data is an important subject. Especially for network analysis which elucidates the relationships between nodes, random extraction tends to lose relevance between nodes. Therefore, it is necessary to extract data while maintaining the network structure as much as possible.

Based on the above, we focused on the cryptocurrency projects. Many cryptocurrencies are developed as OSS on GitHub. We used the follow-network to study their influencers.

The features of the cryptocurrency follow-network are as follows.

- Since it is a cluster of projects and the users of the same domain, network division is small.
- Currently, there are over 600 projects on GitHub, and all major currencies are included.[1]
- Thanks to the attention on cryptocurrency, there are many prominent users, and their information is easy to obtain from the internet. Thus, it is possible to compare this information with the results of our analysis.

The research questions we try to analyze are:

RQ 1: How do we identify an influencer of the cryptocurrency follow-network? There are two kinds of influencers, i.e., an influencer for the cryptocurrency follow-network and an influencer for GitHub as a whole. The data contains a mix of both. We tried to ignore the data of GitHub influencers who have low relevance to cryptocurrency by only selecting influencers followed by users who are relevant to cryptocurrency projects. We compared various algorithms to choose an appropriate method to identify influencers from the cryptocurrency follow-network.

---

[1] http://coinmarketcap.com (accessed 2018-02-12).

RQ 2: Do influencers contribute more than other contributors?

To be an influencer on Twitter, a lot of effort is required, such as tweeting frequently [3]. On the other hand, research on GitHub states that the rate of contribution does not impact the rate of influence [2,10]. We would like to confirm whether these results are also applicable to cryptocurrency projects.

RQ 3: Can each project gain more contribution through the presence of an influencer?

In other words, can the influencer for a cryptocurrency gather new contributors for the OSS project?

As an indicator of influence, we used the in-degree centrality, PageRank and HITS algorithm scores. These metrics were devised to rank important sites in WebGraph (graph formed based on web page link relations), and are mainly used for the network analysis of directed graphs. They are described in detail in Sect. 5.

2 Related Work

Substantial research has been conducted on OSS projects till date. Originally, they were analysis of a single project or projects under common governance such as Apache, Linux, etc. Since 2010, social coding platforms such as SouceForge and GitHub have appeared, and a large number of projects began to be analyzed together.

Network analysis has also started. Thung et al. constructed a project network tied to a common developer and a developer network tied to a common project on GitHub. They compared both network features and investigated the influential projects and developers using the PageRank algorithm [12]. They used the first 100,000 projects obtained by the GitHub API (Application Programming Interface) as their dataset. Yu et al. created a follow-network from the data of about 1.8 million users extracted from GitHub's archive data site, GHTorrent, and analyzed the kinds of patterns that exist [14]. Both studies extracted data without considering the network structure, and there exists a possibility that the relevance between the nodes was compromised.

Numerous studies have been done on influencers of projects on GitHub. Their main themes are: 1. What is the indicator of a influencer, 2. How to be an influencer, 3. What is the effect of an influencer? GitHub has various collaborative functions. "Follow" is a linkage function between users. Between users and projects there are "fork" (source code copy), "watch" (follow a project) and "star" (Bookmark). Blincoe et al. studied the number of followers as an indicator of influence [2]. There is a study that considers whether the number of forks and number of watchers of projects (owned by users) are to be taken into account in addition to the number of followers [1]. In terms of theme 2, users with a lot of activity on GitHub are not necessarily influencers [2,10]. Activities such as promoting yourself on blogs and Twitter using the same user name as on GitHub are necessary to become influencers [6].

Positive research exists on the effect of influencers. Users tend to select a project that has high status developers [13]. By estimating which projects will prosper in the future from participants and deliverables on GitHub, the user decides which project to join [6]. Influencers will guide followers to new projects [2].

All the above studies adopted qualitative analysis such as surveys or interviews or quantitative analysis using randomly extracted subsets of GitHub. In this research, we analyze the cryptocurrency follow-network quantitatively and compare it with the results of the previous research. We don't perform random extraction of follow-network to retain the network structure as much as possible.

3   Description of the Dataset

GitHub provides an API. Using this API, we got the contributors to cryptocurrency projects (users who committed to the project at least once), the number of commits and the activity period. A list of cryptocurrency projects was acquired from a cryptocurrency market ranking chart website.[2] Data on 554 projects and 2434 contributors were gathered. Using the same API, we got the follower data of each contributor. The total number of contributors and followers (total number of users) was 70,217 and the follow linkages were 129,841. Many users act as both contributor and follower. We cleaned this data with the following procedure:

1. Several projects are created by forking or reusing major cryptocurrency source code such as Bitcoin. In such cases, the contributors and activity history of the original project is also inherited. It is necessary to delete the duplicate data. We examined the derived projects and deleted duplicate contributors and their commit records.
2. The GitHub API does not provide all activity data [5]. For instance, the activity history of only up to the top 100 committed users in each project is provided. As the market value of cryptocurrency soared in March 2017, contributors to cryptocurrency projects have also increased sharply, and some projects exceeded 100. This data was acquired in February 2018 and does not include minor contributors with a few commits. Only the main contributors to be analyzed are covered. We consider that it does not affect the conclusion of the analysis.

Figure 1 shows the follow relationships among contributors. It turns out that major currencies, such as Bitcoin and Ethereum form big clusters. On the other hand, about half of the contributors do not use the follow function.

4   Features of Cryptocurrency Follow-Network

Before proceeding to the research questions, this section explains the structural features of the cryptocurrency follow-network in comparison with related work about the GitHub follow-network and Twitter's follow-network.

---

[2] https://www.coingecko.com (accessed 2018-02-12).

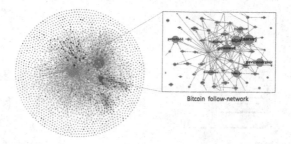

Bitcoin follow-network

Fig. 1. Cryptocurrency follow-network. A node is a contributor. A directed edge shows a follow relationship from a follower to a followed user. The color indicates the project which contributors mainly belong to. Bitcoin: green, Ethereum: blue. The node size indicates the number of followers. There are many nodes that have no edges, which means the contributors don't use the follow function. (This data was obtained on 2018-02-12) (Color figure online)

The average degree is the total number of followers divided by the total number of users. The average degree of cryptocurrencies was 1.85, which falls in the middle of the values 0.74−1.01 [14] and 3.02 [10]. Yu et al. uses a sampled subset of GitHub data [14], and the data seems be impaired, i.e., some links were ignored from the data. This makes the average degree smaller. On the other hand, Lima et al. constructed a network (especially edges) from the relevant follow events [10]. Thus, the network structure was almost completely remained, and the average degree was higher. In these cases, the average degrees were much smaller than Twitter's 35.2 [9]. While Twitter is an information service site and follow is a central function, GitHub is a collaborative development site for source code and follow is a secondary function. Therefore, the average degree becomes smaller because the ratio of using the follow function is low. In addition, as described below, it was affected by the fact that the ratio of mutual followings was low.

The percentage of contributors that follow each other was 13.6%. It is lower than Twitter's 22.1% [9]. As explained in the next section, the top influencers follow only a few users. They seem to be in a so-called "rockstar" state. For example, the creator of Etherium, vbuterin, is followed by more than 6000 people. However, he doesn't follow anyone.

Figure 2 shows the logarithmic distribution of in-degree and out-degree in our dataset. The out-degree distribution is close to a straight line and follows a power-law distribution. The scaling index, which is the value of the slope, is 2.4. The in-degree distribution is biased downward toward the lower range, i.e., range of less than 10. It is common in actual networks that such deviation occurs in the lower range [11]. The scaling index was also 2.4. Since the scaling index of a real-world graph such as WebGraph and Citation Network is between 2 and 3 [4], the results of this study are within range.

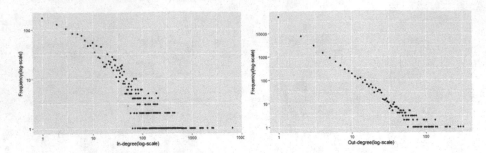

Fig. 2. Follow-network degree distribution; in-degree(left), out-degree(right).

5   RQ 1: How Do We Identify an Influencer of the Cryptocurrency Follow-Network?

Following a user in GitHub means being interested in that user's programming skills and activities [6]. Followers are affected by the followed user. To be followed a lot means the user has considerable influence (influential user). The quantitative measure of this is in-degree centrality, that is, the number of followers. In addition, if he/she is followed by influential users, the rate of influence become greater because he/she will indirectly affect many users through those influential users. PageRank, and Authority of HITS are centrality algorithms that consider indirect influence. These scores are in the range of 0−1.

The outlines of PageRank and HITS algorithms are as follows:

– PageRank was introduced by Brin and Page[3] for weighing the importance of web pages using their link structures. The page rank PR(A) of a certain page A is defined by the following equation:

$$PR(A) = (1 - d) + d \sum_{i=1}^{n} \frac{PR(T_i)}{C(T_i)} \tag{1}$$

Here, $PR(T_n)$ is the page rank of the page T_n linked to page A. $C(T_i)$ is the number of links from page T_n to other pages. d is the probability that a web surfer continues to surf (a.k.a. the damping factor). Usually, it is set to 0.85.
– HITS is a centrality algorithm that rates web pages [8]. In the HITS algorithm, there are two centrality scores - Authority score and Hub score for all nodes(p). Authority score (auth(p)) is the degree of followings from users with high Hub score. Hub score (hub(p)) is the degree of followings from users with high Authority score. Each score is updated by iterative calculation. To begin the rating, $\forall p$, auth (p) = 1 hub(p) = 1.
We update $auth(p)$ to be the summation:

$$auth(p) = \sum_{i=1}^{n} hub(i) \tag{2}$$

then $\forall p$, we update hub(p) to be the summation:

---

[3] http://infolab.stanford.edu/~backrub/google.html (accessed 2019-01-20).

Table 1. Top10 Influential users on In-degree, PageRank, Authority algorithm

	In-degree	PageRank	Authority
1	vbuterin	vbuterin	vbuterin
2	*soulmachine*	DavidVorick	laanwj
3	bytemaster	sipa	sipa
4	laanwj	*soulmachine*	gmaxwell
5	*graydon*	laanwj	gavinandresen
6	gavinandresen	bytemaster	luke-jr
7	*jonathanong*	lukechampine	petertodd
8	sipa	*AndrewScheidecker*	jonasschnelli
9	*jedisct1*	*chrisdone*	bytemaster
10	gmaxwell	gmaxwell	gavofyork

$$hub(p) = \sum_{i=1}^{n} auth(i) \tag{3}$$

As mentioned above, there are two types of influencers: cryptocurrency influencers and influencers of GitHub as a whole. We verified which centrality algorithm is best to extract cryptocurrency influencers by trying to find an appropriate centrality algorithm which can ignore the data of GitHub influencers who have low relevance to cryptocurrency. Table 1 shows the influential users of each centrality algorithm. We examined the profiles of each user on GitHub, blogs and information available on the internet. Then we examined whether they are cryptocurrency influencers. The usernames in bold in Table 1 are not influencers for cryptocurrency. The top users of Authority were all influencers for cryptocurrency, while the top users of the in-degree centrality and PageRank were mixed with different types of users. In-degree centrality includes users who have low relevance to the cryptocurrency but have very large followers. In addition to the above, PageRank also includes users with not many followers.

The attributes of users with high Authority scores are shown in Table 2. It is seen that the out-degree of each user is extremely small. This allows us to conclude that influential users hardly follow other users. Since the PageRank score is the sum of the score of the followers divided by their out-degree, followers who have a very large score and a small out-degree significantly distort the PageRank score. For example, AndrewScheidecker has 181 followers, which is not as much as an average influential user. However, since bytemaster, who has 2506 followers, follows only him, all scores of bytemaster are assigned to him and he becomes the eighth most influential user on PageRank.

According to Fig. 3, PageRank has many similar users with a low number of followers, but high scores (within blue circle). No such user can be seen for Authority.

Table 2. Attributes of Top 10 Influential users by Authority

	ID	In-degree	Out-degree	Score	Commit	Activity period	Currency
1	vbuterin	6472	0	1.000	24	546	ETH(Etherium)
2	laanwj	2033	1	0.309	1544	2464	BTC(Bitcoin)
3	sipa	1493	3	0.269	939	2471	BTC(Bitcoin)
4	gmaxwell	1133	0	0.220	159	2184	BTC(Bitcoin)
5	gavinandresen	1590	0	0.213	485	1855	BTC(Bitcoin)
6	luke-jr	980	0	0.198	326	2485	BTC(Bitcoin)
7	petertodd	1089	0	0.189	102	1771	BTC(Bitcoin)
8	jonasschnelli	671	3	0.156	428	1743	BTC(Bitcoin)
9	bytemaster	2506	1	0.153	563	1715	BTS(Bitshare)
10	gavofyork	1026	0	0.143	40	364	ETH(Etherium)

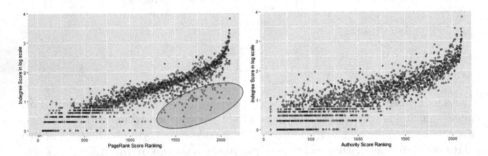

Fig. 3. Score ranking of PageRank(left) and Authority(right). (Color figure online)

In conclusion, Authority is an algorithm suitable for the extraction of influencers from cryptocurrency follow-networks in which the out-degree of superiors is extremely small.

6   RQ 2: Do Influencers Contribute More Than Other Contributors?

To investigate the relationship between a user's influence and the amount of contribution, multiple regression analysis was performed. The centrality scores were the dependent variables. The number of commits, activity period, and the number of participating projects were independent variables. Each variable is log transformed. The results are shown in Table 3. In all algorithms, the p-value was less than 5% significant for all independent variables. However, each adjusted coefficient of determination is from 0.07 to 0.08, which means its explanatory power is extremely low.

Figure 4 is a cryptocurrency follow-network diagram. The size of the circle represents the Authority score (left) and the commit number (right) of each user. Superior users from the view of authority score are at the center of large projects.

Table 3. Regression analysis between centrality scores and influencer's attributes

	log(In-degree)	log(PageRank)	log(Authority)
(Intercept)	2.04 (0.07)***	−10.30 (0.07)***	−8.18 (0.11)***
log(Commit)	0.10 (0.03)***	0.09 (0.03)***	0.12 (0.04)**
log(Day)	0.11 (0.02)***	0.10 (0.02)***	0.18 (0.03)***
Project	0.09 (0.04)*	0.09 (0.04)*	0.14 (0.06)*
R^2	0.09	0.07	0.08
Adj. R^2	0.08	0.07	0.08
Num. obs	2055	2101	1960
RMSE	1.56	1.55	2.40

$***p < 0.001$, $**p < 0.01$, $*p < 0.05$

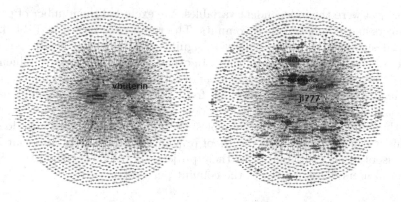

Fig. 4. Cryptocurrency follow-network. A node is a contributor. A directed edge shows a follow relationship from a follower to a followed user. The color indicates the project they mainly belong to. Bitcoin: green, Ethereum: blue. The node size indicates Authority score (left) and the number of commits (right). (This data was obtained on 2018-02-12) (Color figure online)

Superior users of commits are scattered in many projects. Figure 4 visually shows the difference between these two. In summary, active contributors and influencers do not match. These results are consistent with the result of previous research on GitHub [10], but different from previous research on Twitter [3].

7 RQ 3: Can Each Project Gain More Contribution Through the Presence of Influencer?

Is it possible to gain more contributions to a project if an influential user exists in the project as a member among the contributors? To answer this question, we performed multiple regression analysis. The centrality score of the project influencers, i.e., contributors who have the highest centrality score in each project, was the dependent variable. The sum of commits and the sum of contributors of

Table 4. Regression analysis between centrality scores and project attributes

	log(In-degree)	log(PageRank)	log(Authority)
(Intercept)	2.49 (0.16)***	−9.91 (0.17)***	−7.35 (0.21)***
log(Commit)	0.08 (0.06)	0.08 (0.06)	0.13 (0.07)
log(Contributor)	0.90 (0.11)***	0.97 (0.11)***	0.85 (0.14)***
R^2	0.44	0.46	0.33
Adj. R^2	0.43	0.46	0.33
Num. obs	317	318	312
RMSE	1.32	1.34	1.68

***$p < 0.001$, **$p < 0.01$, *$p < 0.05$

each project were the independent variables. We excluded the number of project influencers and number of their commits. The results are shown in Table 4.

In all algorithms, contributors were significant at p-value < 0.001, but their number of commits was not significant. In other words, if the rate of influence of a project influencer increases, the number of contributors increases. The adjusted coefficient of determination is also high from 33% to 46%. Thus, its explanatory power is high. The slope of the independent variable is also large. For example, when the number of contributors doubles, the number of followers also doubles.

This is consistent with the results of previous studies on GitHub that influential users bring contributors to their projects [2, 6, 13]. On the other hand, influential users doesn't increase the commit per contributor.

8   Conclusion and Future Work

In this study, we analyzed the follow-network of cryptocurrency projects on GitHub quantitatively, and found:

- By comparing three centrality scores, i.e., in-degree, PageRank, and Authority, we found that the Authority algorithm is most relevant to finding the influential users from the cryptocurrency follow-network. The Authority algorithm is effective in extracting influencers in specialized areas with extremely low out-degree data.
- The rate of a user's contribution correlates with their rate of influence. However, the explanatory power is small. The amount of activity on GitHub is not as essential for OSS influencers as it is on Twitter, which requires a lot of activity to be an influencer.
- The rate of influence of an influencer in the project correlates with the number of contributors. It suggests influential users contribute to gather contributors to their projects.

This study has analyzed a network of cryptocurrency projects. There are other specialized projects on GitHub as well. It is necessary to confirm whether they produce similar results.

In addition to the number of followers, there are other influence indicators like the number of forks and watchers [1]. Information outside GitHub such as market capitalization, news, blogs, SNS, etc. can also be obtained. By using them, it might be possible to analyze influence in more detail.

References

1. Badashian, A.S., Stroulia, E.: Measuring user influence in GitHub. In: Proceedings of the 3rd International Workshop on CrowdSourcing in Software Engineering - CSI-SE 2016, pp. 15–21 (2016). https://doi.org/10.1145/2897659.2897663
2. Blincoe, K., Sheoran, J., Goggins, S., Petakovic, E., Damian, D.: Understanding the popular users: following, affiliation influence and leadership on GitHub. Inf. Softw. Technol. **70**, 30–39 (2016). https://doi.org/10.5935/0004-2749.20180056
3. Cha, M., Haddadi, H., Benevenuto, F., Gummadi, P.K., et al.: Measuring user influence in Twitter: the million follower fallacy. ICWSM **10**(10–17), 30 (2010)
4. Clauset, A., Shalizi, C.R., Newman, M.E.J.: Power-law distributions in empirical data. SIAM Rev. **51**(4), 661–703 (2009). https://doi.org/10.1137/070710111
5. Cosentino, V., Luis, J., Cabot, J.: Findings from GitHuB: methods, datasets and limitations. In: Proceedings of the 13th International Conference on Mining Software Repositories, pp. 137–141. ACM (2016)
6. Dabbish, L., Stuart, C., Tsay, J., Herbsleb, J.: Social coding in GitHuB: transparency and collaboration in an open software repository. In: Proceedings of the ACM 2012 Conference on Computer Supported Cooperative Work, pp. 1277–1286. ACM (2012)
7. GitHub: Celebrating nine years of GitHuB with an anniversary sale. https://github.com/blog/2345-celebrating-nine-years-of-github-with-an-anniversary-sale
8. Kleinberg, J.M.: Authoritative sources in a hyperlinked environment. J. ACM (JACM) **46**(5), 604–632 (1999)
9. Kwak, H., Lee, C., Park, H., Moon, S.: What is Twitter, a social network or a news media? In: Proceedings of the 19th International Conference on World Wide Web, pp. 591–600. AcM (2010)
10. Lima, A., Rossi, L., Musolesi, M.: Coding together at scale: GitHub as a collaborative social network, pp. 295–304 (2014). https://doi.org/10.13140/2.1.4625.4880
11. Newman, M.E.: Power laws, Pareto distributions and Zipf's law. Contemp. Phys. **46**(5), 323–351 (2005)
12. Thung, F., Bissyandé, T.F., Lo, D., Jiang, L.: Network structure of social coding in GitHub. In: Proceedings of the European Conference on Software Maintenance and Reengineering, CSMR, pp. 323–326 (2013). https://doi.org/10.1109/CSMR.2013.41
13. Tsay, J., Dabbish, L., Herbsleb, J.D.: Social media in transparent work environments. In: 2013 6th International Workshop on Cooperative and Human Aspects of Software Engineering, CHASE 2013 - Proceedings, pp. 65–72 (2013). https://doi.org/10.1109/CHASE.2013.6614733
14. Yu, Y., Yin, G., Wang, H., Wang, T.: Exploring the patterns of social behavior in GitHub. In: Proceedings of the 1st International Workshop on Crowd-based Software Development Methods and Technologies, pp. 31–36 (2014). https://doi.org/10.1145/2666539.2666571

A Cross-Domain Theory
of Mental Models

Sara Todorovikj$^{(\boxtimes)}$, Paulina Friemann, and Marco Ragni

Cognitive Computation Lab, University of Freiburg, 79110 Freiburg, Germany
{todorovs,friemanp,ragni}@cs.uni-freiburg.de

Abstract. Cognitive models for human reasoning are often specialized and domain-specific. So the question whether human reasoning across domains shares the same (or at least a similar) mental representation and inference mechanism is still an unexplored territory, as is the endeavor to create cognitive computational models for multiple domains of human reasoning. In this paper, we consider the theory of mental models for conditionals as a test-case and aim to extend it towards syllogistic reasoning using a formal translation. The performance of this new cross-domain theory is comparable to the performance of state-of-the-art domain-specific theories. Potentials and limitations are discussed.

Keywords: Predictive modeling · Human reasoning · Conditionals · Syllogisms · Mental models

1 Introduction

How do people produce conclusions from prior information? Humans do not always follow the steps proposed by formal logic, and often make logical errors [14]. One of the goals of cognitive science is to have a better comprehension of the way that humans reason. One mean of doing so is by developing cognitive models that would account for the errors and ultimately predict the way an individual would reason. That is very important for predicting human behavior, which, in turn, helps with successful interaction and collaboration with intelligent systems.

Highly specialized cognitive models of human reasoning are developed for various domains, e.g.: conditional [8,12], syllogistic [9], spatial [3]. These cognitive models tackle the specific reasoning domain for which they are designed using different approaches, such as heuristics or probabilistic updating mechanisms. A generalizability to explain human reasoning in a different domain is often not given. However, the question whether human reasoning processes share specifics across domains is still an open question.

© Springer Nature Switzerland AG 2019
K. Ohara and Q. Bai (Eds.): PKAW 2019, LNAI 11669, pp. 184–194, 2019.
https://doi.org/10.1007/978-3-030-30639-7_16

Example 1. Conditional and syllogistic reasoning problems:

Conditional	Syllogism
If the number on the card is 3, then the card is colored red. The number on the card is 3.	Some artists are bakers. All bakers are chemists.
Therefore, the card is colored red.	Therefore, some artists are chemists.

A widely acknowledged account of human reasoning is the Mental Model Theory (MMT) [5–7]. The MMT suggests that humans construct mental models of the given information, and inspect and possibly manipulate them mentally to reach a conclusion. We consider the MMT-based cognitive model for conditional reasoning proposed by [8], and develop a generalization for syllogistic reasoning based on a conditional reformulation of the quantifiers. Similar work has been done by Bara et al. [1], where they created a computational model, also based on mental models, which is used to make predictions in the syllogistic, relational and propositional domain. They make an assumption that individuals always construct the correct mental representation of the premises that they are given. Since that assumption is rather unlikely to be true, we have a different approach – we try to reverse engineer the construction of the mental representation, by adapting to the individuals' responses. That way we also account for logically erroneous representations individuals might construct, and even different interpretations of the same premise by the individuals, e.g., the case when some individuals interpret a conditional as a bi-conditional.

The remainder of this article is structured as follows: First, we give a brief introduction to conditionals and syllogisms, followed by an introduction to the relevant points of the Mental Model Theory and its application in both domains, conditional and syllogistic. A proposal for a generalized cross-domain model follows. Finally, we present the results in a prediction task for both domains.

1.1 Conditionals

Conditionals are statements, usually of the form "If X then Y" (also written as $X \rightarrow Y$, where X is called the antecedent, and Y, the consequent), often used to describe a causal relationship between any two propositions. In this paper,

Table 1. The four inference forms for "If X then Y" (short: $X \rightarrow Y$)

Inference form	Conditional	Minor premise	Conclusion
Modus Ponens (MP)	$X \rightarrow Y$	X	Y
Modus Tollens (MT)	$X \rightarrow Y$	$\neg Y$	$\neg X$
Affirmation of the Consequent (AC)	$X \rightarrow Y$	Y	X
Denial of the Antecedent (DA)	$X \rightarrow Y$	$\neg X$	$\neg Y$

we also consider the form "If X then *possibly Y*". Research on conditional reasoning often relies on acceptance rates for the four inference forms (see Table 1) that can follow when given a conditional along with a minor premise. The conditional in Example 1 is an example of the logically valid *Modus Ponens* (MP). The other logically valid inference form is the *Modus Tollens* (MT). Logically invalid inference forms are *Affirmation of the Consequent* (AC), and *Denial of the Antecedent* (DA).

1.2 Syllogisms

Syllogisms are quantified assertions consisting of two premises and a conclusion. They are used to reason about properties of entities by using quantifiers. Here we take into consideration only the standard quantifiers: "All", "Some", "Some not" and "No". The syllogisms have been a popular psychological research target for over 100 years [9], and their general analysis goes all the way back to Aristotelian times. Example 1. gives an example of a syllogism.

Table 2. Moods of premises and figures of a syllogism.

(a) Moods of a premise/conclusion.

Mood	Premise
Universally affirmative (A)	All X are Y
Particular affirmative (I)	Some X are Y
Universal negative (E)	No X are Y
Particular negative (O)	Some X are not Y

(b) Figures of a syllogism.

Figure	Premise 1	Premise 2
1	X-Y	Y-Z
2	Y-X	Z-Y
3	X-Y	Z-Y
4	Y-X	Y-Z

Each premise in a syllogism (and the conclusion) can be in one of the four moods shown in Table 2a. The research done on syllogistic reasoning is focused on acceptance rates for the possible conclusions. Conclusions contain two terms, a subject and a predicate ('artists' and 'chemists' in Example 1). The premises contain the conclusion's subject and predicate and relate them to a middle term, that appears in both premises ('bakers'). A syllogism can have four different figures, based on the order of the terms, as shown in Table 2b. In the syllogism example in the introduction, the moods of the two premises are I, and A, respectively. The order of the terms in the premises is: X-Y, and Y-Z, which is Fig. 1. This syllogism is of type IA1. The conclusion is in the mood I, and the order of terms X-Z, which we denote as IXZ.

1.3 Mental Model Theory

The theory of mental models [5–7] is a cognitive theory that assumes that an individual reasoner constructs an analogous mental representation of the state of affairs. A reader more familiar with formal logic may think of a truth-table like representation that is iconic [5]. Let us consider first a mental model for the conditional "If X then Y". According to the mental model theory (MMT), a reasoner who processes this information constructs an initial mental model consisting of the antecedent X and the consequent Y, i.e., the reasoner represents first the case where both are true (and nothing is false): the model X Y. Other possible interpretations, e.g., the case where X is false (written as $\neg X$) are abbreviated by an ellipsis.

Premise	Mental model	Fleshed-out models
If X then Y	X Y	X Y
	...	$\neg$X $\neg$Y
		$\neg$X Y

The mental model represents what is true according to the information, but not what is false. This can be fleshed-out in a second process, leading to all possible interpretations (see right column). This can explain why the inference processes MP and AC can be immediately inferred, while for MT and DA the flesh-out process is necessary. The processes of the Mental Model Theory for Conditional Reasoning have been formalized as a multinomial process tree by Oberauer [12] (see Fig. 1)[1]. The MPT can be interpreted as a binary decision diagram with parameters on its edges (see Fig. 1). Specifically, in the case of MMT,

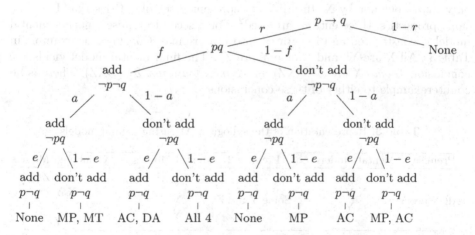

Fig. 1. Oberauer's formalization of the MMT [12] for the conditional "If p then q". The parameters r, f, a, e take on values in the interval $[0, 1]$, indicating the probability of taking the respective decision path in the model. The leafs represent the responses.

---

[1] In the original model by Oberauer [12], the parameter $1 - r$ describes the probability that an individual will not reason, but guess. In our implementation of the model we do not use guessing.

the decisions correspond to whether a human reasoner will add a certain model to their mental representation of the conditional or not. Given a conditional "If p then q", there are four possible mental models that an individual can add to their mental model representation of the conditional (pq, $\neg p \neg q$, $\neg pq$, $p \neg q$). For each one of those mental models, there is a certain parameter that describes the probability of that model being added to the mental representation.

Individuals aim to maintain the information that is provided to them with the conditional or syllogism and try to reach a conclusion based on that. Often, individuals would engage in a search for counterexamples. If their search is successful, the conclusion is no longer accepted by the individual [9]. Quantifiers are interpreted by the representation of single entities, representing the respective set. Consider the premise "All X are Y".

Premise	Mental Models
All X are Y	X Y
	X Y
	X Y
	Y
	...

Again, in a mental model, X and Y means that both properties are true, and each line represents an entity and contains the properties which are true for this entity. The first three rows represent a set of entities which are described by the properties X and Y, whereas the fourth row represents an entity described only by Y, but not by X. In order to represent a set of entities that have the same properties, three entities are used[2]. For a second premise, another mental model is constructed and integrated into the original. Consider the example in Table 3 "All X are Y" and "Some Y are Z". The final mental model yields the conclusion *"Some X are Z"* (IXZ), or *"Some X are not Z"* (OXZ). There is no counterexample to either of these conclusions.

Table 3. Representation of the syllogism AI1 using mental models

Premise 1	Mental Models	Premise 2	Mental Models	Combined Models
			Y Z	X Y Z
All X are Y	X Y	Some Y are Z	Y	X Y
	Y		Y	Y
				Y

---

[2] As discussed by Johnson-Laird, no iconic model can show that it represents an entire set, we have no way of knowing whether a model describes the whole set, or just a small number of entities that belong to it [5].

A Common Ground. There is a close relation between conditional premises and the premises of syllogisms [2]. Consider the conditional premise "If it is a dog, then it is a mammal", and the syllogism's premise "All dogs are mammals", their representation using mental models is equal[3].

dog mammal

...

We will build upon this in the following cross-domain modeling.

2   Cross-Domain Reasoning

Our goal is to demonstrate how a cross-domain cognitive theory can be built for conditional and syllogistic reasoning. We take an already existing formalized approach for reasoning with conditionals using mental models (see Fig. 1) and extend its application to syllogisms.

Note that p and q in Fig. 1 stand for the antecedent and the consequent respectively, which can take different forms in the concrete application. For example, for the syllogism AI1 (cf. Table 3), in the first premise, "All X are Y", p corresponds to X and q corresponds to Y, whereas for the second premise, "Some Y are Z", p corresponds to Y and q corresponds to Z.

Example 2. Adding models:

$$\text{"If } X \text{ then } Y\text{"} \xrightarrow{\text{add } pq} X\ Y \xrightarrow{\text{add } \neg pq} \begin{matrix} X\ Y \\ \neg X\ Y \end{matrix} \ (p \text{ being } X, \text{ and, } q \text{ being } Y)$$

$$\text{"If } Y \text{ then possibly } Z\text{"} \xrightarrow{\text{add } pq} Y\ Z \xrightarrow{\text{add } p\neg q} \begin{matrix} Y\ Z \\ Y\ \neg Z \end{matrix} \ (p \text{ being } Y, \text{ and, } q \text{ being } Z)$$

In the following we describe how we apply the principle of adding models, as described above, to syllogisms.

Step 1: Translation of syllogistic premises to a pair of conditionals. The translations of all the possible moods of a syllogism's premise to a conditional premise, based on their equal representation using mental models, are shown below:

Mood	Premise	Conditional
A	All X are Y	If X then Y
I	Some X are Y	If X then possibly Y
E	No X are Y	If X then not Y
O	Some X are not Y	If X then possibly not Y

This process yields two conditional statements which can be treated as conditional reasoning problems, and can therefore be modeled using the formalization in Fig. 1.

---

[3] From now on we use a compressed version of the models representing sets of the same entity, i.e., one unique entity only, as we do not consider quantifiers like "Most".

Step 2: Obtaining mental model representations. Below, we show a representation of the conditionals that describe syllogism AI1. This corresponds to adding the pq model for the first premise in the syllogism, and adding the pq and $p\neg q$ models for the second one.

Syllogistic Premise	Conditional	Mental Models
All X are Y	If X then Y	X Y
Some Y are Z	If Y then possibly Z	Y Z Y

Step 3: Merging. After obtaining the two mental models representing the two premises, the next step is to merge them based on the middle term Y which appears in both premises, in order to construct the final mental model representation. In the table above we have the model X Y for the first premise. We will merge that model with all models of the second premise that also contain Y. The first such model is Y Z. Merging based on Y, we obtain X Y Z. The second model is Y, leading to a merged representation X Y. We obtain the following mental model representation of the syllogism: $\begin{array}{l} X\,Y\,Z \\ X\,Y \end{array}$

Step 4: Answer prediction. Since what we are interested in is the relation between X and Z, once the full representation is obtained, we do not take Y into consideration anymore (e.g. we would only consider $\begin{array}{l} X\,Z \\ X \end{array}$ from the representation shown above). Also, model duplicates are eliminated, and models with both elements being negative are not considered ($\neg X \; \neg Z$). Based on this representation, a prediction of the individual's answer about what follows from the given syllogism can be made. Possible final representations and the corresponding answers can be found in Table 4. In the cases where there is more than one choice for a possible answer, one is chosen randomly.

Table 4. Final representations and corresponding possible answers.

	Number of unique models in the representation							
	0	1			2			3
Models	-	X Z	X (¬Z)	(¬X) Z	X Z (¬X) Z	X Z X (¬Z)	(¬X) Z X (¬Z)	X Z (¬X) Z X (¬Z)
Answers	NVC	AXZ AZX	EXZ	EZX	IZX OZX	IXZ OXZ	NVC	NVC

Note. NVC – No valid conclusion can be drawn from the premises.

3 Results

To test, how good our cross-domain model is able to perform, we used the CCOBRA-framework benchmarking tool[4] which provides empirical benchmark data from psychological experiments for cognitive models in different domains. A cognitive model can be trained on specific training data, and needs to predict for each individual reasoner her putative conclusion for the respective inference problem. In a first step, we trained our model on the conditional data set which yielded the probabilities $P(pq) = 1.0$, $P(\neg p \neg q) = .65$, $P(\neg pq) = .5$, $P(p \neg q) = .05$. In the conditional domain, using these parameters yields an accuracy of 63%, which is only one percent lower than the best performing model (see Table 5b). Applying the same parameter distribution achieved an accuracy of about 21% on the syllogistic data. Therefore, four further parameter optimizations were performed in the syllogistic domain, based on different criteria, in order to examine the relation between mental models and type of syllogism. The criteria taken into consideration are mood and figure of the syllogism, and whether the currently analyzed premise is the first or second one. The last optimization was using no specific criterion, i.e. optimized the four parameters $(P(pq), P(\neg p \neg q), P(\neg pq), P(p \neg q))$ for all criteria at once. For the parameter optimization based on mood and figure, four separate parameters were fit for each mood or figure, respectively, totaling to 16 parameters. In the case of premise number, there is a total of 8 parameters, four parameters for each premise. Optimization was done with a randomized search with 10^6 iterations on values in the interval $[0, 1]$ with an increment of 0.1. All model specific optimizations had only an average accuracy of at most 27% which is lower than the general optimization. For the general optimization, i.e., without differentiation of mood, figure or premise number, we conducted a grid search with the same specifics. The best parameter values for the general optimization were $P(pq) = 1.0$, $P(\neg p \neg q) = 1.0$, $P(\neg pq) = .2$, $P(p \neg q) = 1.0$

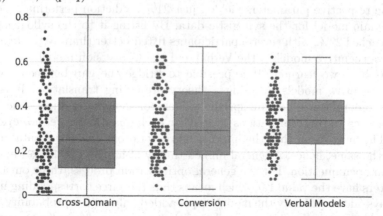

---

[4] orca.informatik.uni-freiburg.de/ccobra/.

The model was tested once again on the conditional data set using these parameters, and its performance dropped down to an accuracy of 38% (compared to the initial 63%). In Table 5, the results of running the Cross-Domain model on a syllogistic and conditional benchmark are shown.

Table 5. Prediction results, given as percentage of correct predictions, and best and worst predictive accuracy for individual reasoners.

(a) Selection of Syllogistic Models

Model[a]	Accuracy	Best	Worst
Verbal [13]	34%	61%	7%
Conversion [15]	32%	67%	3%
Cross-Domain	**29%**	**81%**	**0%**
PSYCOP [16]	29%	70%	6%
Atmosphere [17]	24%	44%	4%

(b) Selection of Conditional Models

Model	Accuracy
Probabilistic [11]	64%
Dependence [10]	64%
Cross-Domain	**63%**
Independence [10]	63%
Suppositional [4]	62%

[a] The models are taken from the meta-analysis by Khemlani and Johnson-Laird [9].

4   Discussion and Conclusion

Our motivation for our paper was the question, if human reasoners employ a similar or a different model representation for conditional and syllogistic reasoning. To analyze this, we used a computational formalization of the cognitive theory of mental models for human conditional reasoning and extended it towards reasoning with syllogisms, by translating quantified assertions into conditionals. While the fitting of our cross-domain model for conditionals demonstrated a performance comparable to other domain-specific models, the initial transfer of the respective parameters yielded just 21% prediction performance of the cross-domain model for the syllogistic data. By fitting it to the syllogisms, the model reached 29%, with several participants fitted better than by the two best-predictive cognitive models – the Verbal and the Conversion model.

What have we learned? It is possible to bridge the gap between domain-specific cognitive models by using a theory-preserving translation. It is even possible to outperform domain-specific models for some individuals. The cognitive processes and interpretations related for each quantifiers are, however, different. This may mean that the internal representations (for our mental model) are not the same, hence, a general unified theory of human deductive reasoning is still an open question. For the general optimization process, three out of four parameters have the value 1.0, which means that the three corresponding models are always added and only the model $\neg pq$ is added only with a probability of 0.2. This needs to be further investigated empirically. Our results indicate, however, that the outlined idea needs to be applied to other cognitive theories as well, such that the cross-domain power (or generalizability) of approaches can be better estimated. For this a general theory of how to generalize a cognitive model across domains is necessary and identifying general principles across formal and cognitive theories might be a first step. Still, this work is only a first try towards successful cognitive modeling of cross-domain human reasoning.

To summarize: Our model has a predictive accuracy comparable to state-of-the-art cognitive models in both domains. However, our model is capable of modeling human reasoning in two different domains, whereas the rest of the models in the benchmark are highly specialized, domain-specific cognitive models. On the basis of our model lies a reduction of the two tasks to a common interpretation. This made it possible to compare the mental representations.

While cross-domain data of individual reasoners is rare, in the future, this type of modeling should be performed on a data set where the same individual gives responses to both, conditional and syllogistic tasks. This way, we can learn more about individual differences in reasoning, which would aid in a more successful simulation of the human mind.

Acknowledgments. This paper was supported by DFG grants RA 1934/3-1, RA 1934/2-1 and RA 1934/4-1 to MR. We are also grateful to Lukas Elflein for helpful comments.

References

1. Bara, B.G., Bucciarelli, M., Lombardo, V.: Model theory of deduction: a unified computational approach. Cogn. Sci. **25**(6), 839–901 (2001)
2. Bucciarelli, M., Johnson-Laird, P.N.: Strategies in syllogistic reasoning. Cogn. Sci. **23**(3), 247–303 (1999)
3. Byrne, R.M., Johnson-Laird, P.N.: Spatial reasoning. J. Mem. Lang. **28**(5), 564–575 (1989)
4. Evans, J.S.B., Over, D.E.: If: Supposition, Pragmatics, and Dual Processes. Oxford Cognitive Science, Oxford (2004)
5. Johnson-Laird, P.N.: How We Reason, 1st edn. Oxford University Press, Oxford (2006)
6. Johnson-Laird, P.N.: Mental models in cognitive science. Cogn. Sci. **4**(1), 71–115 (1980)
7. Johnson-Laird, P.N.: Mental models and human reasoning. Proc. Nat. Acad. Sci. **107**(43), 18243–18250 (2010)
8. Johnson-Laird, P.N., Byrne, R.M.: Conditionals: a theory of meaning, pragmatics, and inference. Psychol. Rev. **109**(4), 646–678 (2002)
9. Khemlani, S., Johnson-Laird, P.N.: Theories of the syllogism: a meta-analysis. Psychol. Bull. **138**(3), 427–458 (2012)
10. Oaksford, M., Chater, N.: A rational analysis of the selection task as optimal data selection. Psychol. Rev. **101**(4), 608 (1994)
11. Oaksford, M., Chater, N., Larkin, J.: Probabilities and polarity biases in conditional inference. J. Exp. Psychol. Learn. Mem. Cogn. **26**(4), 883 (2000)
12. Oberauer, K.: Reasoning with conditionals: a test of formal models of four theories. Cogn. Psychol. **53**(3), 238–283 (2006)
13. Polk, T.A., Newell, A.: Deduction as verbal reasoning. Psychol. Rev. **102**(3), 533 (1995)

14. Ragni, M., Kola, I., Johnson-Laird, P.N.: On selecting evidence to test hypotheses: a theory of selection tasks. Psychol. Bull. **144**(8), 779 (2018)
15. Revlis, R.: Two models of syllogistic reasoning: feature selection and conversion. J. Verbal Learn. Verbal Behav. **14**(2), 180–195 (1975)
16. Rips, L.J.: The Psychology of Proof: Deductive Reasoning in Human Thinking. MIT Press, Cambridge (1994)
17. Sells, S.B.: The Atmosphere Effect: an Experimental Study of Reasoning. Archives of Psychology. (Columbia University), New York (1936)

Author Index

Printed in the United States
By Bookmasters